OFF THE BEAT

Los Angeles

Off the Beaten Path®

Lark Ellen Gould

GUILFORD, CONNECTICUT

Text design by Laura Augustine
Maps created by XNR Productions Inc. © The Globe Pequot Press
Illustrations by Carole Drong
Illustrations rendered from photographs provided by the following: pp. 10, 19, 40, 129, 144 courtesy LA Inc., The Convention and Visitors Bureau; p. 57 from *Where the Bodies Are* by Patricia Brooks; pp. 67, 73 courtesy West Hollywood Convention & Visitors Bureau; p. 83 courtesy Beverly Hills Convention and Visitors Bureau; p. 101 courtesy Catalina Island Chamber of Commerce; p. 117 courtesy Santa Monica Convention and Visitors Bureau; p. 131 courtesy Long Beach Area Convention & Visitors Bureau; pp. 159, 164 courtesy Pasadena Convention & Visitors Bureau

ISSN 1546-6418
ISBN 0-7627-2785-3

Manufactured in the United States of America
First Edition/Second Printing

*To Bubby for all her
wise choices and
enduring strength*

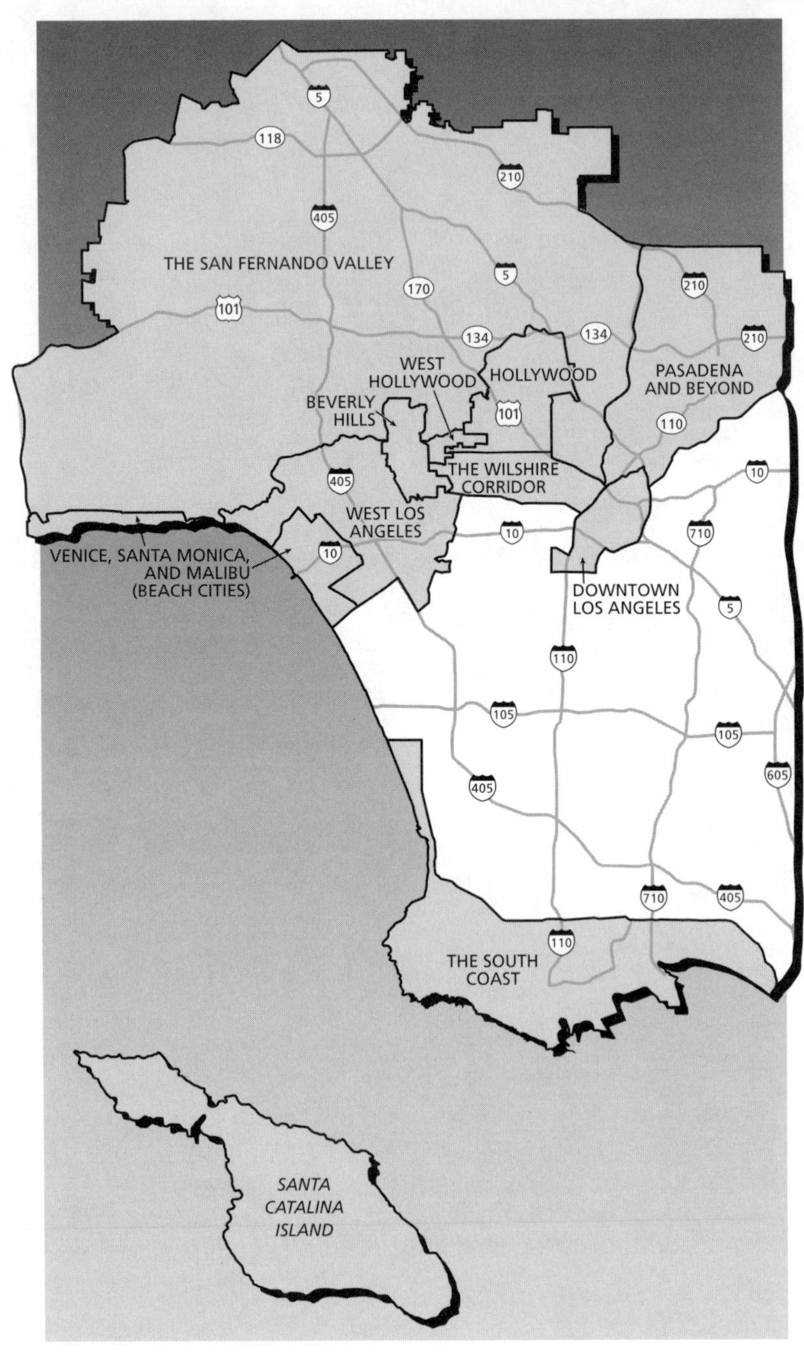
THE SAN FERNANDO VALLEY
WEST HOLLYWOOD
HOLLYWOOD
PASADENA AND BEYOND
BEVERLY HILLS
THE WILSHIRE CORRIDOR
WEST LOS ANGELES
VENICE, SANTA MONICA, AND MALIBU (BEACH CITIES)
DOWNTOWN LOS ANGELES
THE SOUTH COAST
SANTA CATALINA ISLAND
5
118
210
405
170
101
134
110
10
710
105
605

Contents

Acknowledgments

This book would not have been possible without the help of Carol Martinez, a true guardian angel, and the ongoing support I received from the Los Angeles Convention & Visitors Bureau—now LAInc. In addition, the tips and insights from my friend and colleague Amy Reiley proved invaluable to this endeavor as did the patient support of my parents, Norman and Elaine Gould.

Introduction

It's the reel thing, Los Angeles is. It may look like a movie set, but the handful of regions and thousands of neighborhoods that comprise the world's twelfth largest city are chock-full of color, history, and culture. What began as a pueblo in 1781 recast itself in the centuries to follow into a sunny mecca for dream seekers, whether following fortunes in real estate, agriculture, financial empire building, or entertainment. It all boomed here, at the edge of the United States. And the explosion continues.

Today the City of Angels spreads its influence over 467 square miles, down 80 miles of coastline, across immense valleys to the foothills of five mountain ranges. At night the city shimmers in a mesmerizing grid of lights cut by thick rivers of red and white along ever-moving freeways. Los Angeles is a city of light, of spotlights, neon, and low, tropical shadows that keep it forever in its golden years when movies were monumental.

Its past is its present with preservation and detailed restorations of such icons as the Beverly Hills Hotel, the Egyptian Theater, the Max Factor building, the Bradbury building, Angel's Flight, Mann's Chinese Theatre, Farmer's Market, the Hollywood Roosevelt, and the Biltmore Hotel. Los Angeles is alive with history, mystery, and hauntings. Neighborhoods near and far reflect the city's 1930s and 1940s salad days with odd architectural diffusions ranging from Gothic to ornate Art Deco, Mission Revival, and post–World War II chic. Kitsch got its start amid the wide car-filled boulevards with cafes topped by giant plaster hot dogs or doughnuts. Everything had to have an element of entertainment attached, something to get noticed.

And it still does. Check out the confluence of La Brea and Melrose Avenues, marked by the giant rooftop chili dog at Pink's, then grab your dripping piece of L.A. manna and head west on Melrose where each cheesy boutique outdoes the next in an unwritten competition of kitschy facades and interiors. Run down Robertson Boulevard's presentation of designer showrooms, galleries, and famous eateries. Steal an hour or two to discover Beverly Hills and find out what the stars are wearing from among Paris and Milan's latest entrees, then head for It's a Wrap in Burbank for the latest in star-worn and studio wardrobe releases. Cruise down Sunset Boulevard and up to the heights of Doheny Avenue for a film noir look at the lights of L.A. Set aside a day for the beach with a walk or roll down the boardwalk at Venice to the century-old canals that gave the neighborhood its name. Los Angeles is a series of neighborhoods and enclaves, one after another, each offering its own character, personality, history, and fascination to those willing to explore.

For the readers of this book, a Candy Land of off-color kitsch, wild and hidden artistic masterworks, savory secret sauces sampled in secluded gardens, and addictive dishes from a world of undiscovered ethnic cuisine awaits in the chapters to come. Los Angeles was built on dreams, visions, and fantasies found today, neighborhood to neighborhood, cafe to cafe, heaped with love and sweat by a century of talented and tenacious fortune seekers. And it's you who'll reap the benefits, seeing the city with fresh eyes and interest with this book as a compass.

While I may take you down some well-trodden paths to attractions you likely know well, I'll also show you what the travelogues and commercials omit. You can shop at Nordstrom or Bloomingdale's, but I'll show you where the one-of-a-kind clothing stores lie as well as the dumping spots for designers' and stars' once-worn gowns. You might dine at Spago, but I'll show you where celebrities go to get the best blue-plate special or cinema magnates head for their clam chowder fix. You may choose to tread the Hollywood Walk of Fame or browse Rodeo Drive, but I'll show you the hidden cracks and crannies, the history and the humor wedged into the walls as well. Whether you have a day or a week, *Off the Beaten Path* will bring you a magical Los Angeles you might otherwise miss, one worthy of a crowded postcard or mark in your peak experiences profile. Anything else is just facade.

Los Angeles can be divided into a dozen areas of interest and exploration that I have compressed into ten chapters: Downtown, the Wilshire Corridor, Hollywood, West Hollywood, Beverly Hills, West Los Angeles, Santa Monica and the beaches, the south coast, the San Fernando Valley, and Pasadena. A three- or four-day visit will usually satisfy the sojourner without causing an asthma attack. But plan your schedule carefully, and do leave time for distances and traffic. The thirty-minute flow from Downtown to Santa Monica on the Santa Monica Freeway during the day can take more than an hour in the morning or evening rush hour. The San Diego Freeway between the Santa Monica Freeway and LAX is nearly always jammed; try taking Century Boulevard to La Cienega to get into town instead. Also remember to watch for traffic-control photo boxes at major intersections in West Hollywood, West L.A., and the Mid-Wilshire area. Going through a yellow light will run you $278! Warning signs are posted ahead of the intersection, and it's a good idea to mind them. Finally, if you park on the street, note that parking cops take their jobs very seriously. Watch for permit parking areas, feed the meters, parking no farther than 18 inches from the curb—take a Department of Motor Vehicles study guide with you—or park in a lot. A $5.00 bill can buy a lot of peace of mind.

Getting Around

Some four million people live in the City of Angels, extending to sixteen million in the eighty surrounding cities and towns of greater L.A. County. There are 1.3 million commuters on the 527 miles of roadway at any given hour, and the average speed on the freeways during rush hour is a pokey 20 miles per hour.

But Los Angeles did not miss the train completely when it comes to public transportation. Although the Metro buses and DASH services are the preferred method of local transport for the few carless folks in the area, more than 400 miles of tracks join the Metrolink from Union Station with points as far as Oxnard, Lancaster, Riverside, and San Juan Capistrano. For the rest of the green-minded hoofers, it's the Metro Rail, a modern and spankingly clean subway system that connects Downtown with Pasadena, Long Beach, Norwalk, Redondo Beach, Hollywood, North Hollywood, and the Wilshire Corridor. Hours are 5:00 A.M. to midnight every day, and fares (it's the same for buses) run $1.35 one-way plus 25 cents for a transfer. Maps can be found at www.mta.net.

For the mere toss of a quarter, the Downtown DASH will take you to or near anywhere you want to go in the Downtown area. Six lines run from Chinatown to the Los Angeles Convention Center, stopping at hotels, Olvera Street, the Garment District, Bunker Hill, and most other points of interest. Maps are available at most kiosks Downtown.

Taxis

Distances are long in Los Angeles, and cab fares can run high. Even a short trip—say from the airport to an off-site car rental depot—can cost $10 or more. Taxis charge $1.90 at the flag drop, plus $1.60 per mile. A service charge is added to fares originating at LAX, and fares can run to more than $60 one-way for trips to Long Beach, Pasadena, or the Valley. Average fares from LAX to Downtown L.A. run $40; it's $30 to Mid-Wilshire, and $25 to Santa Monica.

Outside of the Downtown Financial District, a whistle and a wave won't get you far. At LAX as well as Union Station and hotels, cabs line up at a certain spot and are summoned by a station manager or valet. Or you can order a taxi from your cell phone through Checker Cab at (323) 654–8400; L.A. Taxi, (213) 627–7000; or United Taxi (213) 483–7604, among other companies.

When you land at LAX, you're landing in the world's fourth largest airport. Even Terminal 1, which services mostly the regional lines like Southwest Airlines and America West, is larger than the entire airport in Tampa, Florida. This airport has seven primary terminals, all served by hotel shuttles, parking shuttles, car rental shuttles, local bus service, airport bus service, taxis, and shared van rides. It's chaos on the sidewalks, because cars are not allowed to stop and wait for their parties but must circle the airport until eye contact is made and a quick stop and load can be accomplished under the ready pen of a ticket officer. A color-coded island separating curbside traffic from through traffic marks where to wait for shuttles, buses, and vans. Taxi stands and transportation kiosks are located right outside each terminal.

For an easy at-a-glance guide to transportation from LAX, check the airport Web site at www.lawa.org, or call (310) 646–5252.

Area Codes

Like New York City, which was well known for its 212 designation until just a few years ago, Los Angeles has endured its share of phone fracturing and is no longer simply 213. The 213 designation is now given to Downtown Los Angeles. West of Downtown, through Hollywood, and all the way to West Hollywood, you'll find the 323 prefix in effect. From West Hollywood to Santa Monica, down to San Pedro, over to Long Beach, and up to Malibu is the 310 area code. The San Fernando Valley is 818, Long Beach east to Whittier is 562, Orange County is 714 and 949, and Pasadena and parts east become 626. Need a number anywhere in L.A. or Orange County? Just call 411.

Sources of Information

The most comprehensive place to go for information on visiting Los Angeles is the Los Angeles Convention and Visitors Bureau. The phone is (800) 366–6116, and the events hotline (213) 689–8822; or you can log on to www.lacvb.com or www.visitlanow.com. In addition, the bureau provides walk-in visitor centers at 685 South Figueroa Street, Downtown (open Monday through Friday from 8:00 A.M. to 5:00 P.M., and Saturday from 8:30 A.M. to 5:00 P.M.); and in Hollywood, on the main floor of the new Hollywood & Highland complex right at the confluence of Hollywood Boulevard and Highland Avenue and adjacent to the Metro station.

Many Los Angeles–area communities also have their own information centers, and often maintain detailed and colorful Web sites. Try the Beverly Hills Visitors Bureau, (800) 345–2210 or (310) 271–8174, www.bhvb.org; the West Hollywood Convention and Visitors Bureau, (800) 368–6020 or (310) 289–2525, www.visitwesthollywood.com; the Santa Monica Convention and Visitors Bureau, (310) 393–7593, www.santamonica.com; the Pasadena Convention and Visitors Bureau, (626) 795–9311, www.pasadenavisitor.org; the Long Beach Convention and Visitors Bureau, (800) 4LB–STAY or (562) 436–3645; or the Catalina Island Visitors Bureau, (310) 510–1520, www.catalina.com.

The Hollywood Arts Council is a good place to get attraction, entertainment, and dining information as well as maps to the celluloid city: contact (323) 462–2355 or www.discoverhollywood.com. But to find out what's really making the buzz about town, pick up an *L.A. Weekly* at any news kiosk and most trend boutiques. The *Los Angeles Times* runs a comprehensive calendar section on Thursday and Sunday that offers the entire roundup of theater, music, museums, clubs, events, and films in the city. The cultural events listings can also be accessed online at www.calendarlive.com.

Touring Around

Get oriented, get educated, and get going. L.A. is full of wacky, wonderful history and stories—not to mention plenty of wild tours to bring it all into focus.

Architours. Los Angeles is home to a collection of architectural masterworks, and Architours finds them, explains them, and gives you the backstory. Frank Lloyd Wright and son, Richard Neutra, Frank Gehry—much design history is made here from Downtown to Santa Monica. Contact (323) 294–5821 or www.architours.com.

Off'n Running Tours takes off on L.A. the old-fashioned way—on foot. Joggers can have a running tour through Santa Monica, Beverly Hills, or Downtown. Tours are designed for runners and walkers of all levels. Call (310) 246–1418.

Don't like the organized thing? Do your own tour on in-line skates. Rent them from ***Perry's Beach Café*** or other rental spots on the boardwalk in Santa Monica and find the beach to be your perfect playground. Contact Perry's at (310) 372–3138 or www.perryscafe.com.

Get Cultural with the Watt shuttles visitors to the famous 100-foot-high Watts Towers built by a single person with a vision. This guided tour also visits eighteen other sites that capture the colorful heritage of this city. Call (323) 563–5639.

Red Line Walking Tours is the most comprehensive way to get a taste of L.A. The tours run Downtown and Hollywood and go behind the

More Tours

Here are some other tour options to consider:

- ***L.A. Tours and Sightseeing,*** *(323) 937–0999, www.latours.net, offers half-day bus tours to the stars' homes and the sights of L.A.*
- ***L.A. Bike Tours,*** *(888) 775–BIKE or (323) 466–5890, www.labiketours.com, offers bikes to rent and buy and privately led interpretive tours by pedal power through the backstreets of L.A.'s prime neighborhoods.*
- ***Los Angeles Conservancy Tours,*** *(213) 623–2489, www.laconservancy.org, puts well-trained docents in charge to tell the story behind the details of the city's monumental movie palaces, ghostly hotels, and ornate office buildings.*
- ***Starline Tours of Hollywood,*** *(800) 460–8331, www.starlinetours.com, is the bus tour of choice for those seeking the on-the-path tours of Los Angeles for a bargain. The tour is free when you purchase an L.A. City Pass (details in the Hollywood chapter).*
- ***Take My Mother, Please!,*** *(323) 737–2200, www.takemymotherplease.com, puts menopausal tour maven Anne Block in charge of the middle-age mothers who come in tow. Whether it's shopping, museums, dining, ethnic havens, or good spots to kvetsch, no one knows L.A. like Anne.*

scenes at historical icons off-limits to the public. Tours last one and a half to three hours and deliver much more than rich entertainment. 6773 Hollywood Boulevard, (323) 402–1074, www.redlinetours.com.

Annual Events

January

Tournament of Roses Parade. L.A.'s famous New Year's Day parade, with floats, bands, and equestrian units. The parade begins on Orange Grove Boulevard, turns onto Colorado Boulevard, then finishes on Sierra Madre Villa Avenue. (626) 449–7673, (626) 795–4171 (for grandstand seats; call February through December), (310) 454–3511 (for grandstand seats; call May through December), www.tournamentofroses.com.

Greater Los Angeles Auto Show. More than 1,000 automobiles are featured in five different exhibition halls, highlighting the newest in foreign and domestic sedans, coupes, roadsters, and sport utility vehicles and trucks, as well as automotive accessories and performance products. Los Angeles Convention Center, 1201 South Figueroa Street in Los Angeles, (213) 624–7300, www.laautoshow.com.

February

Golden Dragon Parade. Floats, dances, and marching bands parade through Chinatown, Downtown Los Angeles. Contact (213) 617–0396 or www.lachinesechamber.org. (Check the Web site three months before the event for more details.)

Street Fest Carnival. Entertainment, food, and booths at the corner of Broadway and Cesar E. Chavez Avenue in Los Angeles. Contact (213) 617–0396 or www.lachinesechamber.org.

March

City of Los Angeles Marathon. Along with the marathon, an Acura L.A. Bike Tour and 5K run are held. Contact (310) 444–5544, www.lamarathon.com.

South Bay St. Patrick's Day Parade & Festival. The festival features a parade, Irish bands, food, vendor booths, a children's carnival, and a petting zoo. The parade includes bagpipe bands, high school bands, local service clubs, Irish warriors, scouting units, and floats. The festival is held at Pier Plaza in Hermosa Beach at Pier and Hermosa Avenues. Contact (310) 374–1365 or www.stpatricksday.org.

City of Santa Clarita Cowboy Poetry and Music Festival. Cowboy poetry readings, rope tricks, music, food, and demonstrations, all found at Melody Ranch Motion Picture Studio on Placerita Canyon in Santa Clarita and other locations. Contact (661) 286–4021 (tickets) or www.santa-clarita.com/cp.

April

Toyota Grand Prix of Long Beach. A professional automobile street race, a celebrity race, and other activities begin in downtown Long Beach, adjacent to the Long Beach Convention and Entertainment Center at 300 East Ocean Boulevard. Contact (562) 436–9953, (888) 827–7333 (tickets), or www.longbeachgp.com.

Blessing of the Animals. An Easter procession of pets and exotic animals, as well as displays and exhibits, centers on El Pueblo de Los Angeles (Olvera Street) at the intersection of Main and Alameda Streets in Los Angeles. Call (213) 625–5045.

Los Angeles Times Festival of Books in Association with UCLA. Booths, book sales, children's activities, and panel discussions are held at the UCLA campus on Hilgard Avenue in Westwood. Contact (800) 528–4637 or www.latimes.com\festivalofbooks.

McDonald's Fiesta Broadway. Music, booths, and food are found along thirty-six blocks of Downtown Los Angeles, including Broadway and Hill and Spring Streets between First Street and Olympic Boulevard. Contact (310) 914–0015 or www.fiestabroadway.la.

May

Cinco de Mayo at El Pueblo de Los Angeles. Traditional music, culture presentations, dance, and food are offered at El Pueblo de Los Angeles (Olvera Street) at the intersection of Main and Alameda Streets in Los Angeles. Call (213) 628–1274.

Topanga Banjo Fiddle Contest & Folk Festival. An old time, bluegrass, folk song, folk dancing, and crafts festival held in the Santa Monica Mountains. Contact (818) 382–4819 or www.topangabanjofiddle.org.

June

San Fernando Valley Fair. At this lively event you'll find a carnival, a rodeo, pig racing, agricultural and gardening exhibits, educational and technological exhibits, home arts, food vendors, entertainment, an academic competition, a festival of choirs, livestock auctions, a petting zoo, and pony rides. Hansen Dam Sports Center, 11770½ Foothill Boulevard in Lakeview Terrace, (818) 557–1600 or www.sfvalleyfair.org.

Long Beach Bayou Festival. Live music, food, arts and crafts, dance lessons, and a costume parade all located at Queen Mary Events Park, 1126 Queens Highway in Long Beach, (562) 427–8834, www.LongBeachFestival.com.

Great American Irish Fair and Musical Festival. Look for music, dancing, food, storytellers, an art contest, a photo competition, a Shamrock Carnival, heritage centers, language programs, sheep-herding shows, an Irish dog show, and a horse exhibit. Festival Fields at Woodley Park in Encino, (818) 501–3781, www.irishfair.org.

Galaxy Soccer Game & Fireworks Extravaganza. This event features, well, a soccer game and July 4 fireworks. Find it at the Rose Bowl, 1001 Rose Bowl Drive in Pasadena. Contact (626) 577–3100, (626) 535–8300, www.rosebowlstadium.com, or www.lagalaxy.com.

Marina del Rey July 4 Fireworks Extravaganza. A Zambelli pyrotechnic extravaganza at the main channel off the breakwater—although the fireworks are visible from locations throughout the marina. Call (310) 305–9545.

First Independence Day Celebration in Los Angeles. Entertainment, a musket salute, historical portrayals, and an outdoor dance at El Pueblo de Los Angeles (Olvera Street) at the intersection of Main and Alameda Streets in Los Angeles. Call (213) 625–5045.

September

Brazilian Street Carnaval and Independence Day Celebration. Enjoy a parade and Brazilian dance, Brazilian music, and craft and food booths at the Promenade from Third Street to First Avenue in Long Beach. Contact (562) 438–3669 or www.carnaval.org.

Manhattan Beach Arts Festival. This free participatory cultural event features art workshops, a community mural, international dance instruction, interactive performance theater, music, dancing, crafts, food, and a children's area. It's all found at Manhattan Beach Boulevard between Valley Drive and Highland Avenue in Manhattan Beach, (310) 802–5417.

Los Angeles County Fair. Horse racing, exhibitions, a carnival, fine arts, flowers, livestock, entertainment, a skate park, contests, and pig races are held at Fairplex, 1101 West McKinley Avenue, Pomona. Contact (909) 623–3111 or www.fairplex.com.

Art's Alive Festival. This event celebrates visual, performing, and literary arts with free hands-on art activities, live entertainment on two stages, crafts booths, food vendors, art exhibits, and a juried art show. Torrance Cultural Arts Center, 3330 Civic Center Drive, Torrance, (310) 781–7150, www.tcac.torrnet.com.

September–October

Alpine Village Oktoberfest. You'll find a live German band, along with a stein-holding contest, wood sawing, food, and beverages, at Alpine Village, 833 West Torrance Boulevard, Torrance. Contact (310) 327–4384 or www.alpinevillage.net/oktoberfest.htm.

October

Port of Los Angeles Lobster Festival. Live entertainment, dancing, rides, games, a lobster-calling contest on Friday, and a Lobster Dog Pet Parade on Saturday. It's located at Ports o' Call Village in San Pedro, (310) 366–6472, www.Lobsterfest.com.

Los Angeles Times Festival of Health. Family health screenings, music, workout sessions, and cooking and alternative medicine demonstrations are all held at USC's University Park campus, Figueroa and Hoover Streets in Los Angeles, (800) 528–4637, www.latimes.com/extras/festivalofhealth.

Bella Via. Professional and budding artists chalk 15-foot creations on a pavement "canvas." The event, named for an Italian street-painting festival, also features vendors, food, and entertainment. It's found at Valencia town center's Main Street at Town Center Drive, Santa Clarita; call (661) 287–9050.

Discover Marina del Rey. The kids can enjoy inflatable games, face painting, story time, crafts, magicians, and clowns while their parents take in crew and outrigger races; U.S. Coast Guard helicopter sea-rescue demonstration; pet adoptions; displays and demonstrations by the Los Angeles County sheriff, lifeguard, and fire departments and environmental groups; health exhibits; and live music. The location is Chace Park, 13650 Mindanao Way, Marina del Rey, (310) 305–9545.

November

Doo Dah Parade. This spoof on the traditional Tournament of Roses Parade doesn't feature floral pageantry or a queen and her court. Instead, entries have included such comical notables as the Briefcase Marching Drill Team, the Ocean Beach Geriatric Surf Club, and Gidget

Patrol and the West Hollywood Cheerleaders. The route begins at Raymond Avenue and Holly Street, travels down Raymond, turns right onto Colorado Boulevard, and ends at Pasadena Boulevard. Contact (626) 440–7379 or www.pasadenadoodahparade.com.

December

Hollywood Christmas Parade. Floats, bands, marching groups, and various celebrities follow a procession that begins at Mann's Chinese Theatre, 6925 Hollywood Boulevard in Hollywood, and goes east, then south on Vine Street, west on Sunset Boulevard, and ends at Orange Drive. Contact (323) 469–2337 (information), (626) 795–4171 (grand stand tickets) or www.hollywoodchristmas.com.

Marina del Rey Holiday Boat Parade (Marina del Rey Tournament of Lights). At least seventy boats with holiday illuminations light up the main channel of the Marina del Rey Marina. Some of the best views are from Fisherman's Village, 13755 Fiji Way, and Chace Park, 13650 Mindanao Way. Call (310) 822–9455 or (310) 305–9545.

Climate

Los Angeles does, indeed, have seasons, although you sometimes have to search for them.

Whether you're timing your visit with winter or summer, the weather in Los Angeles is bound to be temperate and bright. The south coast "monsoon" season runs November into February, starting with the welcomed overcast clouds of September and usually resulting in much-needed rain by the time the warm Santa Ana winds take hold from February to April. Winters can get chilly, with temperatures in the high forties at night and low sixties during the day. But periods of seventy- and eighty-degree sunshine-filled days are more the rule than the exception. Summers, too, are comely and kind, with dry warm days in the upper eighties and low nineties and nights in the low seventies. Late August brings the heat waves: Temperatures could climb to triple digits, though rarely for more than five days in a row.

Distances from Downtown

Disneyland: 26 miles

Beverly Hills: 10 miles

Burbank Airport: 13 miles

Hollywood/Griffith Park: 6 miles

Los Angeles International Airport: 17 miles

Pasadena: 9 miles

Santa Monica: 15 miles

Universal Studios Hollywood: 9 miles

Venice Beach: 16 miles

The weather by the beach can be considerably cooler—ten degrees or more—and usually starts with fog and haze that burn off by late morning. After that, days remain comfortably dry, if sultry—but they can reduce to chilly nights faster than the roll of credits at a movie. (Follow your mom's advice and bring a sweater.) Nights are invariably moist as well; indeed, L.A. wreaks havoc on frizzy hair.

The key to L.A. is not trying to do it all, or at least not all at once. True to its reputation, L.A. often is a great big freeway, and if you don't plan your time according to location, time, and type of activity you're likely to spend most of it on the road rather than at your intended destination. But then you can crank up the tunes and take in the palms and billboards along the way. When it comes to Los Angeles, you have to enjoy the ride.

The prices and rates listed in this guidebook were confirmed at press time. We recommend, however, that you call establishments to obtain current information before traveling.

Downtown Los Angeles

If Los Angeles has a center, it's here, in Downtown L.A. The skyline alone might be the most photographed on the planet, with its celebrated composition in steel and glass standing in as Anycity USA for film directors. Still, urban architecture aside, this is where it all began—it's where Los Angeles can trace her every era, and where new eras in her evolution continue to take shape.

From the eighteenth-century pueblo settlements on Olvera Street, to the Victorian elegance of Bunker Hill; the Art Deco grandeur of the first movie palaces; the thriving commerce in textiles, toys, clothing, and jewels; the evolving centers of Chinese, Japanese, and Hispanic culture; and the continual renaissance in fine arts, architecture, music, and performance—this is Downtown L.A. The city unfolds in a very walkable and fascinating 4 square miles, every block bearing a story.

Los Angeles begins at ***Union Station*** at 700–900 North Alameda Street. This was the end of the line for many and the start of a life for others, where seductively warm days, the riches of Hollywood beckoning from

Walls of Wonder

Los Angeles would not be Los Angeles without its walls, and in L.A. that means murals. With more than 2,000 murals decorating the exterior landscapes of Los Angeles, all you have to do to experience this profusion of color and culture is keep your eyes open and look up. While many murals focus on the art, history, and culture of Latin Americans and their resettlement in the north, a number of whimsical paintings, trompe l'oeils, and California Dreamin' scenes make their mark. Examples include the Fifty-one Bees *endeavor at the Flower Mart between Seventh and Eighth Streets or the Flight of Angels on Third Street in Little Tokyo. Downtown is awash in sidewalk poetry, secret-corner sculptures, and sensational fountains. For information, contact the city's Murals Program—part of its Cultural Affairs Department—at (213) 473–8344 or www.culturela.org.*

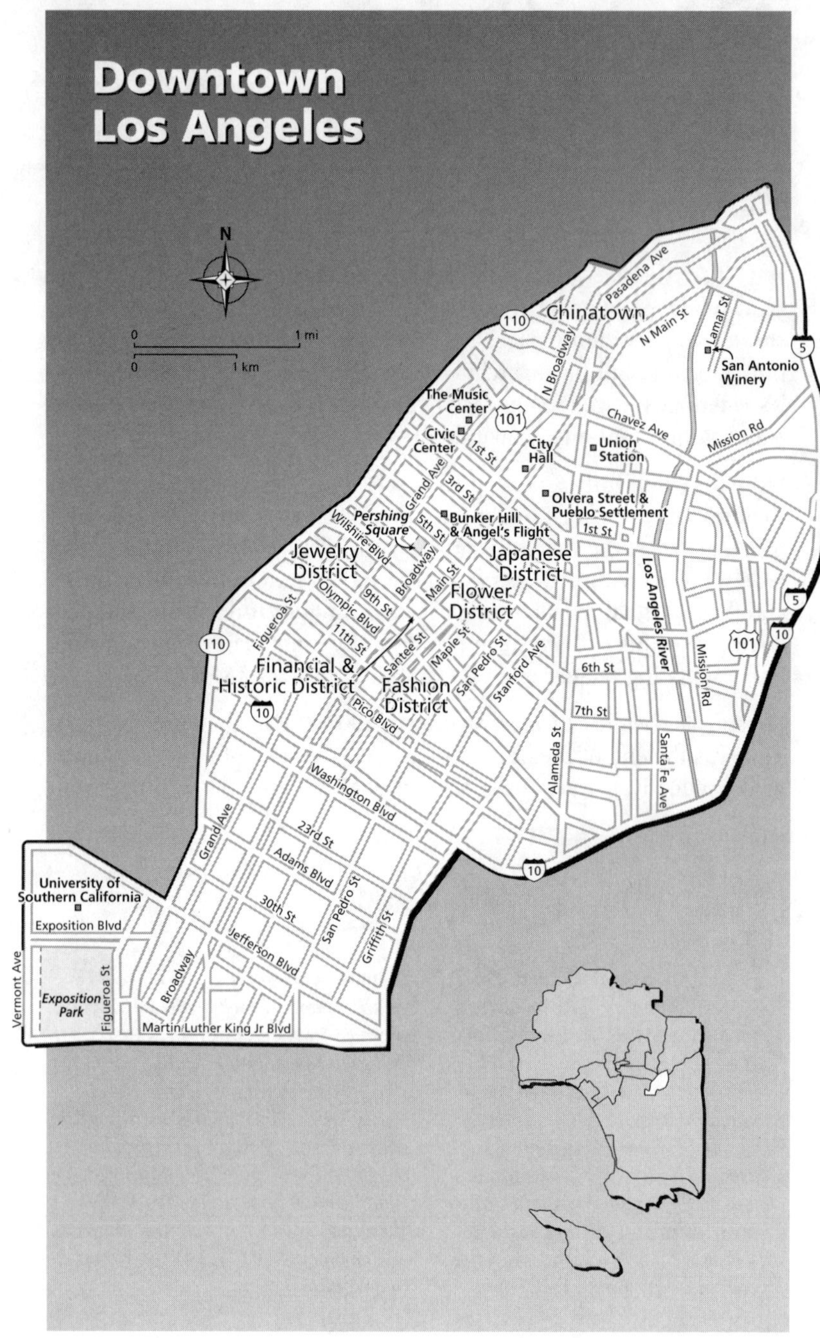
Downtown
Los Angeles
N
0
1 mi
0
1 km
Chinatown
Pasadena Ave
N Main St
Lamar St
San Antonio Winery
N Broadway
The Music Center
Civic Center
1st St
City Hall
Union Station
Chavez Ave
Mission Rd
Grand Ave
3rd St
Olvera Street & Pueblo Settlement
Pershing Square
5th St
Bunker Hill & Angel's Flight
1st St
Wilshire Blvd
Jewelry District
Broadway
Japanese District
Main St
Los Angeles River
Olympic Blvd
9th St
Flower District
Figueroa St
11th St
Santee St
Maple St
San Pedro St
Stanford Ave
Mission Rd
Financial & Historic District
Fashion District
6th St
7th St
Pico Blvd
Alameda St
Santa Fe Ave
Washington Blvd
Grand Ave
23rd St
Adams Blvd
University of Southern California
San Pedro St
30th St
Griffith St
Exposition Blvd
Jefferson Blvd
Vermont Ave
Broadway
Exposition Park
Figueroa St
Martin Luther King Jr Blvd
110
101
5
10

Author's Top Picks Downtown

Old Chinatown

Cathedral of Our Lady of the Angels

Bradbury Building

Grand Central Market

Millennium Biltmore Hotel

Santee Alley

burgeoning movie palaces, and the promise of abundance in all its forms turned more than a few people into bright-eyed dreamers.

By 1887 the transcontinental railroad had already whisked more than 120,000 people west to the Los Angeles basin with tickets costing $125 one-way from St. Louis. A fare war between railroad companies took hold a year later, and suddenly the city of 10,000 or so was having its first big real estate boom, and if you looked closely, you could see the first tentacles of sprawl. By 1939 Los Angeles was more than an outpost of cattle barons, con men, and celluloid cowboys: It was Wall Street West, with its own industries and gateway trade. This was the year Union Station was built, as perhaps the last of the great railroad stations, to the tune of $13 million.

A tour of L.A. begins here as well, for the station neatly reflects the history, the philosophy, the pace, the possibilities, the aesthetic priorities, and the precision of a city built on the backs of dreamers. Step inside the Streamline-Moderne-Meets-Southern-Spain foyer and find yourself in 1939, the heavy leather-and-wood chairs resting squarely in sun-dusted rows. Its center is a cross—whether the crossroads of travel, the intersections of time, the confluence of styles, or an industrial call to a higher order. Muted earth tones and elaborate Spanish tile work lend a sense that is half hacienda, half adobe cathedral, under a firmament of Euclidian wood frames and Navajo patterned etchings illuminated by wrought-iron chandeliers. The elaborate structure has served as a backdrop for a long litany of films, including *Guilty by Suspicion, The Way We Were, My Best Friend's Wedding,* and *Pearl Harbor.*

Unbelievable Bargain

Widespread relocation to Los Angeles actually began in the 1880s, when competition between the Santa Fe and Southern Pacific Railroads led to intense price wars. At one point the trains were actually ferrying forward-looking farmers from the American heartland to the new frontier for a single dollar. The war came to an end in 1888, but skillful land speculators, con men, and real estate boosters took over, and the city became its own advertising engine. Now the land of sunshine, sea, orange blossoms, and health sprawls for 467 square miles, with 3.7 million people in the city alone.

Built on what was once the site of vineyards and then the city's first Chinatown, today the station serves passengers heading toward Seattle, San Diego, and points east on Amtrak lines as well as those headed west into parts of L.A. on the Red Line, south to Long Beach on the Blue Line, and north to Pasadena on the Gold Line. The light rail entrance in the ***East Lobby*** may be an attraction in its own right. Here an installation of twelve light sticks by kinetic sculptor Bill Bell warns of incoming trains by producing ghostly images of a train, a city bus, famous faces, and a Chinese written character.

To the right of the entrance is ***Fred Harvey Restaurant,*** now used for special events only but still a nod to the famous eateries along the Santa Fe Railroad. The real dining treat is right inside: ***Traxx Restaurant*** is a favorite with travelers and the L.A. business community alike. Martinis are shaken in dimly lit Deco surroundings while white tablecloths inside and alfresco patio dining outside host dressed-up patrons in the mood for jazz tracks and corn-fed fillets. The cafe extends to an outdoor garden that also serves as a waiting area for passengers looking for a bit of peace and quiet. An Andalusian tile fountain brings soothing water and birds sounds. As the sun angles in on the benches and grass, you could think you're in a vizier's courtyard rather than a train station. 800 North Alameda, (213) 625–1999, www.traxxrestaurant.com.

A sweet holdout from the vineyard era in these parts is found a few blocks east of Union Station on Lamar Street. ***San Antonio Winery*** is L.A.'s only wine producer; California grapes have been fermenting in its cooled oaken barrels since 1917. A tasting room offers a sampling of any number of Merlots, Cabernets, and Pinots from California's central coast. A restaurant serves lunch and dinner, as well as wines by the glass for $4.50 to $7.00. A gift shop for baskets, gadgets, and wine-minded specialty foods is also located in this unlikely spot between the train docks and the Los Angeles River. 737 Lamar Street; call (323) 223–1401 for information on free tastings and tours.

Just across from Union Station is ***Philippe's Original Sandwich Shop.*** This 1908 L.A. icon found fame when a server accidentally dropped a roast beef sandwich in a plate of run-off juice. The result: the French dip—the original—and no one does it better. Open twenty-four hours, the sawdust floors, the L.A. Dodger and pal pix on the wall, the wooden booths and communal seating have not been touched in decades, and lamb, pork, and turkey sandwiches benefit from the original server's mistake as well. 1001 Alameda Street, (213) 628–3781.

Head a few blocks northwest on Alameda and you'll find yourself in

Tree Truths

Palm trees are not native to Los Angeles. The city grows more than twenty-five different varieties of palms, and most got their L.A. roots during the 1932 Summer Olympics.

"Old" Chinatown—this was once, of course, the "new" Chinatown, back in the 1940s. Chinatown is inching block by block westward and northward from its current site, however, as its Vietnamese, Cambodian, and Hmong communities expand. Most of the moneyed Chinese families have resettled over the past decade to Monterey Park near Pasadena, but the true spirit of the Old Country is still alive across Alameda Street from Spring Street west to Hill Street, and from Ord Street to the Pasadena Freeway.

Amble westward on Ord Street toward Broadway and find yourself under the cinnabar-colored ***Chinatown Gateway,*** festooned in luck-bringing roof curves; its Cantonese inscription labels it the GATE OF MATERNAL VIRTUES. Enter and find yourself in 1940s L.A. in one of the many neighborhoods created over the last century as a segregated ethnic enclave. But separation has its virtues. The Chinese population that settled in L.A. to lay the railroad lines, dig canals, and mine gold built their own empire of imported treasures, laundries, produce houses, restaurants, and precious elements. Not much has changed from those days, and you could just as easily be walking the alleys of Shanghai as the streets of L.A.— at least for a moment or two.

The shops, restaurants, fortune-tellers, bookshops, herbal emporiums, and financial institutions of Old Chinatown exude a colorful sort of chaos by day and a romantic radiance by night. The sidewalks along ***North Broadway Avenue*** are lined with the best Chinese cuisine within a 10-mile radius, with all its sights and smells. Here you'll find live chickens stacked in an alley in back of ***Superior Poultry*** at 750 North Broadway—selling chickens for the last half century and the only place in L.A. to find live fowl—as well as seemingly depressed fish awaiting their fate in car-sized aquariums, and roasted whole ducks stuck on the hook-covered walls of rotisserie bars. All is a-bustle here, whether you choose ***Sam Woo's*** famed Peking Duck and Pig Trotters, the succulent Slippery Shrimp of ***Yang Chow,*** or the fabulous Dim Sum of the ***Empress Pavilion.***

A recent addition to the street is a spate of Vietnamese eateries serving piquant fisherman's soups and elegant spring rolls. Every day is market day along ***Saigon Plaza.*** The corridor flows with outdoor stalls selling electronics, Mexican fruit snacks, golden rings, plastic children's toys, and polyester shirts in no particular order, all day, every day.

While the western side of North Broadway teems with restaurants, the east is a jewelers' alley where store upon store lures with finely crafted gold chains from Singapore, India, and China. Diamonds, too, weigh heavily among the offerings, sold with accompanying paperwork and buy-back guarantees.

Continue westward toward Hill Street and ***Chung King Court*** to find the art, antiques, and souvenir shops, the bonsai boutiques, and the pagodas that epitomize the character of this containment. Hill Street's ***Niming Books*** and ***Great Wall Books*** offer detailed wall charts of acupuncture energy meridians, reflexology, and other exotic therapies, along with the latest newspapers from Beijing. A small selection in English can be found among the character-filled tomes. Herb apothecaries sell potions and herbs mixed to specification with potent grades of ginseng root sent all the way from . . . Wisconsin (and officially certified by the Ginseng Board of Wisconsin!). Food markets sell dozens of grades and shades of tea amid cans and plastic packages of indecipherable nourishment. Take a plastic bag and dig into the barrels of dried wood ear mushrooms, desiccated shrimps and oysters, shriveled octopus, dried snails and jellyfish. A slicing machine produces fresh paper-thin slices of ginger and ginseng root, while aquarium tanks bubble with carp and crabs. To keep things even more interesting, English is barely spoken here.

Tucked into a corner of this area between Broadway and Hill Street near College Street is ***Quon Bros. Grand Star Restaurant.*** This is the Rat Pack dive of Chinatown with darkly lit red vinyl booths, tropical drinks that should have fire extinguishers attached, and live entertainment—Saturday features jazz from 9:00 P.M. to 2:00 A.M., no cover. 943 Sun Mun Way, (213) 626–2285.

The Central Plaza of this neighborhood is alive with slanting rooftops, paper lanterns, crowded antique window displays, paper lantern and bamboo souvenir shops, and Chinese string sounds. Wander into ***Sun Yet Sen Square,*** where the ***Wonder Bakery*** sells lotus seed mini pies, preserved duck egg pastries, and steamed pork and chicken buns by the half dozen. ***Sincere Imports*** beckons across the courtyard with a chest-high Ho Tai or good-luck Buddha begging to be rubbed as you walk in. Besides bowls of beads and good-luck amulets, the store carries a display case full of antique hand-painted mud men or porcelain statues costing up to $1,000 apiece.

The court contains a number of dark and cluttered antiques shops forever boasting "going out of business sales" with items up to 70 percent off. Ogle a mother-of-pearl floor panel for $200 or a faux Ming vase for

$60. Grab a pair of silk slippers or Chinese pajamas fr(***Dragon Imports,*** where embroidered silk dresses start a saunter over to the ***Seven Star Cavern Wishing Well*** by a 50 pagoda where a properly tossed coin can land you a future ity, love, happiness, well-being, health, and fertility.

As you make your way through the crowd of cafes and stores, head toward Chung King Court across Hill Street where the "New" Chinatown seems to be taking root—literally—with three-story department stores like ***T S Emporium*** at 835 North Broadway. Here you can buy twenty species of ginseng root, herbs mixed for what ails you, two dozen types of cured teas, and all the fake jade dragons you can lift. This store might be as close to modern Hong Kong as you're going to get in L.A.—and chances are you'll find a store clerk who speaks English, too. In the corridor plaza outside are more restaurants, bookshops, herb shops, exotic therapy offices, and teahouses as well as the ***F. See On Company*** antiques import shop as made famous in Lisa See's family saga, *On Gold Mountain* (St. Martin's Press). Movies, too, have had their moment in Chinatown. The list includes: *Rush Hour, Lethal Weapon 4, Primal Fear, Eight Millimeter, 48 Hours, Ring of Fire,* and *Golden Child.* A good place to stop in this plaza is ***Pho 79*** at 727 North Broadway; the phone is (213) 625–7026. Here is a Vietnamese noodle shop with excellent spring rolls and fisherman's soup. The tariff will come to less than $10 for two—and you can even throw in a Thai coffee. Beware, however, of other Vietnamese restaurants in the area that present a very confusing menu, overcharge for the orders, and push high-priced off-the-menu offerings onto unsuspecting customers.

Moving south on Spring Street, adjacent to Chinatown is the world's oldest theme park of sorts. ***El Pueblo Settlement***—featuring ***Olvera Street***, a living, themed remake of a thriving nineteenth-century Mexican plaza—has been around in one form or another since 1781, L.A.'s official birthday.

Start with the ***Plaza de Los Angeles*** and a rest under a ***130-year-old ficus tree,*** which creates thick shade over the circle of benches that surround it. From there make your way to ***Firehouse No. 1,*** an 1884 relic that served as the city's first firehouse as well as a saloon, hotel, and store. The century-old fire-fighting equipment and horse-drawn fire dowser are on view with photos of the day in a free and accessible museum open daily. Then check out ***Pico House*** next door—a formidable Italianate structure as old as the ficus tree that stands as the first "luxury" hotel in Los Angeles (named for the last Mexican governor of California). While the exterior is preserved, the only standing aspect of its former interior grandeur is the staircase. Behind lies the ***Merced Theater,*** 1870, a preserved three-tiered Italianate structure of arched openings and pilasters with a cast-iron balcony off the third floor. The ***Masonic Temple*** next door also reflects the ornate Italianate tastes of the time. Other than lending atmosphere to the plaza, neither building sees much use anymore.

The plaza, however, also is the gateway to Olvera Street, site of the surviving pueblo and the original center of Spanish culture. *Olvera* means "vineyards," which describes the area during the first settlement of Los Angeles in the 1780s, when a ragtag assembly of Africans and mestizos was lead by Spanish conquistadores to this area to build a village in the middle of the floodplain that is now Union Station. The current site, several floods later, is on the plateau of a hill, out of harm's way and home to the last surviving adobe structures from these founding wanderers.

Whether or not you are waylaid by the greasy tacos, overpriced serapes, or photo-with-papier-mâché-burro opportunities that call along the way, do see ***Avila House.*** The adobe tour is quick and free, and besides providing a respite from the Olvera Street crowds in the peaceful courtyard out back, it offers a certain perspective on the area that you can't get anywhere else—one of how slow and peaceful life might have been in L.A. in 1818. Simply furnished, well-preserved rooms cast an eye back 200 years to 1818, while a "zanje" exhibit sheds light on how water was lifted out of the Los Angeles River near what is now Dodger Stadium and sent several miles through a crude aqueduct system to the settlement. 125 Paseo de la Plaza.

Across from Avila is the ***Sepulveda House,*** an 1887 structure housing a visitor center and screening the eighteen-minute film *Pueblo of Promise.* This Victorian building was used as a boardinghouse during the 1880 L.A. land boom, and a bedroom (one of the original fourteen) and kitchen are preserved and on view. The building itself merits mention as an emblem of the transformation beginning to take place at that time, from distinctly Mexican to American architectural designs.

Olvera Street got its start in 1928 and today remains pretty much the same lively, kitschy block it has always been. Though the margaritas may be more mix than spirit and the dishes high in fat but low in taste, the street still lights up at night and offers plenty of great browsing with its lineup of candle shops, hammock stores, pottery and notions spots, and Mexican rug stalls. ***Casa Carolina*** at W21 Olvera Street specializes in velvet paintings, with and without Elvis; ***Casa Bernal*** at W23 is the place to go for serapes, sombreros, and those embroidered cotton blouses. For unusual pottery and masks mixed in with hokey wind chimes and souvenir-issue Mexican rugs, it's ***Casa Sousa*** at W19 Olvera Street.

After filling up on the tastes and colors, head across the plaza to ***La Iglesia de Nuestra Senora La Reina de Los Angeles de Porciuncula*** (Church of Our Lady, Queen of the Angels of Porciuncula) built in 1818, also known as La Placita. The thing to see here is the mosaic placed above the front door in the year of the city's bicentennial, 1981. The elaborate panel of the Annunciation copies a swath of the St. Francis of Assisi's Porciuncula chapel in Italy. A focus of ongoing restoration and modification, the church provides a refreshing outdoor waterfall of flowing holy water and holds regular Masses, mostly in Spanish. Find here the largest Roman Catholic congregation of Latinos in North America. And when it comes to important holidays, don't leave Rover at home: The church is the center site for the sacred blessing of the animals on the Sunday before Easter. The plaza area in front is a crush of pets at that time, from hamsters to horses, seeking the blessings of the Los Angeles Archdiocese.

Babes in Toyland

Los Angeles is the birthplace of the Barbie, the hula hoop, the Mazda Miata, the DC-3, the Fender Stratocaster, the chaise lounge, the space shuttle, and Mickey Mouse.

The church is still known for having been a sacred place for refugees escaping repressive regimes in the El Salvador and Guatemala of the 1980s. Father Luis Olivares tempted fate over and over in sheltering immigrants of the El Norte movement and offering them safety and healing, until he, himself, died of AIDS in 1993, supposedly from a needle used for immunization shots.

From Olvera Street head southwest and into the twenty-first century with a visit to the $300 million masterwork ***Cathedral of Our Lady of the Angels.*** Bordering Hill and Grand Streets along Temple Street, the new cathedral might be considered the Getty of Downtown. It opened its doors in 2002—and that was a feat in itself, because these ***doors,*** made of bronze, weigh 50,000 pounds and need the help of a Rolls-Royce motor.

Crafted to represent a bridge that is traversed to help us in our journey through the ages, they offer carved images of forty ancient pagan symbols as a nod to the forty years the Israelites wandered the deserts, Jesus' forty days in the desert, and the forty days of his ascension after Easter. Each is scored with seven diagonal lines, perhaps suggesting the seven cardinal virtues or the seven sacraments.

Cathedral of Our Lady of the Angels

The terra-cotta-and-alabaster cathedral itself is the latest work by the Madrid-based, Pritzker Prize–winning architect Jose Rafael Moneo. It features a flood of detail, including symbolic engravings and stories in the walls, windows, and doors, and a point to be made in every flow, function, and angle. A ***6,000-crypt mausoleum*** lies beneath for those so impressed with the cathedral they want to stay a while. For others the lure is the ***meditation gardens,*** the art and education exhibitions, the twice-daily Masses celebrated in forty-two languages, the massive, 6,019-pipe organ concerts, or the solving of the numerological symbols found in everything from the doors to the artworks, floors, ceilings, and windows. 555 West Temple Street, (213) 680–5200, www.olacathedral.org.

Just to the east along Temple Street emerges the biggest ***Civic Center*** area outside the nation's capital. With San Pedro and Grand at its north and western borders and First and Temple Streets running south and east, the sprawl is anchored by two veritable icons of film fame: City Hall and the Los Angeles Times building. The ***Los Angeles City Hall*** building, which harks back to 1928, may be better known by the general public than it is by locals for its roles in such black-and-white classics as *War of the Worlds,* the original *Superman,* and the *Dragnet* series. The well-recognized twenty-seventh-floor pyramid-capped tower was, until 1957, the only exception to the city's thirteen-story limit on buildings and still has its Empire State Building wannabe ***observation deck*** on the twenty-sixth floor for the public to amble through and marvel at the early-twentieth-century skyline around them. Floor-to-ceiling windows towering more than 30 feet line the walls beneath an interior frieze that reads, THE CITY CAME INTO BEING TO PRESERVE LIFE. IT EXISTS FOR THE GOOD OF LIFE. Tours are offered on Monday, Wednesday, and Friday from 9:00 A.M. to 1:00 P.M. and take in the Art Deco elevators and elaborate murals of L.A.'s cultural evolution decorating the lobby ***rotunda.*** The floor here is paved in 4,000 pieces of cut marble depicting a Spanish ship in full sail. It's said that the builders used sand from every county in California and water from the wells of each of the state's twenty-one missions. At the opening in 1928, Irving Berlin sang and Calvin Coolidge pressed a key in the White House to light the tower beacon that beamed *L–A* in Morse code until security concerns during World War II stopped the practice. Tours are free and last about thirty minutes. Reservations can be made by calling (213) 978–1995.

Interesting Cathedral Facts

Our Lady of the Angels has some fun measurements:

- *It's 1,000 feet smaller than Notre Dame in Paris.*
- *It's 21 feet higher than the Washington National Cathedral.*
- *It's 32,000 square feet larger than San Francisco's Grace Cathedral.*
- *And it's 1 foot longer than St. Patrick's in New York.*

This final note was not part of the original plans, but topping New York by 1 foot was too much fun to avoid and remains an inside joke even among the clergy.

Across the street enter the ***Los Angeles Times building,*** aka Times-Mirror Square. The modern and Art Deco edifice of 1935 exudes all the prestige that power and ruthlessness could raise at the time. It was built by *Times* founder Harrison Gray Otis and son-in-law Harry Chandler, also known for originating the trend toward unchecked urban sprawl that marks the city today as well as nefarious union-busting practices, water rights manipulation, and public funds profiteering. Tours of the historic building (and its printing plants if curiosity takes over) run three times a day during the week at 9:30 A.M., 11:00 A.M., and 1:30 P.M.; they last about an hour and require reservations a week in advance. The tour that continues from the 1935 structure over to the connected late-century steel-and-glass operation next door also gives heartening insight into the workings of daily journalism through a peek at the different editorial departments and news sections that together put out California's largest daily newspaper. Children must be at least ten years old to join a tour. 201 West First Street; call (213) 237–5000 or (800) LA–TIMES to arrange for this tour and any tours of the company's two printing plants.

Nearby on West First Street, find a wacky world from another time and planet: the ***Bob Baker Marionette Theater.*** Puppet master Bob Baker has been pulling the strings in this uninspiring cinder-block hall for forty years. The theater features nearly a hundred puppets in the shape of bears, penguins, clowns, kids, circus animals, banjo-strumming primates, and space aliens, all set to recorded kitschy music. Shows happen Tuesday through Friday at 10:30 A.M. and weekends at 2:30 P.M. The hour and a quarter of captivating children's entertainment set in a Candy Land ambience of sparkles and stars costs $8.00 to $10.00 and includes a cup of ice cream. 1345 West First Street, (213) 250–9995.

Continuing east on First Street, once again the cityscape changes. Low, slanted roofs, gentle meandering courtyards, a burst of ginkgo trees, and suddenly you're in ***Little Tokyo,*** once a thriving community of 200,000 Japanese Americans and now a dozen blocks or so of sushi bars, tearooms, groceries, and lacquerware stores. Bordered by Third Street to the south, Alameda Street and Central Avenue to the east, First Street to the north, and Los Angeles Street to the west, the hot spots here are not exactly tourist magnets. ***The New Otani Hotel***—the highest structure in the vicinity—is *the* place to go for an expensive evening of fine Japanese sushi, tempura, and teppan grill at ***A Thousand Cranes.*** The dining room overlooks the hotel's fourth-floor ***Japanese roof garden,*** a tranquil gem that is open to the public. The restaurant is also known for its Sunday brunch, a lavish Japanese-American buffet served with champagne for $27 inclusive. The property also offers several Japanese-style suites with shoji screens and deep soaking tubs that overlook the roof garden. 120 Los Angeles Street, (213) 629–1200, www.newotani.com.

Another Japanese garden to note is ***James Irvine Garden*** or Seiryu-en (Garden of the Clear Stream) at the ***Japanese American Cultural Center***—an oasis of beauty and meditation in a sunken garden along a three-part stream. At the top, the water is turbulent, as were the times endured by the issei or Japanese immigrants. In the middle, the stream divides, as did this population's relationships and loyalties with the United States during World War II. In the end, the stream flows to a calm finish. Hours are Tuesday through Friday noon to 5:00 P.M. and weekends, 11:00 A.M. to 4:00 P.M. 244 South San Pedro, (213) 628–2725.

Around the corner at 315 First Street is the oldest store that has been in continuous operation in Little Tokyo: ***Fugetso So.*** This sweets shop, founded in 1913, is run by the grandson of the original owner, Seiichi Kito. As a bonus, the block where the store is operating, between San Pedro and Central, is also a designated National Historic Landmark and one of the few blocks in L.A. that has carefully preserved its row of turn-of-the-twentieth-century buildings.

Two museums in this area are worth a detour. The ***Japanese American National Museum,*** housed in the converted 1925 Nishi Hongwanji Temple, is the only museum in America dedicated to the issei experience. The Japanese were brought here by Henry Huntington in 1903 to lay tracks for the Pacific Electric Railway, and were later joined by thousands more fleeing the heightened racial tensions in San Francisco following that city's 1906 earthquake. The museum's collections include 15,000 photographs, movies, manuscripts, and objects from the original immigrations and subsequent internment camps, all put to use in revolving presentations on particular aspects of this volatile history. You'll also find a bookstore and gift shop with unusual folk art and focus. Hours are Tuesday through Sunday 10:00 A.M. to 5:00 P.M., and Friday from 11:00 A.M. to 8:00 P.M. with a $6.00 admission (free the third Friday of each month). 369 East First Street, (213) 625–0414.

The second museum is the ***Geffen Museum of Contemporary Art (MOCA)***—or, as the locals like to say, the Temporary Contemporary. Part of the larger ***Museum of Contemporary Art*** at the California Plaza, MOCA was intended to be used as a temporary facility while the permanent one was being built a few blocks away. But this is L.A., and little happens without at least a modicum of fanfare and star power. So in came renowned architect Frank Gehry to take what was a hardware store and police garage in the heart of Little Tokyo and convert it to a world-class exhibition space. And with a little help from movie mogul David Geffen, the building is now a museum in its own right with freewheeling mini to mega installations by twentieth-century artists. If you don't have time to take in the exhibits, make time to take on the gift shop, a repository for unusual, creative, and artful jewelry, crafts, and notions you won't find anywhere else. Hours are Tuesday through Sunday 11:00 A.M. to 5:00 P.M., and Thursday 11:00 A.M. to 8:00 P.M. Admission is $8.00 and is good for both MOCA museums; free every Thursday from 5:00 to 8:00 P.M. 152 North Central Avenue, (213) 621–2766.

Look upward toward the setting sun and you'll see the now shaved heights of L.A.'s Downtown at ***Bunker Hill.*** This was once the stomping grounds of the white-gloved set and crowned with sprawling Victorian residential spreads and elegant hotels. To carry its well-heeled residents up the hill from Hill and Third Streets, a sort of elevator was created—the ***Angel's Flight*** funicular, actually—and it continued ferrying folks from the lower plains to the heights for sixty-eight years until it stopped service in 1969. "A leveling of the levels" took place in the 1980s during the same building boom that created the smashing skyline of Downtown, with its skyward glass-and-concrete shapes in odd angles and cascading circles dwarfing the lower echelons of ziggurat and Art Deco rooftops. The funicular, clearly a focal point of Bunker Hill, was torn down and reassembled a few yards away in 1996, but closed again in recent years following a fatal accident. The 25-cent rides up the hill are expected to resume sometime in 2004.

For the view, check out the rotating cocktail lounge at ***L.A. Prime*** on the thirty-fifth floor of the ***Westin Bonaventure,*** with its much-filmed indoor atrium overlooked by glass-tower hotel accommodations. The view of Downtown L.A. is complete and romantic enough to average a marriage proposal a day from a window seat, as reported by hotel staff. 404 South Figueroa Street (see also page 25 for a hotel description).

At ground level the ***Spanish Steps*** are a bustling place to watch the noontime office parade or read a book. The promenade links the ***Library Tower*** (the tallest building west of the Mississippi at a fifth of a mile in the air) with ***Wells Fargo Plaza*** and the adjacent ***Watercourt*** near the hill's Fifth Street boundary with L.A.'s ***lower Financial District.*** The step path is also a stream that leads into soft shaded pools and sculptures and is surrounded by courtyards. In the summer months concerts, performance art, and festivals transform the area from a deserted business district after 5:00 P.M. into a hot spot for local arts and international music.

Within this area lies an offbeat and underutilized museum in the bowels of Wells Fargo Plaza, which fills the block between Third and Fourth Streets: the ***Wells Fargo Museum.*** The big thing here is the stagecoach—an original from the 1850s when Henry Wells and William Fargo teamed up to serve the communications and banking needs of the mother lode pioneers and founded American Express. A seventeen-minute video of Wells Fargo's part in the settling of the West, an animated audiotape of a journal left by a twenty-one-year-old British traveler in 1859 taking the stage between St. Louis and San Francisco, plenty of documents under glass, and some renderings of the way things were shed light on just what it took to transport money and goods across a hostile and seemingly endless expanse 150 years ago. Admission is free and spans banking hours. 333 South Grand Avenue, (213) 253–7166.

If banks are your thing, the ***Federal Reserve Bank,*** L.A. branch, about four blocks away at Ninth and Grand, may be just the ticket. Here you can indulge in managing the money supply and setting fiscal policy as you would have it without fear of getting fired by the White House. The principles of money supply, M1 and M2, unemployment, inflation, tax-and-spend habits, and growth restraint are all explained in user-friendly interactive computer exhibits geared toward kids and their parents. In addition, take a free tour of the Fed on Monday, Wednesday, and Friday at 10:00 A.M. or 1:00 P.M. Reservations required. 950 South Grand Avenue, (213) 683–2904.

Culture Sightings

California Plaza *presents free concerts at noon and (usually) on Thursday evening during the warm months. The fountains that submerge the plaza recede to expose a sophisticated soundstage surrounded by a seating arena of granite benches. Performers ranging from famous African juju bands to classical quartets deliver first-rate shows for free. 350 South Grand, (213) 687–7159, www.grandperformances.org.*

Walking south between Third and Eighth Streets, Downtown L.A. becomes New York in the 1930s, Mexico City's Zona Rosa of today, and the Golden Era of Hollywood all wrapped in one bustling, pigeon-packed, wedding-dress-and-diamond-bazaar-filled package that could be the setting for *Seinfeld, NYPD Blue,* and *Rush Hour II* all at the same time. This is L.A.'s historic core if ever there was one, and a microcosm of its cultural core at its mercantile essence. The American Dream started here with the better-life promises made by the real estate hustlers of the 1900s trying to sell orange groves and sunshine to burned-out midwestern farmers, and it continues today in a phalanx of languages, foods, herbs, clothes, music, and luxuries squeezed into aging office buildings and warehouses and sold by newly arrived immigrants giving it all they've got.

Here you'll find the largest concentration of once grand movie palaces in the world. Still called the ***Great White Way*** (west), the relics that were once the ***Million Dollar Theater, United Artists Theater,*** the ***Tower Theater, The Orpheum, The Palace,*** and ***The State*** have all been closed and boarded up for a good forty years now, looking for a buyer or cache of redevelopment funds. Walking tours through the ***L.A. Conservancy*** ($8.00 a person, 213–623–2489, www.laconservancy.org) or through a ninety-minute, well-narrated program with ***Red Line Tours*** ($20.00, 323–402–1074, www.redlinetours.com) are the only way to get behind the velvet rope and in front of the velvet curtain in these entertainment halls. They lie waiting in a state of grace, like Miss Havisham's wedding cake, with little altered beyond the dust and cobwebs. Springy seats with no room to spare between rows (were people that much shorter back then?) still have underseat hatracks. Art Deco plumes outline ladies' room doors, while Merlot-hued velvet lobby furnishings, crystal chandeliers, and grand staircases are still intact.

One theater that is still open for business is ***The Mayan Theater*** at 1038 South Hill Street between Eleventh Street and Olympic Boulevard. Seven Mayan priests look down on you from above when you enter. Pre-Columbian kitsch at its finest, this 1927 structure's brightly painted cast-concrete facade and interiors are reminiscent of an excavated Mayan tomb. In 1989, the theater was turned into an elaborate nightclub and concert hall that still rocks. If you get hungry, ***Tony's Burger*** across the street grills patties in a 1932 log cabin structure. Call (213) 746–4287.

While the Great White Way theaters work their Art Deco, Beaux-Arts, and Baroque magic along the cityscape from Broadway and Third to Ninth Streets, where the United Artists Theater stands, the scene at sidewalk level is just as intense. A quick segue into the ***Bradbury Building*** (304 South Broadway, 213–626–1893), brings you to 1893 and the recognizable background to dozens of movies, most notably *Bladerunner.* Inside is a lobby atrium of five flights, with a caged elevator to take you up. Architect George Wyman, it is said, consulted a Ouija board to discuss the project with his dead brother before taking on the job. The result was a masterpiece that has been preserved as part of L.A. lore and—true to the word of the Ouija board—Wyman's only significant

The Biddy That Could

*B**iddy Mason Park** is a little oasis in the midst of the bustle of the Broadway marketplaces. With myriad metal sculptures and water designs created by UCLA artists and comfortable park benches on which to sit, the park offers a tree-shaded sojourn into art and a little bit of history. It's all about Biddy Mason, an African American woman who was born a slave in 1818 in the plantation south. She walked from her home in deep Mississippi with her Mormon master and the three daughters she gave him. The 2,000-mile journey landed them first in Utah and then in California, which unbeknownst to her master had been admitted to the Union in 1850 as a free state. Biddy won freedom for herself and her daughters and moved to Los Angeles to work as a midwife and nurse. After saving up for ten years she bought the very site of the park with $250 and became one of the first black women to own land in Los Angeles. In 1884 she sold a piece of the land for $1,500 and began developing an empire of commercial real estate with the remainder that amounted to a worth of more than $300,000 by the time she died in 1891. 331 South Spring Street.*

work, but a crowning one. The building continues to house offices, including Red Line Tours, but also contains the ***A + D Architecture and Design Museum*** (213–620–9961, www.aplusd.com), a two-room exhibit space that keeps snapshots of twenty-first-century design along the walls to maintain a continuous flow of thought about L.A. design plans for the future.

Salsa on the Side

For the best burritos in Downtown, check out the **Taco House,** *serving up every kind of burrito and taco imaginable from its order window since 1962. The stand is next to Grand Central Market's second entrance on Hill Street and provides a no-hassle breakfast or lunch with a quiet and shaded patio for the price of a latte at any cafe—and at 85 cents, the coffee is a bargain, too. 340 South Hill Street, (213) 625–2700.*

A few steps south on Broadway, find the true soul of Downtown's present at ***Grand Central Market.*** The warehouse-sized space is the great Angeleno kitchen with stalls upon stalls of burritos, tostados, and even a tortilla factory, surrounded by today's (and yesterday's) produce, all manner of unrecognizable fried morsels served up in paper, herbs in Español that cure anything from gout to gonorrhea, tamarind and horchado juice stands, and even a diner counter area for fast and dripping Chinese food. The push through the throngs is worth it if only for the people-peeping and eye entertainment. The market was established in 1917, and little has changed but the food choice and faces.

Another down-and-in lunch spot not to miss is the scene at ***Clifton's Cafeteria.*** This bilevel chow chamber is part national park kitsch, part Disney nightmare, part Grandma's house with fake squirrels, taxidermied deer, stuffed moose, and faux waterfalls. Stretch out in a sort of picnic table plastic forest full of Astroturf and synthetic foliage as you dine on hot, mushy buttered peas and mounds of from-the-flake mashed potatoes. They still serve up the best hot, cheap cafeteria meals in the city—if canned vegetables, meat loaf, and grilled chicken legs aren't a problem. The restaurant was first established by a Salvation Army officer in 1931 as a puritan dining establishment. The philosophy continues, artfully written up in a little monthly pamphlet you can find in the entrance called "Food for Thot." 648 Broadway, (213) 627–1673.

Make your way past the cheap electronics boutiques, the polyester wedding dress parlors, and the gold-plated jewelry windows to ***Pershing Square,*** bordering Fifth and Hill Streets. This is as close as Downtown L.A. comes to a town square and provides access to the subway's Red Line and parking. At ground level a number of modern artwork displays and fountains make this a good resting spot and bridge between the cultures of historic Broadway and the more upscale Jewelry District to the south. The park design by Mexico City architect Ricardo Legoretta might

Mall Art

Seventh Avenue Market Place*—also known as 7th + Fig, because it abuts Figueroa—is a three-level subterranean shopping mall with a soul. You may find fashion and fancy at Macy's and Robinsons-May here, but you'll also find a grassy park one flight above street level. Known as Poet's Walk, it's adorned with poetry and artwork.*

be recognizable in some Mexico City establishments, such as the Camino Real Hotel, but in L.A. his contemporary shapes and colors are bunched with turn-of-the-twentieth-century bronze statues and sculptures from World War I.

Across from Pershing Square is the grande dame of L.A. accommodations, the eighty-year-old ***Millennium Biltmore Hotel,*** home of the original Academy Awards and one of the last places visited by the Black Dahlia, focus of a still-unsolved murder on the dockets since 1947. A tour of the hotel reveals the original Renaissance and Churrigueresque murals and ceiling designs by Giovanni Smiraldi, and some interesting extras: a lobby-level ballroom containing a secret door to a speakeasy joint in between the walls and a quick escape to the sidewalk, as well as secret panels within the walls of the top suite to hide and store liquor. The pool, featured in the film *Bugsy,* among others, is a soft-sung gem. The indoor, Olympic-sized pool room is in its original Beaux-Arts-inspired design with its nod to Pompeii in blue terra-cotta tiles. 506 South Grand Street, (213) 624–1011, www.millennium-hotels.com.

Across from the Biltmore on its Grand Street side lies the ***Hilton Checkers*** in a century-old tower built by Chinese laborers concerned about the location's bad luck. Originally a dead-end street, this spot's feng shui was so bad that the superstitious builders added a large mirror over the door to dissuade undesirable spirits from entering. That mirror gets missed by the untrained eye but is still there, large and looming in its original spot over the entrance in a strange segue from the rest of the building design. 535 Grand Street, (213) 624–0000, www.checkershotel.com.

From the upper floors of the Checkers you can see east to the golden pyramid of the ***Los Angeles Central Library*** at Fifth and Flower Streets—square one for those researching their family genealogy. The original building harks back to the early 1920s and borrows from Egyptian, Roman, Byzantine, Spanish, and Moorish styles to make its crossroads-of-learning point. From exterior to interior to the modern addition built after a 1986 fire, all is art, space, meditation, and beauty in this unlikely spot. A dozen murals in the ***second-floor rotunda*** describe the sordid and glorious history of California. Other murals in the ***children's wing*** and the ***history wing*** relate episodes in history and literature. Outdoor gardens designed in the English, Mediterranean, and Islamic traditions provide quiet respite for reading. Unlike other

Los Angeles Central Library

public libraries, however, this one comes with a gift shop bearing an impressive collection of hard-to-find California- and Los Angeles–focused literature and texts as well as humorous and art-quality novelty items. The new wing is eight stories of glass and open space, known locally as the Grand Canyon of Books. From time to time the library presents world-class exhibits, such as the *Pop-up Book* exhibit installed by Frank Gehry, which offered an enchanting selection of pop-up books from all over the world, printed and cut over the last two centuries. 630 West Fifth Street, (213) 228–7000, www.lapl.org.

While the library's exhibits are usually free, dining alfresco on California-French fusion cuisine in its patio gardens or in the glass encasement of its ***Café Pinot*** can be a costly—but magical—experience. The cafe is hosted by master chef and restaurateur Joachim Splichal and is a gastronomic take-in whether for take-out sandwiches or his latest treatment of foie gras. 700 West Fifth Street, (213) 239–6500.

Just down the street find a little-known, inexpensive, and fun eatery that's also full of chances for celebrity sightings. This is ***Flix Café*** at the ***Los Angeles Center Studios.*** The cafeteria-commissary is used by one of the busiest film studios in L.A. The studio itself is not open to the public, but Flix Café is, and alongside the salad bar, fresh grill, deli counter, homemade soups, and pizzas you're likely to spot hungry film and TV stars on break from the next *Terminator* sequel or *NYPD Blue.* The cafe is open Monday through Friday 8:30 A.M. to 2:30 P.M. 1201 West Fifth Street (at Bixel Avenue going west from Downtown), (213) 534–3000, www.lacenterstudios.com.

For a little more class, there's ***The Pacific Dining Car.*** This is one of Downtown L.A.'s odder venues—a plush and upscale restaurant in an old train car in the middle of a parking lot, all set in a district perhaps better known for crack deals than veal chops. But the velvet-and-vinyl establishment has been at it since 1921 serving Filet Oscar and Roquefort Steak to royalty, gamblers, garment magnates, and rogue politicians looking for privacy, big plates, a martini atmosphere, and upper-crusty waiters. The car itself is the last of a breed—the only remaining nod to the California Red Car days, when the streets were filled with trolleys running along tracks that extended 1,200 miles around the southland. Open twenty-four hours, moon or shine, seven days. 1310 West Sixth Street, (213) 483–6000.

Back in central Downtown, the ***Jewelry District*** starts on Fifth and Hill Streets and resembles a modern gold souk in Abu Dhabi, with prices that are good enough to match. Blocks of aging high-rise office buildings house some 60,000 jewelers, mostly from Eastern Europe and the Middle East. Commercial rooms with endless counters handle the wholesale and retail sales and easy repairs. Discounts from regular retailers average about 70 percent for good customers, though diamonds can be the real bargain if you know what you're doing. Most merchants are certified gemologists and can provide proof that the item of interest has been certified by the Gemological Institute of America (GIA) or European Gemological Institute (EGI). The seller should note in writing the properties of the Four C's: color, clarity, cut, and carat weight, and if there is a name attached to the finished piece of jewelry, who is the designer. Unlike shops in the Middle East, items are sold by the piece, not the weight, but a minor amount of bargaining is tolerated.

Another dining attraction that incorporates plenty of Deco-dappled eye candy is ***Cicada,*** located in the ***Oviatt Building.*** The circa-1928 former haberdashery still bears all the emblems of its former beauty, from oak-lined walls and shelves to intricate René Lalique glass-work details and even an elevator that goes up to the top two floors, where the original owner had a bilevel penthouse now used for parties. Cicada is among L.A.'s most exclusive dining establishments, with northern Italian delicacies served in an opulent spread of overstuffed couches and Italian landscape murals. A visit here, however, is mostly an excuse to admire Art Deco design in its original and preserved grandeur. 617 Olive Street, (213) 288–9488.

Before you hoof southward toward the designer bargains of the Garment District, head around the corner at Fifth Street and Grand Avenue to ***Caravan Books,*** open Monday through Saturday. On the endangered list of independent bookstores, this is the top source for both old and current literature on California and Los Angeles history and culture. Call (213) 626–0044.

The L.A. Fashion District begins at Seventh and Los Angeles Streets and sprawls fingerlike for some eighty-three blocks and alleyways. Make a quick first stop at the ***Museum of Neon Art (MONA),*** straddling Ninth Street and Olympic Boulevard with an entrance on Hope. The $5.00 entrance fee gets you into a space that is forever ticking, scratching, blinking, sighing, and exploding with kinetic color. Preserved signage from the 1960s shares space with new and retro creations, all leading to a clever and imaginative gift shop selling $18 touch-sensitive blinking pins (battery included), original luminescent pottery, and plastic rocket lamps. 501 West Olympic Boulevard, (213) 489–9918.

Finally you're ready to step into what is a strange combination of New York's Seventh Street, Beverly Hills' Rodeo Drive, Mexico City's Zona Rosa, and Morocco's Marrakech bazaar. ***Los Angeles's Fashion District*** (213–488–1153, fashiondistrict.org) runs up Eighth Street to the north, Twelfth Street to the south, Main Street to the west, and Maple Avenue to the east, housing 10,000 clothing brands and 15,000 showrooms in between. The catchphrase here is *Fashion Forward* and the area's four design marts deliver on that promise, presenting and selling at rock-bottom prices—to retailers only—what the finer department stores will be featuring on their floors in seasons to come. But on secret Saturdays and scattered days during the week, these same showrooms open their doors to the public, giving you the chance to buy at wholesale rates and get a leg up on what the world will be wearing in a few months. All the name brands are here: Guess, Gucci, Prada, Fendi . . . and all their knock-offs are here as well, selling briskly. A Kate Spade bag by any other name still looks like a Kate Spade, and even though the fashion police make their raids with uncompromising regularity, the merchants do well despite the laws.

The locals know the territory—where to go for $10 Hawaiian shirts and where to go for authentic Versace jeans at 70 percent off department store prices. Showrooms in the ***Cooper Building, CalMart, California Mart,*** and ***New Mart*** serve as the core of the district and present fashion's crème de la crème in what is now the largest clothing mart in the United States. But boutiques along Santee Street between Eleventh and Pico provide the secret selling spots for St. Johns knits, Carole Little, Calvin Klein, Armani, and other upscale clothing brands. For petites and plus-sizes, it's Wall Street; for designer jeans, it's Los Angeles Street between Twelfth and Fifteenth. Need shoes? Check out Olympic and Main. Kids' clothes? Pico and Wall. Into leather? Look to Los Angeles Street between Olympic and Eleventh. Perfumes? Go to Seventh and Los Angeles Street.

The Fashion District runs Saturday tours on an irregular basis; these are well worth the time if you hit it right. A trolley circles the area, while two shopping experts tell you what's what. (Call the Fashion District for times: 213–488–1153.) In addition, the four primary design buildings that anchor the district with designs for major national couturiers open their doors to the public on the last Friday of the month starting at 8:00 A.M. for sales on sample items. It's possible to get a $400 blouse from Nicole Miller for $40 or a designer accessory for a fraction of its retail worth.

The district is nearly 90 percent ma-and-pa stores, run mostly by immigrants from the Middle East and Asia, and four-fifths of the merchandise to be found is women's wear or women's accessories. But it all mixes with menswear, electronics, plastic toys, and the tastes, sounds, and smells of Mexico at "The Alley."

Santee Alley is anything but L.A. It is a writhing, pushing, crowded, colorful mass of human shopping passion; it is every chaotic street market in the world, and if you see something you like, you grab it off the rack and buy it. Trying it on is not an option—though at $10 for a pair of khakis or track shorts, it may be well worth the risk. The snacks of mango with chili and lime are worth the risk as well.

Lofty Plans

In an effort to revitalize the Downtown area of L.A., public and private partnerships are busy at work renovating the broken-down buildings of the 1920s and 1930s in core commercial areas and turning them into luxury artists' lofts—with rents starting at $1,200.

The Fashion District is a cash-and-carry market to the public. Bring your dollars, your shopping cart, and your sun hat. It's a fun day, and a safe one—plenty of foot and bicycle patrols around. Come here early enough (like 5:00 A.M.), and you can also witness the ***Los Angeles Flower Mart*** in full swing. The clearinghouse for all the flowers sold in this city happens daily (except Sunday) in an overflowing warehouse on Wall Street between Seventh and Eighth Streets, usually winding down around 10:00 A.M. on weekdays and noon on Saturday. After that it can be a French toast breakfast at ***Angelique*** (840 Spring Street, 213–623–8698), coffee at the ***Coffee Bean and Tea Leaf*** (210 East Olympic, 213–749–5746), or a snack from any of the seventy international dining and refreshment spots in the area.

Moving westward, check out ***The Pantry*** at 877 South Figueroa Street—the prison food capital of the city. Currently owned by L.A.'s former mayor Richard Riordan, The Pantry has been serving meat loaf and mashed potatoes to L.A. fat cats since 1924—on the same tables and chairs, at the same linoleum bar, and using the same rounded ceramic dishware. Only the prices have changed: A New York strip with mashed carbs now costs $13.95. Breakfast is served around the clock. There are no menus; all specials—such as they are—appear in heavy chalked script on a blackboard in the back. It's all at Nineth and Figueroa, two blocks north of the Los Angeles Convention Center. Never closed. Never without a customer. Don't bother to call.

Continuing on a southwest-angled tack from central Downtown, consider a stop at ***Exposition Park*** across the street from the University of Southern California at the confluence of Figueroa and Jefferson Boulevard. The sprawling twenty-five-acre site dates back to 1872, when it operated as an agricultural fairground. The central egress is lined with imported palms planted for the 1932 Summer Olympics held at the ***Memorial Coliseum,*** also located here. This venue has hosted the 1959 baseball World Series, two Super Bowls, and the 1984 Summer Olympics as well.

The Classical–Art Deco structure was built in 1923, and although it holds 106,000 people, it's rarely used these days. Rather, visitors pay the $6.00 all-day parking fees and spend their time on the grounds, where fairs are often held and several museums cluster.

Outside, the pulling attraction is the Rose Garden, free for the wandering and offering 150 varieties of its namesake bloom amid gazebos and marble fountains.

Adjacent to the garden is the solid 1913 Spanish Revival edifice that is the ***Natural History Museum of L.A. County.*** Inside is a veritable Smithsonian-quality layout of exhibits detailing the earth's evolution starting four and a half billion years ago. Skulls and skeletons of dinosaurs, ice age mammal dioramas, gems and mineral interpretive cases, and even a preserved Megamouth—a 14.5-foot shark that is the world's rarest—are the stuff of this museum. Bugs are big here, too, with a butterfly pavilion, intermittent bug fairs, and a well-stocked insect zoo. It costs $8.00 and is open daily. 900 Exposition Boulevard, (213) 763–DINO, www.nhm.org.

Next door along the park promenade is the ***California Science Center,*** where the gift shop alone is worth the visit. Admission to the museum is free, although special exhibitions and IMAX admissions are not. See fantastical kinetic sculptures of DNA helixes and something called a hyperbolic parabola as well as an up-close lesson in interactive anatomy in a celebrated exhibit called *Gertie's Guts.* The museum is dedicated to active learning and interactivity; most exhibits are hands-on in some way and able to be shared with family members. The science of life and reproduction can be found on the second floor in the permanent *World of Life* exhibit, which features such entertaining elements as a drop-in surgical theater and a busy chick hatchery. *Creative World* focuses on what life can do, including human innovation and advancement in transportation, communications, and invention. Across from the museum is the IMAX Theater, designed by Frank Gehry and a treasure trove of amusement. The theater's screen measures seven stories in height and 90 feet in width with six-channel digital surround sound and technology that masters 3D projection and clarity. The 1.5-kilowatt xenon projector lamp is bright enough that if it were located on the moon and facing earth, it would be easily visible to the naked eye. Admission costs $7.50, with revolving features. Like the museums in the park, the IMAX runs shows daily. Call (213) 744–7400 or (323) SCIENCE (323–724–3623), or visit www.casciencectr.org, for information on the science museum or IMAX.

Just past Exposition Park where Jefferson Boulevard meets Crenshaw Boulevard is L.A.'s own ***Catfish Row.*** Several soul food restaurants clustered along a four-block strip serve up some of the best barbecue in the business in a casual, friendly ambience. These include ***Steve's on the Strip*** (3403 Crenshaw, 323–734–5975) for oxtail gumbo and black-eyed peas; ***Tasty Q Barbecue*** (2959 Crenshaw Boulevard, 323–735–8325), a drive-through or walk-in establishment that specializes in ribs; ***Louisiana Pete's*** (3701 West Jefferson, 323–735–7470), for supreme sausage; ***Mel's Fish Market*** (4046 West Jefferson, 323–735–7220), where "U-Buy, We Fry" is the motto; and my own favorite: ***The Kobbler King*** (3622 West Jefferson Boulevard, 323–721–9286). The King creates individual-sized cobblers in thick, rich crusts that contain saucy seafood, veggie, or chicken interiors. But the Cajun, Jack Daniels, and spicy honey barbecue chicken fingers are truly addicting.

Places to Stay Downtown

Luxe: $250+
Deluxe: $150–$249
Good deal: $79–$149

The Downtown L.A. Standard
550 South Flower Street, (213) 892–8080.
This is Downtown's newest hotel and a work of deft design by owner Andre Balazs, who took an abandoned office building and put it to good use. Interiors are très chic and simple with modular sofas, international music, and a rooftop pool and bar scene that is second to none in the City of Angels. Deluxe.

Figueroa Hotel
939 South Figueroa Street, (213) 627–8971, www.figueroahotel.com.
One of the city's unsung gems, the Figueroa harks back to 1925. It features a Moroccan lobby that's more Tangiers than L.A. and a series of large, high-ceilinged rooms in Moorish Deco supporting a celebrated, bougainvillea-filled rooftop pool. Some rooms come with a kitchenette. It's located close to the L.A. Convention Center and the twenty-four-hour Pantry cafe. Good deal.

Author's Favorite Places to Stay Downtown

Millennium Biltmore Hotel
506 South Grand Avenue
(213) 624–1011
(see page 18 for more information)

Westin Bonaventure
404 South Figueroa Street
(213) 624–1000
(see page 14 for more information)

New Otani Hotel & Garden
120 Los Angeles Street
(213) 629–1200
(see page 12 for more information)

Westin Bonaventure Hotel
404 South Figueroa Street, (213) 624–1000, www.westin.com.
This is easily Downtown's largest four-star hotel, with 1,354 rooms in five 35-story glass towers (and glass elevators to match). A dramatic six-level atrium overlooks a five-story shopping gallery and one-acre indoor lake. The beds are among the most comfortable in the city. Deluxe.

Places to Eat Downtown

Expensive: $25.00+
Reasonable: $15.00–$24.00
Bargain: $8.00–$14.00

Café Pinot
700 West Fifth Street, (213) 239–6500, www.patinagroup.com.
California French cuisine by Joachim Splichal in a Moorish garden on the grounds of Los Angeles Central Library. Reasonable. See page 20 for more information.

CBS Seafood
700 North Spring Street, (213) 617–2323.
Classic Chinese in a modern, design-conscious setting. The midday Dim Sum is excellent, and the Hong Kong–style dinner menu with Shark's Fin Soup and crispy Peking Duck get the buzz. Bargain.

Cicada Restaurant and Bar
617 South Olive Street, (213) 488–9488, www.cicadarestaurant.com.
Dine in style here—1930s style, that is, in the amazing Art Deco surroundings of a former fashion haberdashery. The menu is northern Italian and northern California. Soups are a daily specialty, with simplicity at the source. Expensive. See page 21 for more information.

Ciudad
445 South Figueroa Street, (213) 486–5171, www.millikenand feniger.com.
Fun is Ciudad. Latin music fills the dining room as patrons sip on rum drinks. Dining is creative Spanish, Miami, and south of the border—at times very south—from Central American seviches to Argentine empanadas and all with the famed twists of L.A.'s "Two Hot Tamales," Sue Milliken and Susan Feniger. Expensive.

Clifton's Cafeteria
648 Broadway, (213) 627–1673.
Bargain. See page 17 for more information.

Empress Pavilion
988 North Hill Street (at Bernard Street in Bamboo Plaza), (213) 617–9898.
Empress Pavilion brings on the dragons, the freshwater aquarium with hapless catfish, and all the pomp and circumstance of a large and atmospheric Chinese restaurant in the heart of Chinatown. Specialties are Dim Sum and fresh seafood—but be prepared to wait for a table. Bargain.

Engine Co. No. 28
644 South Figueroa Street, (213) 624–6996, www.engineco.com.
The scene is an authentic 1912 firehouse saved from urban overlay and preserving all but the alarms. Even the original brick, pressed-tin ceiling, and fire pole are in place. Comfort food is king in this all-American restaurant, whether you're sitting in a white-clothed booth or at the classic wooden bar. Bargain.

Epicentre Restaurant
200 South Hill Street (in the Kawada Hotel), (213) 625–0000, www.kawadahotel.com.
This is a watering hole and feedlot to the working press and those they source. The food is fine, fun, and affordable with a thinking man's menu of fusion dishes. Reasonable.

Flix Café
1201 West Fifth Street, (213) 534–3000.
Bargain. See page 20 for more information.

Frying Fish
120 Japanese Village Plaza (in Little Tokyo), (213) 680–0567.
Frying Fish serves sushi prepared to your order. The restaurant has just twenty-nine seats, all of which are set around a circular sushi "conveying" bar counter that winds its way among the diners as they pick and choose from the fresh and constantly replenished options. Bargain.

Market Place Restaurant
1102 Lawrence Street (one block east of Eighth Street and Alameda), (213) 622–7285.
This spot opens at 4:00 A.M. and is way off the beaten path in the heart of the Produce District. Cuisine is inexpensive and runs the gamut from pizzas with crusts made from scratch to al dente pastas, fresh catches, and gourmet breakfasts. Bargain.

Oiwake
122 Japanese Village Plaza Mall, (213) 628–2678, www.oiwake.com.
You can't go wrong with unabashed karaoke and sushi for under $5.00. A buffet of noodles and hot and cold dishes runs until 9:00 P.M. and costs $8.00. Bargain.

Pacific Grill
601 South Figueroa Street (in Sanwa Bank Plaza), (213) 485–0927, www.paradise restaurants.com.
Pacific Grill is lunch for people in suits—usually the lawyers, bankers, and politicians with offices in the area. But the food is imaginative and California at its core, served in serene surroundings and often with soft piano accompaniment. Expensive.

The Pantry
877 South Figueroa Street.
Bargain. See page 23 for more information.

Philippe's Original Sandwich Shoppe
1001 Alameda Street, (213) 628–3781.
Bargain. See page 4 for more information.

R23
923 East Second Street, Suite 109, (213) 687–7178.
Opened nearly eleven years ago, R23 is a staple for sushi lovers in these parts. It sits in a difficult-to-find ware-

Author's Favorite Places to Eat Downtown

The Pacific Dining Car
1310 West Sixth Street
(213) 483–6000
(see page 20 for more information)

Yang Chow
819 North Broadway
(213) 625–0811
(see page 5 for more information)

Traxx
800 North Alameda Street
(213) 525–1999
(see page 4 for more information)

R23
923 East Second Street
(213) 687–7178

house in the Arts District, and serves eye-catching dishes that are as much art as gourmet. Chef's specials change daily and are the ones to watch. Reasonable.

A Thousand Cranes
120 Los Angeles Street, (213) 253–9255.
Expensive. See page 12 for more information.

Water Grill
544 South Grand Avenue, (213) 891–0900, www.kingsseafood.com.
Paradise found for fish lovers. The trademark raw bar only adds to the appeal of dining, which takes place in a blond-wood-paneled space of simple sleek lines and comfort. Specialties to note here are the seafood platter, clam chowder, jonah crab salad, and bluefin tuna tartare. Expensive.

Yang Chow
819 North Broadway, (213) 625–0811.
Yang Chow, at the entrance to Chinatown, is high on service, moderate on atmosphere, and over the top on taste. It serves superb Mandarin-Szechwan cuisine but is best known for its dish of Slippery Shrimp, a crispy honey-and-batter-caked treatment that can become addicting. Bargain.

The Wilshire Corridor

The history of L.A. sprawl begins with the Wilshire Corridor. Downtown Los Angeles began inching west into the ranches and bean fields that defined the land beyond the town at the turn of the twentieth century. While prehistoric mammoths and saber-toothed cats ran paths between the inland areas and the tar pits at La Brea 10,000 years ago, the Yang-Na Indians settled at the Los Angeles River and cut the formal swath to the tar pits in more recent history.

The path eventually became the Camino Viejo or Old Road during the pueblo settlements of the 1790s and the path of speculation for the land boom-and-bust years a century later.

Then along came a daring young petroleum magnate with a Marxist bent in 1885, and the corridor was created. Henry Gaylord Wilshire was a man with a vision—to link Downtown Los Angeles with the ocean with a line of commercial purpose. He bought a thirty-five-acre site around what is now MacArthur Park, turned what was a dump into a city park, and made plans for developing the land around it.

The gesture prompted families to move out of the city, tracks for the electric trolley to move west, and a movement of California architecture to take shape. By the 1920s Los Angeles was turning into the quintessential linear city, with commercial districts extending as far west as Western Avenue, beyond which a rolling sprawl of bungalows and bean fields took over. A history of urban design unfolds along this line, starting with Downtown's grand Beaux-Arts-meets-Mission styles, then moving on to the ornate Deco, Egyptian, and pre-Columbian Revivals of the 1920s; the neon explosion of the 1930s; the WPA Streamline and Classical Moderne structures of the late 1930s; the eye-catching kitsch of the late 1930s and 1940s; and finally the steel-and-glass high-rises of the 1950s and 1960s.

The Wilshire Corridor continues to serve the city as its most commercial and centralized east–west street and offers a good place to start in any

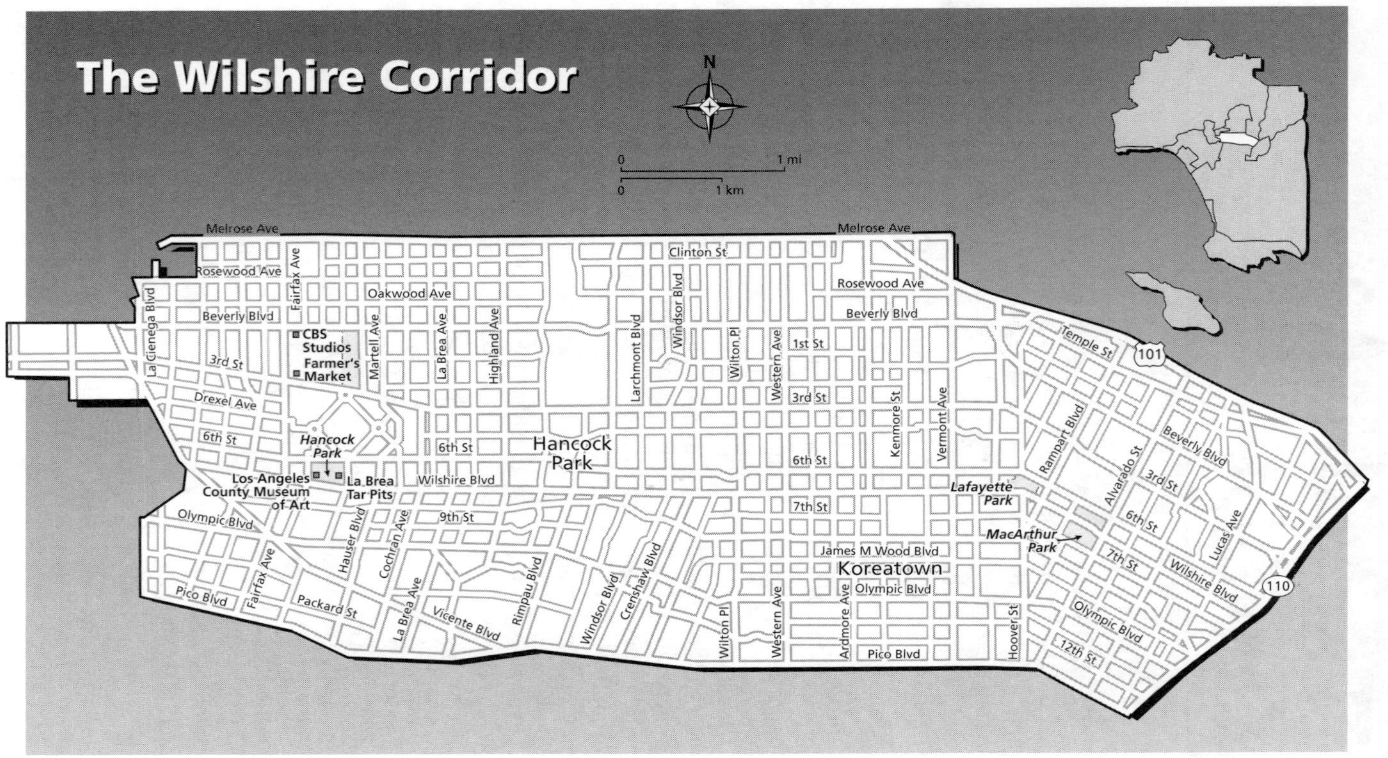
The Wilshire Corridor
N
0
1 mi
0
1 km
Melrose Ave
Melrose Ave
Clinton St
Rosewood Ave
Rosewood Ave
Fairfax Ave
Oakwood Ave
La Cienega Blvd
Beverly Blvd
Beverly Blvd
CBS Studios
Farmer's Market
Martell Ave
La Brea Ave
Highland Ave
Larchmont Blvd
Windsor Blvd
Wilton Pl
Western Ave
1st St
3rd St
3rd St
Drexel Ave
Kenmore St
Vermont Ave
6th St
Hancock Park
6th St
Hancock Park
6th St
Los Angeles County Museum of Art
La Brea Tar Pits
Wilshire Blvd
Lafayette Park
Olympic Blvd
Hauser Blvd
Cochran Ave
9th St
7th St
MacArthur Park
James M Wood Blvd
Koreatown
Fairfax Ave
Rimpau Blvd
Windsor Blvd
Crenshaw Blvd
Olympic Blvd
Pico Blvd
Packard St
La Brea Ave
Vicente Blvd
Wilton Pl
Western Ave
Ardmore Ave
Pico Blvd
Hoover St
Temple St
101
Rampart Blvd
Alvarado St
Beverly Blvd
3rd St
6th St
Lucas Ave
7th St
Wilshire Blvd
110
Olympic Blvd
12th St

Author's Top Picks in the Wilshire Corridor

Grier Musser Museum

Atlas Supper Club

La Brea Bakery

Illiterature

Friday Jazz Nights at the LACMA

Los Angeles Craft and Folk Art Museum

L.A. exploration. It's still possible to take a bus from Downtown Los Angeles straight down Wilshire Boulevard to Santa Monica and the ocean, a distance of about 16 miles. Currently, the Red Line of the Metro runs from Union Station in Downtown L.A., through Westlake and MacArthur Park, to Wilshire and Vermont, on to Wilshire and Normandie, and as far west as Wilshire and Western Avenue. Plans to extend this service to Santa Monica are in the works but going nowhere at present. For now the adventurous walker will have to trade off among foot, bus, car, and rail to explore this area.

An exploration of the Wilshire Corridor, however, comes with some cultural adventures. The road travels through neighborhoods where only Spanish is spoken and others where Korean is the tongue; in some you'll hear Yiddish, and in others, Hebrew, Russian, and Farsi. Continuing west, the road passes some of the most exclusive neighborhoods in Los Angeles abutting some of the hippest and most up and coming. For this chapter's purposes, the Wilshire tour runs from west of Downtown, detouring here and there to take in some worthy finds along the way and ending at La Cienega Boulevard, the doorstep of Beverly Hills.

For a strange museum experience, start with the ***Grier Musser Museum*** just west of Downtown. In a neighborhood of imposing Queen Anne–style mansions set off from the street in what may clearly be one of the oldest preserved neighborhoods in the city, a thirteen-room home that was bought by a doctor in 1898 and turned into a maternity clinic is now the home and museum of Susan Tejeda, whose family bought the stead in 1984.

Grandmother, daughter, and granddaughter lived here and counted themselves as avid yard-sale collectors. While they each eventually moved on, the house has become the repository for all of their hard work and is a veritable treasure trove of historical kitsch. Tours are by appointment only and cost $6.00. The house itself is a window into the Victorian world of turn-of-the-twentieth-century Los Angeles, and the collections—which change with the season or holiday—offer plenty of ocular entertainment, whether it's a plethora of silk Chinese dolls, clothes, lamps, umbrellas, shoes, you name it, for Chinese New Year or piles of Santas, reindeer, candlesticks, trees, ornaments, the works, for Christmas. Each room of the two-story home is decorated separately and most of the items would likely fetch hefty sums on the *Antiques*

Road Show. A gift shop at the end of the tour sells knickknacks like Howdy Doody dolls for $24, ceramic boxes for $10, and all manner of snow domes for varied prices. 403 South Bonnie Brae, between Wilshire and Third Street; appointments can be made by contacting (213) 413–1814 or www.isi.edu/sims/sheila/exhibits.html.

Next stop, ***Tommy's,*** the legendary home of the original chili burger. Tommy's has been scooping out the grease-laden flavor to the fast-food market for nearly sixty years. On May 15, 1946, a young Tommy Koulax introduced Los Angeles to a new kind of burger—this one with a chili con carne base and a bastion of hot chili spices—from a ramshackle little stand on the corner of Beverly and Rampart Boulevards. The original stand remains as the one and only original Tommy's, although the company has long since branched out to twenty-three locations all over the southland. While Tommy's is credited for bringing the burger to the car culture, its reputation has grown to become for L.A. what pizza is for Chicago. Hot dogs, tamales, and french fries are on the menu, but the burger is it and available twenty-four hours. 2575 Beverly Boulevard.

Back to Wilshire and continuing west is ***MacArthur Park***. The thirty-five-acre parcel purchased by Wilshire himself was turned into a park in 1890 and named Westlake Park. The park ran along Wilshire between what became Sixth and Eighth Streets and Alvarado and Park View Streets around a marsh that was cleaned and landscaped for the gentry class. It was renamed for General Douglas MacArthur after World War II and served as a central gathering spot for Sunday amblers, families, and the romantically engaged for the next forty-five years. Once described as L.A.'s Champs-Elysées, this was the desirable neighborhood of aging stars and sophisticated heiresses like Norma Talmadge and Gloria Swanson. The fountain still springs from the center of a lake that swans and ducks once shared with paddleboaters and scraps of bread thrown by children. The Otis College of Art and Design that was formerly nearby contributed artworks and sculptures to the park. A looming sculpture of rusted found objects called *Clock Tower: A Monument to the Unknown* by George Herms honors the old men who once played chess on the park's tables and benches. The former beauty of the park is well in evidence. Little has changed in form and structure, but the area has become quite run down and dirty and is no longer a pleasant place to feed ducks and read the paper—it tends to be crowded, busy with ad hoc flea markets, loud with portable music, and dangerous when the sun goes down. At night the gangs come out, the dealers move in, and the park that once was seems to melt away.

Vestiges of the park's former glory can be gleaned from a quick pan of the area. The surrounding buildings were some of L.A.'s most luxurious in the 1930s and 1940s. Designs from Art Deco (Zigzag) Moderne to 1920s Beaux-Arts, California Craftsman, and Spanish Churrigueresque evoke the varied personalities of the time and were some of the first buildings in the United States to get neon.

Neon came to Los Angeles in 1923 and, along the Wilshire Corridor, never quite left. A number of the original neon remains in what is locally considered ***a neon museum*** on the rooftops of buildings surrounding MacArthur Park and along Wilshire. The signs light up at night on top of the Astor Arms, The Town House, the Asbury, the Ansonia, Barbizon, Bryson, and Park Wilshire buildings, among others, and create a sedate, historical complement to the modern neon overload of Koreatown just ahead. An enjoyable drive around the park will provide all the views.

Praising the Pastrami

Langer's Deli *has been serving hand-cut mounds of pastrami on fresh rye bread for nearly sixty years right above the MacArthur Park exit on the Red Line. The half-pound sandwich, with or without Russian dressing, with or without Dr. Brown's Celery Tonic, was good enough to get the attention of the sixteen-member James Beard Foundation Awards Board recently. Meantime, this has been the lunch spot of knowing Angelinos for decades. 704 South Alvarado and Wilshire Boulevard, (213) 483–8051.*

The most historically significant building along Wilshire Boulevard, however, isn't neon lit at all. It's the ***Bullock's Wilshire*** building at 3050 Wilshire Boulevard, a striking example of the leaking riches Zigzag Moderne meant to imply and the mark of what it meant to be a city centered on the car.

In 1929 Bullocks Wilshire, dubbed the "cathedral of commerce," was built at Wilshire and Westmoreland as the city's first branch department store in the suburbs. Its Art Deco architectural style was modeled after designs that had recently premiered at the Paris Exposition des Arts Decoratifs et Moderne. That same year the Academy Awards ceremony was moved from the Hollywood Roosevelt to the Ambassador Hotel a few blocks north on Wilshire. The store's exquisite interiors are gone. Only the exterior attests to its past these days. It's now a law school.

Continuing west, the area between Alvarado and Vermont is mostly a hodgepodge of grocery stores, car repair shops, and indecipherable bars, restaurants, and notions shops—although a few do stand out for their historical perseverance.

Cross Vermont Avenue and enter Koreatown. In a not-so-dramatic metamorphosis, the signs that had been advertising street pharmacies and madre's tamales in Spanish now promote accountants, lawyers, acupuncturists, and kim chee in Korean neon. The blocks that run from Vermont to Western are modern and clean, evoking a certain prosperity of the people and reflecting a little Seoul. At night the transition is as dramatic as it is electric: Towering glass-and-steel high-rises take over the space above, while what promise to be good food and healing medicine shops divide the visual space on the street.

A search for the old L.A. in this neighborhood does bring a couple of noteworthy attractions. The historic ***La Fonda*** restaurant has been serving up fajitas, margaritas, and mariachis in ornate Mission Revival ambience since 1969, although the building dates back to the 1930s. The cavernous cafe on the second floor brings lively musical entertainment and occasional Ballet Folklorico performances Thursday through Sunday to a motley crowd of offbeat fun seekers willing to enjoy what comes their way. 2501 Wilshire Boulevard, (213) 380–5055.

Farther up the block, a stop into the ***HMS Bounty*** will put you back in the 1960s the proper way: with Manhattans up and with a cherry around a nautical-themed bar with a model tall ship illuminated in a glass case on the rear wall, fishermen's lanterns for light, paintings and photos of schooners at sea above red vinyl booths, fresh catch on the menu, and Tony Bennett on the jukebox. 3357 Wilshire Boulevard, (323) 385–7275.

Where the infamous ***Brown Derby*** used to reside at Wilshire and Kenmore now sits a modern Korean mini mall with a cybergames cafe and

Korean Hot Spot

Deep in the center of Koreatown is a one-spa wonder that celebrities and pretty people seem to have discovered but not too many others know about. ***Beverly Hot Springs*** *is L.A.'s only geothermal spa. It has an unfancy room containing a hot mineral pool continuously replenished by a Spanish fountain in the center piping in the natural artesian waters. Experienced Korean masseuses apply no-holds-barred acupressure and shiatsu manipulations that will crack as much pain as they give, and a soothing post-massage rest can be had in the rock and jungle room adjacent to the mineral pool. Soaking is not cheap: $40 to $50 just to use the waters. Treatments cost $110 to $125 and do not include the water charge. 308 North Oxford Avenue, (323) 734–7000, www.beverlyhotsprings.com.*

a juice bar, teahouse, and a few ever-present nail and hair salons and CD stores. Across the street a sad shadow of the ***Ambassador Hotel*** sits behind rubble and link fencing, the ***Coconut Grove*** nightclub standing out in front in some strange defiance of this ignoble deterioration. The hotel was *the* scene in Hollywood VIP and celebrity life from the 1920s to late 1940s and was the focus of films like the original two versions of *A Star Is Born* as well as Academy Awards ceremonies. Its recent past may supersede its glory days, as this is the spot where Bobby Kennedy was assassinated. The fate of the building remains a question; the city is considering turning it into a school.

At Western the scene on Wilshire begins to switch back to original L.A., marked by the ***Wiltern Theater*** and ***Atlas Supper Club,*** both housed in the 1930 ***Warner Brothers Theater.*** The grand Art Deco structure of zigzag towers and aquamarine tiles was remade twenty years ago into the current Wiltern Theater, where popular international rock and blues bands play.

While a few gems of ornate Deco and whimsical fairy design crop up here and there as you continue west along Wilshire, the area doesn't get interesting again until ***Hancock Park.*** This neighborhood was the creation of another oilman, G. Allan Hancock, who bought the original parcel in the 1920s, but his interests were not so altruistic. The area was developed as an elite suburb of Tudor, Mission, and Neoclassical mansions exclusive of blacks, Jews, Mexicans, and any other non-white Anglican group that could be identified. Today the charm remains, but the original bloodlines—which included names like *Doheny, Crocker,* and *Van Nuys*—have long since left for the suburbs. The area now is a comely mix of religions, ethnicities, lawyers, and rock stars.

Jazz and Jerk

*A**tlas Supper Club** in the blue-tiled Deco surroundings of the Wiltern Theater building is a big fat L.A. secret for people who love to listen to great blues and jazz with a piquant piece of Caribbean jerk chicken in front of them. The Atlas serves Caribbean influenced dishes prepared by a resort-trained chef on white-clothed tables as the combo at hand belts out ballads and blues in riveting performances. At 10:00 P.M., the tables disappear and the floor becomes a hip-hop and salsa dance club. 3760 Wilshire Boulevard (at Western Avenue), (213) 385–8062, www.clubatlas.com.*

Hancock Park's broad boulevards, tree-shaded streets, and large manicured front lawns are a welcoming segue from the teeming sidewalks and traffic of Wilshire. There are a few houses worth a look. One is ***The Getty House,*** at 605 South Irving, also known as the mayor's residence. This mock Tudor home underwent a total renovation, which was completed in 1995, and sticks out with a green-and-cream kind of garishness that's not the usual order of mayoral haunts. The ***Rothman House*** at 541 Rossmore Avenue is a tamer English manor dwelling that seems transported from some European hamlet. The ***Meade House*** at 350 June Street is considered the finest example of the Spanish Colonial Revival style among homes in Los Angeles. The ***Sisson House*** at the northwest corner of Hudson and Sixth Street brings a strange medieval French touch to the neighborhood with its central three-story round tower and gloomy facade.

On the corner of Third Street and Muirfield, ***The House of the Davids***—as it is known locally—catches the eye with its front fence lined from one side to the other with mini *David* statues standing guard on top of the fence. The crowded backyard, though hidden by a wall, shows more of the same with white metallic and cement mock Italian wonders peaking into the viewline. The neighborhood, which starts roughly at Van Ness and Wilshire, runs west to Highland Avenue and north to Beverly Boulevard. It's best experienced at Christmas, when the residents go all out to top each other on extravagant and excessive Christmas lights and yuletide scenes such as behemoth silver reindeer eating up the front lawn, little electric elf villages, and Santa and entourage ready to crash through the roof. The *Davids* are usually wrapped in red velvet ribbons for the season. The streets are ablaze in all manor of lights and colors, and usually at least two huge pines are given the star treatment with decorations that might otherwise be seen at Disneyland in the Small World ride.

Central to the charm and appreciation of Hancock Park is ***Larchmont Village,*** a local gathering spot that retains its former simple, unhurried charm. For two full blocks moving southward from Beverly Boulevard and Larchmont, strollers have their day with bagel shops, latte shops, precious outdoor French cafes and indoor Italian bistros, independent bookstores, magazine kiosks, boutiques, and beauty and spa product boutiques. The village seems right out of the 1950s, with angled parking spaces and, in the middle of the block, the local family-owned hardware store where shopkeepers know the neighbors and have been selling them duct tape for decades. This is Saturday-morning people-watching territory. The outdoor sidewalk tables fill at Starbucks (206

Larchmont) and across the street at Café Chapeau (236 North Larchmont), and life just seems to slow down all around.

Meanwhile, back on the Wilshire side of the corridor, a massive and impressive museum to Freemasonry opened in November 2002 with little press or fanfare but a lot of history and literature. The ***Scottish Rite Masonic Temple*** and its ***American Heritage Masonic Museum*** presents a 15,000-square-foot space (to be expanded eventually to 45,000 square feet) with exhibits and paintings on everything you could want to know about Freemasons—the who's who list of presidents and kings, from George Washington to Gerald Ford to Juan Carlos of Spain, as well as tomes on the secret society, on its rituals, and on its use of the occult. The purpose is to describe the history of this society and its impact on American history. Few escape the large Eye of Horus and other symbols of Freemasonry in elaborate friezes and sculptures along the wall spaces. The museum is open seven days a week from 11:00 A.M. to 5:00 P.M.; there's a $5.00 admission fee. 4357 Wilshire Boulevard, bordered by Lucerne Avenue, (323) 937–2566.

La Brea Avenue crosses Wilshire Boulevard and, as it moves north, gets funkier and funkier. This street is an unexpected enclave of some of the finest dining in the city, retooled junk and clothing shops, quirky fashion boutiques, celebrity resale clothing stores, and pricey Asian furniture shops. You can spend a day or an hour on La Brea, depending on your appetite and wallet size.

Moving north among newfangled boutiques, the most notable entree is ***La Brea Bakery.*** This is the original—the company recently opened a bread shop in Anaheim at Downtown Disney, and sells brand breads to food stores around the Los Angeles basin. Here you'll find more than just the usual sourdough rosemary bread, potato bread, and olive breads; you can also enjoy brioches that can be cut like butter and breakfast breads full of chunk-sized seeds and nuts. A smell that brings you back to toy chests and freshly washed curtains hangs over the block, and the lines are hefty all day. Sandwiches on breads of the day are a perfect purchase, to be enjoyed down the block with a frappuccino at any of the sidewalk coffee spots. 624 South La Brea.

La Brea Bakery is attached to ***Campanile Restaurant,*** one of L.A.'s preeminent dining spots. Wolfgang Puck protégé Mark Peel took what was once an office for Charlie Chaplin and converted it into a cavernous Italian atrium of fine dining with a California fusion of dishes that center on rare and precious ingredients. The fare here is as fine as it gets, and suitably pricey. Still, the airy and calming ambience of Italian statuary and sun-drenched cathedral ceilings sets it apart from the plethora of other similar L.A. dining options. 624 La Brea, (323) 938–1447, www.campanilerestaurant.com.

A warehouse-sized journey awaits at ***Little Paris Antiques,*** where it's possible to get lost amid the Indonesian woods and French red brocade. This is the place to go for good deals on exotic new and antique furniture, but it's also fun to lose yourself within and just soak up the atmosphere. Tucked in the back is ***China Doll,*** a boutique of tight knit blouses and pants and sparkly open-toed shoes. The clothing is perhaps too L.A. precious in price, but shoes and accessories are usually available on sale in some corner bin. 612 La Brea.

At the corner of Sixth Street, pass an outdoor revamped furniture store in the Shabby Chic style, as well as gem of a spot attached to it called ***Kenza*** that sells all items Moroccan, from massive copper tagine plates, to wrought-iron and ceramic Fez dining tables to Mamluke-style glass lanterns. The lilting conversation of the French-Moroccan proprietress is a bonus.

Continuing north a block, you'll come to ***Illiterature*** at 456 La Brea, a clever book, design, and odd notions shop that requires exploration. Here find rare books on California bathrooms and writer's block aids, as well as a wellspring of romance talismans, odd-shaped vases, strange photo frames, and how-to kits for office survival. Two doors down and owned by the same people is ***Pulp,*** which celebrates elaborate wrapping papers and accessories as well as cards.

Art galleries show up on either side of the street, some with just a buzzer, others with a design-intensive door. Fine-art photographs are celebrated in several of these galleries, with shows revolving around a topic, a celebrity, or a photographer.

These items and more can be contemplated from the flower-shop-cum-cafe of ***Rita Flora Kitchen*** at 460 La Brea, where flowers and food go together in a kind of flourishing bouquet of salad and sandwiches amid the buckets of orchid stands and gladiola blooms. Farther north at 150 La Brea is the ***American Rag Cafe,*** where a menu of salads, pancakes and quiches is served in the back of a boutique selling ripped jeans, cotton shirts, and designer dishes. In between, stop at ***Diavolina*** at 334 La Brea. The decor here is perhaps more interesting than the stiletto Italian shoeware on the shelves and the skimpy Italian ladies' wear on the racks. Check out the leopardskin walls and floors, high-heeled shoe chairs, and draped ceiling.

Although the chic side of La Brea ends more or less at Beverly Boulevard, across the street lie a few more galleries, 1960s-style furniture stores, as well as antiques and contemporary showrooms and a vintage, celebrity, and movie studio resale clothing boutique called ***Cinema Glamour Shop,*** which, from its spot at 343 La Brea, sells barely worn items once used by stars and actors on sets at the surrounding movie studios for vintage-clothing prices.

From La Brea to La Cienega, the streets of Wilshire, Third, Beverly Boulevard, and Melrose—all running parallel to one another east to west and north of one another—offer many Off the Beaten Path finds.

In the Pink's

*It's a plain white shack on La Brea just north of Melrose, but it always has a crush of people in front of it whether it's 9:30 A.M. or 3:00 A.M. It's called **Pink's**, and it has been serving the most delicious and greasiest chili dogs in L.A. since 1939. Parking and benches are in the back. With a slather of onions and fries, it's a meal in a bun. Bring Rolaids and a bib.*

Let's start with Wilshire Boulevard. A quick stop at an unassuming lobby at 5505 brings everything you ever wanted to know about Korea. ***The Korean Cultural Center*** is tucked away amid this hodgepodge of deli bakeries, wig stores, beauty supply shops, drugstores, and office supply warehouses. In a way it signals things to come on this block, because you're now entering ***Museum Row*** in what's referred to as the ***Miracle Mile District.*** The museum at hand isn't particularly well visited, especially by non-Koreans. But the exhibits are impressive: a detailed remake of a 1,000-year-old marriage palanquin in lacquer and silks, tea ceremony items, a wall of dance masks, traditional gold jewelry and accessories, dolls modeling traditional women's clothing. Upstairs is mostly painted scrolls with nature scenes and calligraphy in wall frames. The museum is free and open Monday through Friday until 5:00 P.M., Saturday until 1:00 P.M. 5505 Wilshire Boulevard, (323) 936–7141, www.kccla.org.

Other museums that mark the boulevard along the twelve-block segment between La Brea and Fairfax Avenues include the very worthwhile campus of museums within the ***Los Angeles County Museum of Art.*** A $7.00 ticket buys entrance into the museum's permanent collections of well-curated works that run strong in Islamic art collections, seventeenth-, eighteenth-, and nineteenth-century European movements, and twentieth-century expressionism in Germany and France.

Attached to the art museum along a rambling park of benches, trees, and occasional roiling ponds of pitch are other museums, such as the ***Japanese Pavilion*** (included with the ticket). The ***La Brea Tar Pits*** are located on this land as well, and a look into the pits is a window onto a

Los Angeles County Museum of Art

world roamed by ice age animals and roving hunters 9,000 years ago. A staff guide will take you into the pits on weekend mornings and tell you about all the horrible deaths suffered by saber-toothed felines and sloths looking for water and getting sucked in by the tar. Ambling through the park behind the museum complex, you can still see patches and ponds of this bubbling black pitch as if 9,000 years ago were only yesterday. The ***Page Museum of Natural History*** is the place to go afterward to see the bones dredged out and assembled into towering skeletal exhibits.

The museum runs free jazz nights on Friday from 6:00 to 9:00, with area artists showcased in the campus courtyard. The museum galleries are open and free, and a museum cafe serves well-prepared and reasonably priced gourmet fare cafeteria-style. Often film retrospectives with director or producer commentary run in the ***Leo S. Bing Theater*** at the museum on weekend evenings—$4.00 easily buys a double feature. On Sunday afternoon the Bing often stages a classical quartet ensemble. The complex is found at 5905 Wilshire; call (323) 857–6000.

Across the street is the ***Los Angeles Craft and Folk Art Museum.*** As with the LACMA, one of the top attractions here is the gift shop, in this case filled with one-of-a-kind handmade items from ceramics to greeting cards. The museum runs exhibits on folk art collections, such as an entire floor devoted to Day of the Dead figures and scenes from southern Mexico or exhibits dedicated to Carnaval and nineteenth-century European courtship traditions. 5814 Wilshire Boulevard, (323) 937–4230, www.culturela.org.

On the east side of Museum Row, the ***Petersen Automotive Museum*** is well worth the walk. The former home to Orbach's Department Store of 1960s note is now three floors of auto classics, auto history, and auto dioramas and scenes. It all perfectly fits the passion of a southern California audience that is woefully in love with cars. Guided and unguided tours both cost $10. 6060 Wilshire Boulevard bordering Fairfax Avenue, (323) 930–2277, www.petersen.org.

Fairfax Avenue, which runs north–south, is a feisty little street with a lot of ethnic personality. To the south of Wilshire down to Pico Boulevard, it becomes ***Little Ethiopia,*** a hamlet of Tejj houses, cafes, and African notions boutiques mixed in with junk stores, travel agencies, and strong, aromatic coffeehouses. Try the doro wat with African beer and fresh-poured injera at ***Nyala*** at 1076 South Fairfax Avenue. The restaurant is light on atmosphere, with plain linoleum tables instead of the round table baskets and benches traditional in Addis Ababa. If you like the spices, however, the special "berbere" blend can be purchased at the notions shop next door.

The road north leads to ***Little Israel*** between Beverly Boulevard and Melrose Avenue, a focused few blocks of kosher delis, bakeries, butcher and fish shops, falafel bars, Korean and Romanian greenmarkets, Jewish Yemenite cafes where you can order a bountiful plate of hummus falafal and all the trimmings for $6.00, and Ashkenazi restaurants where matzo balls are thick and light and the pickles do not get any sourer. Interspersed with these Israeli delights are several thrift stores, including an AIDS charity called ***Out of the Closet,*** where a lot of high-end stuff from surrounding elite Jewish neighborhoods ends up. Similarly, some odd cracks in the street include ***Nova*** at 426 North Fairfax—a punker coffeehouse open from 7:00 P.M. to 4:00 A.M. nightly and serving Cosmic Pizzas, Celestial Salads, and Earthling Sandwiches to the spin sounds of guest DJs—and ***Largo,*** two stores over, a local rock and comedy performance room where you can dine on a "home-cooking" menu that includes an excellent honey-glazed chicken and real mashed potatoes and watch up-and-coming performers in a rather intimate setting as performance spaces go.

Across the street at 419 Fairfax is ***Canter's Deli,*** open twenty-four hours for the last seventy years and still a place to go star spotting at the oddest hours. A pastrami sandwich is two meals here, where it's possible to order seltzer from a spritzer and Dr. Brown's by the can. Your waitress is your surrogate Jewish mother if you don't have one already—and don't expect her to take your bill to the register for you.

A few doors up on the corner of Fairfax and Rosewood Avenue is ***Eat-a-Pita,*** an outdoor Mediterranean garden cafe with a walk-up window serving falafel by the ball or pita pocket, all the tahini you can pour, and the best fresh-made lemonade in the city—all kosher, of course.

Running parallel and north of Wilshire is ***Third Street,*** which, from Fairfax west to La Cienega, is chock-full of sights chichi and funk, one cafe after another, one niche boutique after the next. A hulking cup of coffee at ***Doughboys*** at 8136 Third Street with fresh, homemade mega muffins is how a number of professional food writers and caterers in the city start their day—after dropping their pooches off a few doors down at ***Chateau Marmutt*** for doggy day care (this place deserves an impromptu look just to watch dozens of dogs entertaining themselves in the back room). Amble west and pass antiques stores and frilly clothing and accessories shops and end up at two special spots on the Third Street map: the ***Cook's Library*** at 8373 West Third Street and ***The Traveler's Bookcase*** next door. Both stores are owned by the same people and dedicated to their namesakes in every way. Adventurous cooks will find books on Burmese cooking and recipes of the Jewish populations of India in the Cook's Library and travelogues about adventures with Burmese cooks and Indian Jews in the Traveler's Bookcase, along with lightweight travel equipment and gadgets.

Back to La Brea and moving east to west on ***Beverly Boulevard,*** three blocks north and parallel to Third Street, you'll find a richer, more refined package of restaurants and stores leading up to Fairfax. First, find ***Sugarplum's*** at 7122 Beverly Boulevard. The confectionary shop just opened in 2003 and is fast becoming the favored sweet spot in the city—conveniently sitting next to the street's only Starbucks. Continue west and hit ***El Coyote,*** serving up margaritas and chips for longer than Canter's has been dishing out the matzo balls. The place is long on mariachi-style atmosphere, and wait staff who likely served this middle-age author's parents when they were dating, will sally up to your table (when you finally get one—this place is popular as a kitsch meeting spot on weekend nights) in heavily made-up faces and long Mexican hoop skirts to give you the look: *What'll it be and make up your mind 'cause I'm not coming back.* You'll get the evil eye once again and the huffy turnabout if you don't order dinner—but don't order dinner, which tends toward used grease. Still, the chips are warm, with two types of endless salsas.

Timeless Tacos

*Midnight scarfers hit the goods at **Benitos Taco Shop** at 7912 Beverly Boulevard at Fairfax. Home of the rolled taco, this kitchen never stops cooking and can be an entertaining treat at 4:00 A.M.*

Walking west on either side of the street, you'll pass antiques stores and *très* haute couture shops where wedding and Oscar gowns are designed and cut. ***Cantu & Castillo*** at 7415 Beverly Boulevard might be the most interesting—it's housed in an aged brick castle of sorts, with a moat. And the clothing inside is not far from the fairy-tale theme—flowing satin gowns are cut to fit here, and taffeta is revived, but modern, light, and sleek tastes are certainly accommodated. You'll also find a lot of haute couture wannabe shops with preciously priced skimpy off-the-rack knits, art and photography galleries, manicure shops ($18 for a mani/pedi—can't beat that!), and the ***Insomnia*** coffee hut where scripts get written by unemployed, starry-eyed coffee addicts. Next door at 7282 Beverly Boulevard is ***Fifi & Romeo,*** a boutique devoted to selling matching clothing and accessory ensembles for dogs—especially those the size of large rodents.

Continue on for a few blocks. Just before you pass ***CBS Studios,*** turn right onto Stanley Avenue, anchored by an upscale holistic food store called ***Erewon.*** You are now heading out of independent boutique land to chain heaven at ***The Grove.*** The outdoor promenade between Third Street and Beverly leading up to Fairfax Avenue is the latest entertainment retail complex to open in L.A., and it does an excellent job of bringing on the new while energizing the old. Anchored by such commercial giants as Nordstrom, Apple Computer, Nike Goddess, F.A.O. Schwartz, and Anthropologie, it also has the largest Barnes & Noble west of the Mississippi and an eight-screen megaplex cinema with stadium seating and every showcase technology on the books.

The Grove is set up in parklike fashion, with a village green and a singing water ballet central fountain feature; every so often a trolley comes by

Bob Barker Lives

Yes, you can still see a live taping of The Price Is Right *with Bob Barker. In fact, you can get studio audience passes to participate in the live tapings of* Hollywood Squares *and the* Late Show with Craig Kilborn, *too. Simply show up at the ticket booth at CBS Studios at 7800 Beverly Boulevard and Fairfax Avenue anytime between 9:00 A.M. and 5:00 P.M. and you're bound to get a seat for something. For more information, call (323) 575–2624.*

and makes a circle around the promenade. Hidden in the side streets of this Neoclassical village facade are a day spa, a chocolatier, and a store selling olive oils only. Get past the Barbie collection at F.A.O. Schwartz (which doesn't have a trademark window scene here but does have a little song-and-mechanical-mustache act that goes off every hour on its toy-soldier marquee) and head west to the ***Farmer's Market*** at 6333 West Third Street and Fairfax. This L.A. icon (since the 1930s) is now somehow linked to The Grove in a kind of grandparents-meet-the-Y-generation connection. The market is a labyrinth of fruit stands and food stalls selling everything from Kosher Singapore salads to N'awlins seafood gumbo with beer broth. Each stand is independently owned and extremely clean—and the food is good. Most of the stands have been around through the decades and with the same food to match.

Weekend nights are boogie nights at The Grove and Farmer's Market. Stores are open until 11:00 P.M., the cinemaplex is in full tilt, the dating couples are queuing at the outdoor cafes, and all is alive with beat and sound. As many as four bands may be in performance between the green at The Grove and different ends of the Farmer's Market. Russian grandmas are dancing with cooks and stand managers, homeboys are boogying with Kokomo coffee drinkers, the crowds writhe in one big block party, all for free and all for fun.

Finally, backtracking to La Brea, running three blocks north to ***Melrose Avenue,*** and taking those store-lined blocks west to Fairfax, be prepared for an entirely different experience. Refinement turns to youth

Reflective Walk

Directly across from The Grove is an unusual sight for these parts: a park. The seven-acre green of ***Pan Pacific Park*** *is laced with jogging trails and picnic tables and an unusual monument. At the north end of the park is an iron fence with cosmetic barbed wire surrounding a stand of granite obelisks all inscribed with names of people who died in Nazi concentration camps. Sometimes the fence gate is open and it's possible to read the carved inscriptions.*

culture. All is grunge, hip-hop, polyester, and statement making, and whatever can be pierced or tattooed, is.

The colorful, almost carnival atmosphere along Melrose is a fun take-in all by itself. Sit at any number of outdoor wine cafes, coffeehouses, or Mexican cantinas along the way and watch the mixture of over-the-top teenyboppers, soccer moms, Korean cousins, out-of-town families, tattooed Harley hogs, hooker divas, Orthodox Jews, skateboard boys, drag queens, cell phone hunks, and shopping bag starlets hustle by you. The mélange of loud and fanciful shop facades adds to the lively nature of the street, which gets a lot of foot traffic because it's possible to walk a good twelve blocks and be entertained along every foot of it by the bizarre one-of-a-kind boutiques, the shlock shops, and the pockets of class inserted here and there.

Personal Odor Order

Cleopatra had one so why shouldn't you? Your very own perfume scent, that is. ***Ebba*** *mixes your personal perfume based on your personality and what you'd like to attract. What you end up with is an essence that is yours alone to leave where you like. 8164 Melrose Avenue, (323) 651–5337.*

The shops are varying measures of the same stuff: platform shoes and thigh boots, size zero skintight knits, leather, cheap rag racks recycled from the trash boxes in the Downtown Garment District, used-clothing arcades, and CD shops. A few stores are worth the exploration, however. ***Necromance*** at 7162 Melrose sells Gothic chic on the racks and all sorts of dead lizards, bats, snakes, and insects in its cases. Black magic potions and an altar to Satan make this store a unique shopping experience.

Wound & Wound Toy Co. at 7374 Melrose Avenue is a hands-on, wind-'em-up paradise for anyone who has ever loved those plastic chattering teeth. The whole store is devoted to every manner of odd item that can be wound up and made to do something for ten seconds.

Beyond the trash rag stores, designer eyewear, stiletto shoe shops, and superexpensive sneaker boutiques is one more store that stands above the others: ***Drake's*** at 7566 Melrose makes shopping for sex toys almost mainstream. The store is devoted to condoms in all shapes and colors, potions, gels, plastic bosoms, and blow-up items—but all laid out in tasteful presentations with mom-and-pop shoppers milling around and a helpful crew of store managers willing to explain and inform.

Should you be set on voguing for the *Tonight Show,* dine alfresco at ***Louise's Trattoria*** at 7505 Melrose Avenue cornering Gardner Street. Several times a month Jay Leno stands here, mike in hand and camera at the ready, to interview passersby on their lack of worldly knowledge for that night's show. Come between 6:30 and 7:30 P.M.

On Sunday a walk from La Brea to Fairfax along Melrose Avenue, a good twelve blocks of slow ambling and watching, ends up at the ***Fairfax Flea Market*** at Fairfax High School. This outdoor market is one of the best in the city with used Persian carpets, candles, kitschy jewelry, purses, lots of rehabilitated furniture, and a clutter of crafts. The $2.00 admission is a bargain for the live music performance (usually a hot blues band) alone.

PLACES TO STAY IN THE WILSHIRE CORRIDOR

Luxe: $250 +
Deluxe: $150–$249
Good deal: $80–$149

Beverly Plaza Hotel
8384 West Third Street, (323) 858–6200 or (800) 62–HOTEL, www.beverlyplaza hotel.com.
This converted budget motel is now a favorite with the gay population as well as comers who want to be hip but not empty their pockets for it. Cushy rooms with all the upscale pleasantries in the center of Third Street action plus a roof pool and downstairs tapas bar. Good deal.

Elan Moderne
8435 Beverly Boulevard, (323) 658–6663 or (888) 611–0398, www.elanhotel.com.
Sleek lines meet function in this stylish futuristic boutique hotel that's located within walking distance of great restaurants, theaters, and the Beverly Center shopping mall. Deluxe.

Hotel Sofitel
8555 Beverly Boulevard, (310) 657–2816 or (866) 824–9330, www.sofitel.com.
A little Pierre Deux and a lot of je ne sais quois in this hotel that overlooks West Hollywood. French touches are everywhere, and there's a fun little bistro on site. Great location directly across from the Beverly Center and two blocks from designer showrooms on Robertson Boulevard. Deluxe.

Le Meridien Hotel
465 South La Cienega Boulevard, (310) 246–2018 or (800) 300–9147, www.lemeridien.com.
Contemporary Asian fused with ornate European decor creates an upscale feel in this hotel that is a favorite for business travelers and film industry executives. Broad affordability and walking distance to shopping and top restaurants add to the benefits. Deluxe.

PLACES TO EAT IN THE WILSHIRE CORRIDOR

Expensive: $25.00+
Reasonable: $15.00–$24.00
Bargain: $8.00–$14.00

Authentic Café
7605 Beverly Boulevard, (323) 939–4626.
A hip and accessible choice for fresh Mexican cuisine where they make the salsa on the spot. Bargain.

Buddha Belly
7475 Beverly Boulevard, (323) 931–8588.
Healthy cooking with an Asian twist. Tofu done just right, downed with tea spiked with energizing Elixir potions. An outdoor patio under the arbors provides the right touch on warm nights. Reasonable.

Campanile Restaurant
624 La Brea,
(323) 938–1447,
www.campanilerestaurant.com.
Expensive. See page 37 for more information.

Canter's Deli
419 Fairfax.
Reasonable. See page 42 for more information.

Cobras & Matadors
7613 Beverly Boulevard,
(323) 931–4995.
Tapas and an A (to Z) list of Spanish wines in a gypsy setting catering to a hip, young crowd. Bargain.

Hirozen
8385 Beverly Boulevard,
(323) 653–0470.
Hidden in an unsuspecting mini strip mall, this corner sushi bar gets high ratings for affordability and perfection. Go early or late or you'll wait. Reasonable.

HMS Bounty
3357 Wilshire Boulevard,
(323) 385–7275.
Bargain. See page 34 for more information.

La Fonda
2501 Wilshire Boulevard,
(213) 380–5055.
Bargain. See page 34 for more information.

La Paella
476 South San Vicente (between La Cienega and Wilshire), (323) 951–0745.
The best paella in L.A. comes in a tiny townhouse walkdown with a black-and-white floor, low ceilings, candlelit tables, and dark-eyed Spanish waiters. What could be more romantic? Expensive.

Le Chardonnay
8284 Melrose Avenue,
(323) 655–8880.
High-caloried and high-priced French cuisine the old-fashioned way—with a precious wine list and an intimate Art Nouveau ambience. Expensive.

Lucques
8474 Melrose Avenue (at La Cienega),
(323) 655–6277.
California, French Mediterranean fare in a setting right out of *Elle Decor*. Expensive.

Mani's Bakery
519 South Fairfax Avenue,
(323) 938–8800.
An inexpensive counter and sidewalk cafe serving veggie and free-range chicken sandwiches and delectable pastries with natural ingredients, many wheat- and dairy-free and all powered by honey. Bargain.

Mishima
8474 West Third Street,
(323) 782–0181.
Thick and robust udons and ramen bowls, tofu sansai with mouth-melting touches, or delicate tempura as a meal or a side, all inexpensive and washed down with endless cups of buckwheat or brown rice tea in a casual Tokyo-like cafe setting. Bargain.

Opaline
7450 Beverly Boulevard (five blocks west of La Brea),
(323) 857–6725.
Neo-California fusion with an innovative wine list in a neutral minimalist setting. Named for Oscar Wilde's description of the color of absinthe. Expensive.

Tommy's
2575 Beverly Boulevard.
Bargain. See page 32 for more information.

Zen Grill
8432 Third Street,
(323) 655–9991.
Seven spiced salmon, tuna rice tower, sautéed banana, and plenty of Asian intrigue in this dark red, dark wood culinary meditation cafe. Reasonable.

Hollywood

Hollywood, a city of lingerie shops, fantastical movie palaces and streets set right out of a 1940s film noir backdrop, did not have such a glamour-loaded beginning. As a matter of fact, it was started by the Wilcoxes, a couple from the Midwest who, in 1887, bought a fig and apricot orchard and hoped to start somewhere on that 160-acre 'stead, a Christian enclave where no saloons or vices would be tolerated and people of the Bible could pursue their clean utopian dreams. The *Hollywood* name is even more banal—it derived from a conversation the missus had with a very wealthy woman on a train who described her summer estate, which she called Hollywood.

But by the early 1900s, the city of Bibles and churches had become a stop on the Red Car for tourists headed for the gardens and hotels on the edge of the enclave, and Hollywood soon became a part of creeping L.A. Young men from Brooklyn who had seen their future in Broadway nickelodeons followed their visions to the hills of Hollywood with motion picture endeavors that started in 1907. D. W. Griffith stamped these hills and groves as the arising film industry headquarters, and three young immigrants from New York sealed it: Cecil B. DeMille, Jesse Lasky, and a guy named Samuel Goldfish, later to change his name to Goldwyn and form Metro Goldwyn Mayer.

While remnants of these early-century days are still accessible in some parts of Hollywood, the city is nearly perfectly preserved in its golden glory days of 1930s and 1940s. A walk up Hollywood Boulevard—wacky, seedy, and disturbed as it is—is a walk through Hollywood Babylon, Paradise lost and found, where anything is possible on and off the silver screen.

You can still see the teenage boys on the corner hawking maps to the stars' homes for $10 a pop, but the places they'll take you will likely be inhabited by Joe and Jane Smith, scriptwriters from Chicago, since the stars have long since segued to the beach. Chances are, if you do see a star, it won't be someone mowing the front yard. You *will* see celebrities walking on the street, getting a latte, buying a paper, stopping at a red

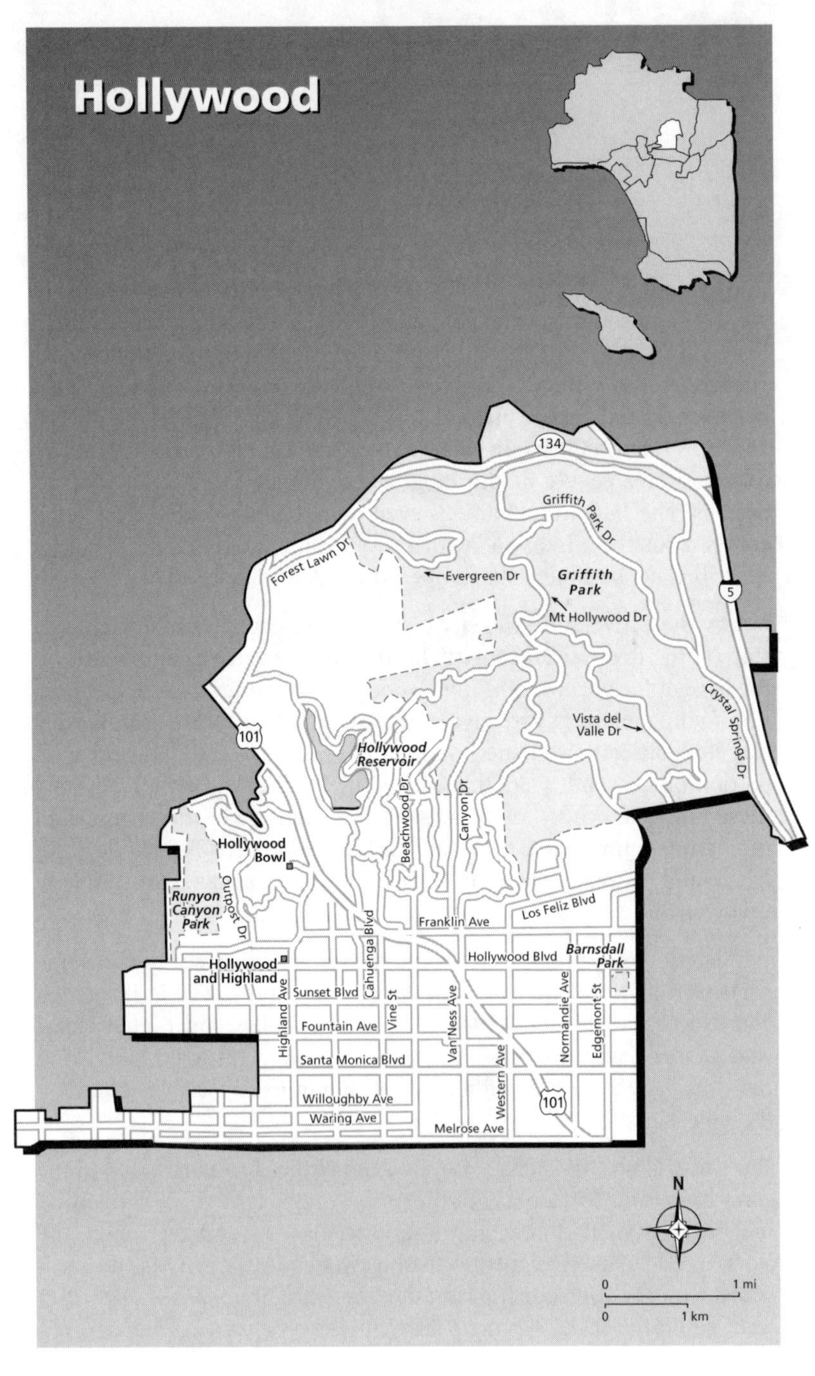

Hollywood
134
Griffith Park Dr
Forest Lawn Dr
Evergreen Dr
Griffith Park
5
Mt Hollywood Dr
Crystal Springs Dr
Vista del Valle Dr
101
Hollywood Reservoir
Beachwood Dr
Canyon Dr
Hollywood Bowl
Outpost Dr
Runyon Canyon Park
Los Feliz Blvd
Franklin Ave
Cahuenga Blvd
Hollywood Blvd
Barnsdall Park
Hollywood and Highland
Highland Ave
Sunset Blvd
Vine St
Van Ness Ave
Normandie Ave
Edgemont St
Fountain Ave
Santa Monica Blvd
Western Ave
Willoughby Ave
Waring Ave
Melrose Ave
101
N
0
1 mi
0
1 km

Author's Top Picks in Hollywood

Hollywood & Highland coffee and poetry court

Frederick's of Hollywood Museum of Lingerie

L. Ron Hubbard Life Exhibition Museum

Sunset Ranch sunset ride

Hollywood Bowl

light behind you, or downing organic dun dun noodles next to you at a local low-fat health bar.

So walking Hollywood is the best way to see it and see the culture that comes from it. A trip through Hollywood comes in two parts: Hollywood at its core along the blocks of Hollywood Boulevard—a stroll that requires a certain sense of humor—and the spots that surround central Hollywood in parks, lots, and legend.

Head for Hollywood on the ***Red Line*** subway system that runs from Downtown Los Angeles along Wilshire Boulevard for a stop at Hollywood's new epicenter location at Hollywood & Highland (see below). A good thing to have in your pocket is a ***CityPass,*** which will get you entrance into Universal Studios Hollywood (two Red Line stops away) as well as American Cinematique at the Egyptian Theater, the Hollywood Entertainment Museum, the Autry Museum of Western Heritage, a 150-minute Starline bus tour of Hollywood and Hollywood star homes, and other museums and attractions outside Hollywood (see below for more on many of these attractions). The $59 pass more than pays for itself between the Universal Studios Hollywood admission—currently $43—and the $29 bus tour. The best way to buy is electronically: www.citypass.net.

Off the bus and more on the unbeaten path, however, are the gems to be found along the boulevard and its environs.

An official start of the ***Hollywood Walk of Fame*** can be found two blocks west on La Brea Avenue. Besides a few entertainers' names on the sidewalk, however, Hollywood really starts at the ***Hollywood Entertainment Museum*** only a block west, where a check of the basement venue brings you face to face with James Dean's leather jacket, Joan Crawford's shoulder pads, and sets from the SS *Enterprise* and *Cheers.* Admission is $8.75 and hours are 11:00 A.M. to 6:00 P.M., except Wednesday. 7021 Hollywood Boulevard, (323) 465–7900, www.hollywoodmuseum.com.

Moving east, you are now at ***Mann's Chinese Theatre*** and likely in the center of throngs of indistinguishable fanny-packed bellies and hyperactive kids. The 1927 movie palace, with some recent renovations in projection technology, screens, and stadium seating, still packs the seats with first-run films and eye display. Between the kitsch Chinese pagoda presentation and the courtyard of famous hands and feet, Mann's is worth the touristic frenzy you may have to endure, if only for a few moments.

The Chinese theater leads up to ***Hollywood & Highland,*** L.A.'s tribute to the evolution of the urban mall. This one tried to be intelligent from the start—once you make it past the T-shirt and souvenir stores. Inside, you are faced with what seems like a grand, interminable staircase in some monster mansion where makeup stores and purse boutiques call mercilessly to the youth demo with must-have glamour tools. The adults, however, can step back and enjoy the coffee—with poetry, that is. Odd poems and commentaries from Hollywood dreamers are burned into the cement to adorn the outdoor flooring. An official city tourism desk is found here, offering assistance and pamphlets on all the other well-trod tourism places to consider in the city before climbing the shop-lined edifice.

Across the street is the ***Hollywood Roosevelt Hotel,*** which still bears the markings of an earlier era when it held the first Academy Awards ceremony in 1929, hosted by Douglas Fairbanks. The lobby retains its Spanish Revival design, with the original tiles and open hacienda setting. A mezzanine walkway brings in the true history of the hotel with a time line of photographs on display and memories of the CineClub—now ***Cinegrill***—that served martinis to such legends as F. Scott Fitzgerald and even Salvador Dalí. The rooms have long since been renovated from dive Murphy-bed configurations with blood on the walls to stylish and comfortable with a touch of Deco. The ghosts remain, however. Marilyn Monroe and Montgomery Clift still appear now and then in mirrors or slamming doors. Sightings of Marilyn have been reported in a wall mirror she used when she lived in Suite 1200. Clift haunts Room 928, his digs for three months in 1952. He sometimes appears as a glimpse or as

A Little Chinese History

When Graumann's Chinese Theatre opened in 1927 to Cecil B. DeMille's King of Kings, *it was the third theater Sid Graumann had built in L.A. The developer believed the theaters should be as grand as the films themselves: His gargoyle-laden 1917 Million Dollar Theater is still standing Downtown at 307 Broadway; it cost $1 million. He opened the Nubia-inspired Egyptian Theater five years later. The footprint factor was an accident. Although no one is certain of the origins, legend likes to have it that Norma Talmadge slipped on wet cement during construction, and Graumann liked the effect. Soon Mary Pickford and Douglas Fairbanks came in for a preview tour and left prints for their time. Since then more than 200 other celebrities have followed.*

Kodak Moment

*The **Kodak Theater,** the new 3,300-seat Academy Award site at Hollywood & Highland, considers the glamour in every detail. A VIP lounge has an undulating glass flow to its design so passersby can look in, just a little, as the angle of the glass shifts with their movement, but the celebrities within cannot see out at all. The bathroom wall mirrors are tilted toward the floor to give a full view of your gown as well as your face. Thirty-minute tours are offered daily every fifteen minutes between 10:00 A.M. and 2:30 P.M., offering these little tidbits for $15 a pop. Contact (323) 308–6363 or www.kodaktheater.com.*

a touch. Psychics called upon to examine the air have noted impressions of Errol Flynn, Betty Grable, Ethel Merman, and Humphrey Bogart. 7000 Hollywood Boulevard, (323) 466–7000, www. hollywoodroosevelt.com.

On the next block sits a strangely little-known icon in movie history past and present: The ***El Capitan Theater*** is easily one of the most glamorous of the preserved film houses in Hollywood and keeps its luster from 1926, when it was converted from a live stage venue to film. The strange intersection of ornate Spanish Colonial with East Indian decor impressed audiences when the original *Citizen Kane* premiered in the 1940s. Today it has had a little Disneyfication done to it with a mezmerizing glitter curtain. It shows Disney films, often with a character stage performance beforehand. 6838 Hollywood Boulevard, (323) 467–7674.

Continuing east, along the next block between Highland and Las Palmas is what could easily be called Kitsch Museum Row. Between the ***Hollywood Wax Museum***—well worth the $10.95 entrance just to see how it's possible to make every figure look like a poor imitation of Michael Jackson's latest face or Elvis with a James Brown wig, no matter whether the figure is supposed to be Frank Sinatra or Frank Zappa (the exhibit labels come in handy here)—***Guinness World Records Museum,*** and ***Ripley's Believe It or Not.*** It's possible to get a combo ticket and down the hefty walk-in tariff. Or you can head onward to all the free entertainment ahead. Aim toward the ***Egyptian Theater,*** now home to the ***American Cinematheque,*** a film organization dedicated to the preservation and presentation of older films and genres, often with talks given by the original directors or cast. *Forever Hollywood,* a film about the city's celluloid history, runs weekends at 2:00 and 3:30 P.M. and costs $7.00. The CityPass includes this attraction or a full feature film at night. 6712 Hollywood Boulevard, www.americancinematheque.com.

Angelyne

You may notice along your traffic-crunched itineraries that you come face to face—or maybe face to chest—with strange broad billboards of a buxom blonde in perky pink looking like she's about to give the world a red-smeared smacker. Meet Angelyne, a strictly Hollywood phenomenon. She's not selling you anything, she's just doing what she loves to do: vamp for the camera. Legend has it that she found a wealthy husband who likes it, too. Confused? Feel free to get your questions answered on www.angelyne. com. More vamping and no sales pitch.

The theater itself recently resurfaced from a painstaking two-year renovation to bring it back, detail by detail, to its original 1922 presence. Inspired by the monumental tombs of Luxor and the treasures of King Tut, you can almost see the caged monkeys and Egyptian toga-clad usherettes that populated the palm-and-pyre courtyard in its 1930s halcyon days.

Walk across the street to ***Musso & Frank Grill*** for some of the meat loaf or brisket they've been serving since 1919. Neither menu nor martini mix, red vinyl booth table, or waiter has changed since it opened. Well, slight exaggerations here. The waiters have been around since the 1970s, okay? But the setting is the same as when William Faulkner lunched here with F. Scott Fitzgerald, and Mary Pickford and Douglas Fairbanks shared cocktails in the corner. 6667 Hollywood Boulevard, (323) 467–7788.

On to ***Frederick's of Hollywood*** and the bras that built Hollywood—but you'll see a tamer Frederick's of today. Trying to travel in the mainstream, the lingerie store is beginning to look a bit more like Victoria's Secret, possibly to separate itself from the plethora of trashy lingerie stores selling fishnet everything as well as vinyl body suits and thigh-high elevator boots. The Museum of Lingerie is a surprisingly healthy history of underwear and costume accoutrements worn by famous singers and actors through the years, from Madonna's bustier in the "Who's That Girl" video to Joan Crawford's hoop slip, Natalie Wood's bra in *Bob and Carol and Ted and Alice,* and Ava Gardner's underskirt in *Showboat.*

Nearby, ***Los Angeles Contemporary Exhibitions*** marks the beginning of another side of Hollywood—artsy, wild, and current. The space is a gallery that runs shows by a number of budding and well-known local artists. It is definitely worth a browse, if only to pay homage to the emerging scene in the art world. A donation of $3.00 is requested. A recent show

Enter Shopping

The first shopping mall was not that institutional geometric cement structure that seems to crown every suburb and freeway exit. It was actually ***Crossroads of the World,*** *circa 1936, at 6671 Sunset Boulevard in Hollywood. The designer, who also designed the Steamship Moderne Coca-Cola bottling plant still standing in Downtown Los Angeles, put a Tudor and Victorian garden arrangement in this project, all tied together with a neat little space-age tower and globe in the center. The quaint shops have long since turned to offices, but the atomic globe is still there.*

by artist Chris Burden titled *Small Skyscraper* presented a "quasi-legal sculpture/building that exploits a loophole the artist discovered in the Los Angeles building codes; the prototype here is displayed horizontally." Was he successful? You decide. 6522 Hollywood Boulevard, (323) 957–1777, www.artleak.org.

The area around North Cahuenga and Hollywood Boulevard rocks with cool boutiques, salons, and devotions to hip culture in an old neighborhood blooming with newly renovated spaces.

Chic ***Christie Martin*** at 1616 Cahuenga sells hand-knitted vamp attire and bitsy bikini designs to celebs like Paula Abdul. The ***Beauty Bar*** next door gives manicures and pedicures 1950s-Hollywood-style with gin martinis sipped on pink vinyl chairs while you dry. Then there is the ***Blest Boutique*** in the same cluster, which sells one-of-a-kind creations and accessories by aspiring local designers on consignment. If you're having e-mail withdrawal at this point, you can stop into ***Badlanz Internet*** down the block at 1602 North Cahuenga or choose to send your messages by spell across the street at ***Panpipes Magical Marketplace,*** 1641 North Cahuenga, which sells ingredients, charms, and custom spells for whatever your wish. Contact (323) 462–7078 or www. panpipes.com.

Moving east down Hollywood Boulevard, check out the ***L. Ron Hubbard Life Exhibition Museum,*** where you can learn everything you've ever wanted to know about the founder of Dianetics and take a test to see if maybe you, too, could aspire to higher being. The revamped Art Deco building also offers some pricey books and videos. Admission runs $5.00. 6331 Hollywood Boulevard, (323) 960–3511.

The cross street of Ivar brings some Hollywood lore and look-worthy elements. The literary ambler will appreciate 1817 Ivar, because this was ***Nathaniel West's residence*** when he was writing *Day of the Locust.* The

No Babble in Babylon

The Church of Scientology inhabits a number of buildings in Hollywood, among them the ***Chateau Elysee*** *at 5310 Franklin Avenue near Ivar. The sprawling Beaux-Arts elephant—rescued by the church from certain destruction three decades ago—had its origins in shady hush money played out in a plot that could only have been hatched in Hollywood. The celebrity hotel and hideaway was built in 1927 by Eleanor Ince, the widow of movie mogul Thomas Ince following his murder on the yacht* Oneida *owned by William Randolph Hearst. The incident remains unsolved to this day but was believed to have involved one Marion Davies, one jealous Mr. Hearst, one absent Charlie Chaplin, one dark and stormy night, and one murdered Thomas Ince. The year was 1924. Put the pieces together, and it is believed that a violently jealous Hearst assumed his mistress was carrying on with Charlie Chaplin. He burst into her stateroom and plugged the man he thought to be Chaplin—who turned out to be producer Thomas Ince. The official cause of death was heart attack.*

nearby ***Knickerbocker Hotel*** at 1714, from whence the *Queen for a Day* series hailed in the late 1950s and early 1960s, includes a famous lobby and bar area that is believed to be possessed by a variety of specters. The lobby was the last thing resident D. W. Griffith saw before his death, and the bar was the favored watering hole of Rudolph Valentino, who would arrive on horseback from his Hollywood Hills estate until he bought the farm in 1926. Other heavy frequenters included Gloria Swanson, Frank Sinatra, Bette Davis, Doris Day, Judy Garland, Cary Grant, and Marilyn Monroe—who would meet Joe DiMaggio here on secret trysts. Elvis Presley stayed at the Knickerbocker in its later days while filming *Love Me Tender.* Now it's a senior living building but sheds traces of its former glory to those who seek. 1714 Ivar Avenue.

Sunday morning is a treat on Ivar moving south toward Sunset Boulevard. The block becomes the open-air ***Hollywood Farmer's Market*** from 8:30 A.M. to 1:00 P.M. Here boutique chefs and bakers sell their flavor of the week, and fresh produce and unusual crafts and body treatments are showcased.

Continuing down Hollywood Boulevard toward Vine, watch for pieces of the area's long and tangled past as you pass such places as the ***Studio Café,*** (6633 Hollywood Boulevard) still selling pancakes, fish of the day, and jukebox tunes to patrons in red vinyl booths, and the ***Snow White*** (6769 Hollywood) palace of burgers, offered with salsa these days. You

The Loved Ones

There's no place like a cemetery to get close to the stars you love—and some you don't. ***Hollywood Forever Cemetery,*** *abutting the backlots of Paramount Studios, is the perfect place to commune with the remains of Tyrone Power, Rudolph Valentino, Jayne Mansfield, John Huston, and Charlie Chaplin—they're all here. Mausoleums that look like ancient European abbeys and a lake filled with lotus leaves and swans add character to any quiet amble. Entrance is free and parking isn't a problem, but a map is necessary if you don't want to be wandering over the remains of every Smith and Jones in the city. A paper place-mat-like map at the gift shop costs $5.00 and is your key to 101 departed Hollywood notables. 6000 Santa Monica Boulevard, (877) 844–3837, www.forevernetwork.com.*

Tyrone Power Gravesite

can get your shoes shined in the littered foyer of a barely used building next door for $3.00 or buy three suits for $299.00 from the Hollywood Suit right across the street, shirts and handkerchiefs included. Try on a monster suit or an outrageous orange wig while learning new magic tricks taught by D'Lite himself at ***Hollywood Magic*** (6614 Hollywood). For more than six decades, ***Larry Edmunds Bookstore*** at 6644 Hollywood Boulevard has been the market for still photos, celeb calendars, those hard-to-find posters like Barbarella and Farrah, and whatever books exist on theater and film past and present. Odd finds like ***Latin Sun*** at 6683 Hollywood Boulevard dot the landscape and would probably find

Vinyl Pisa

Just above Hollywood Boulevard on Vine Street is the tower of records that started it all. ***Capitol Records,*** *now a subsidiary of ABC and Disney, stands thirteen stories like giant pile of stacked LPs with a needle ready to fall onto the revolving table. The Beatles, Johnny Mercer, Frank Sinatra (Frank was the first to record in the tower's studio)—they all recorded here. The 1956 avant-garde structure was one of the coolest things going when it opened and still is, especially since the light beam on the needle still flashes out HOLLYWOOD in Morse code to those lost and in need of a sign. The lobby is worth a look for the mural depicting the legends who have recorded here over the years.*

a more fitting place to sell their hand-hewn crafts, clothes, and tapestries from South America in Santa Monica or Beverly Hills. But then, ***Abyssinia*** nearby at 6727 Hollywood Boulevard is doing a brisk business in the African jewelry, crafts, clothing, and arts trade. And retro clothing stores find their own space on this boulevard that seems to be the great equalizer among chic, trendy, cheesy, and sleazy in the glorious shadows of Babylon.

While the city churns in its mélange of angst and colorful riffraff, all around the celluloid empire are accessible paths to nature and a rare urban peace.

Lacing the havens of Hollywood are the hills that made them happen. From the Hollywood Sign to the Hollywood hideaways are wonderful spaces where nature dares to tread. Start with the ***Hollywood sign,*** found up Beachwood Drive and accessible from Franklin Street just east of Gower (Franklin runs parallel to Hollywood Boulevard, a block north). The sign is visible by mid-Beachwood and good for shots, but a hike to the site is even better. The street ends at ***Sunset Ranch,*** where you can rent a horse to call your own by the hour ($20), take the sunset ride on Friday to unparalleled vistas, and barbecue on a cowboy ride that lasts about five hours ($45). Call (323) 469–5450. Meanwhile, walkers can go where the horses don't—to the sign, reachable by a well-laid path on a pretty demanding ascent that runs 3 miles round-trip. Another path heads east instead of up and takes a more level approach that leads to parts of ***Griffith Park,*** including the Griffith Observatory (closed for renovations until 2005), ***Dante's Gardens*** on top of the mountain that overlooks the Hollywood Bowl and Greek Theater from lush, hidden picnic areas, ***Mount Hollywood*** at the summit just above the Griffith Observatory, and the descending trail to Bronson Caves that leads to a meadow and parking lot. All walks are well marked, all run between 3 and 7 miles round-trip, and there will be plenty of people to consult for directions along the way. It's a local favorite for exercise and views and horses, dogs, and coyotes are welcomed. Watch for rattlesnakes in the warm months.

For those who would prefer to hike with the stars, ***Runyon Canyon*** at the top of Fuller Street just two blocks west of La Brea on Franklin is the path of choice for sky shows and the latest in exercise chic. The 3-mile round-trip hike ascends about 400 feet to views that reach all the way to Catalina Island on a clear day. The paths in this 160-acre park that once belonged to Errol Flynn meander past the Frank Lloyd Wright–designed poolhouse where Flynn's celebrity friends frolicked until it all burned up in 1978. Pieces of the house, garden, pool, and tennis courts are still here and make entertaining diversion from the male and female eye candy airing out their flesh with Rover en route to the summit. It's easy to distinguish the working actors trying to have an anonymous workout from the wannabes hoping to get noticed. Recent sightings: Wynona Ryder, Ellen Degeneris, Elaine Boosler, Adam Arkin, and countless unnamable television profiles.

To catch the divas, however, you'll need to check out the ***Hollywood Bowl*** along Highland Avenue above Franklin Avenue. Although the amphitheater is a famous landmark along the Los Angeles landscape

Sign of the Time

The Hollywood sign has seen better days during its eighty-year watch atop Mount Lee. Originally erected with 50-foot-high letters as an advertisement to get real estate moving in the area, the first go-round actually said HOLLYWOODLAND, *but the last four letters blew away in a storm in 1949. With Black Forest–style homes and real estate offices, the surrounding property, now filled with elaborate glass mansions, woodsy cottages, and modest apartment buildings, remains one of the most desirable places to live in Hollywood. When it was owned by* L.A. Times *publisher Harry Chandler, the letters were lit by 4,000 lightbulbs, all tended by a lightbulb changer who lived in a cottage nearby. The thirteen-letter sign was thought to be bad luck—an idea confirmed in 1932 when a failed starlet jumped to her death from the letter* H. *The sign suffered from disrepair and prankstership over the years and even was spelled* HOLLYWEED *for a while during the 1960s. Eventually, the celebrities came out and rescued it, raising donations of $27,000 per letter. On December 31, 1999, the sign lit up again in its original glory, each letter glowing in 250,000 watts of brilliance. Neighbors put the kibosh on the wattage soon after. The sign has been dark ever since, but still lights up the hills in the California sunshine.*

and has been so since 1919, the magic that happens under the stars is something only the Bowl can inspire. The season runs May through September. Rehearsals are the big local secret here—no crowds, no cost, and work begins around 9:00 A.M. Otherwise, there are two other ways to do the Bowl: the nosebleed cheap seats and the boxes. Box seats are a prize in this town and rarely available without reservations or a connection. Once in, however, come early, around 6:00 or 6:30 P.M., bring the wine, the candles, and the sandwiches, and take it all in. For an off-the-beaten-track attraction, find the ***Hollywood Bowl Museum*** for the full Bowl story. It opens at 10:00 A.M. Tuesday through Saturday and offers a ten-minute movie that features the adagio from *Sleeping Beauty* in a 1928 L.A. Philharmonic performance and clips of Frank Sinatra amid tales of Frank Lloyd Wright Jr.'s two failed stabs at the half shell. Information on performances, tickets, parking, and the convenient park-and-ride options around town can be found by contacting (323) 850–2000 or www.hollywoodbowl.org.

Across the street from the Bowl, just above Franklin and before the Hollywood Freeway entrance, is another odd gem of the area: the original studio barn used by Cecil B. DeMille in shooting *The Straw Man.* The "DeMille Barn," as it's called, is now the ***Hollywood Studio Museum*** and is tucked away in a woodsy area that is otherwise a parking lot on Bowl nights and surrounded by picnic areas. Inside—which is open only on weekends between 11:00 A.M. and 3:30 P.M. or by appointment—a photo and memorabilia tribute to silent film can be found with props from 1913, cameras of the era, and a re-creation of DeMille's office. Admission is $4.00. 2100 North Highland, (323) 874–BARN.

For best of the lights of Hollywood over a Grey Goose martini or Grand Marnier Mai Tai, it's ***Yamashiro's.*** The 1913 pagoda-style palace atop this Hollywood hill sits next to a look-but-can't-touch fantasy attraction, ***The Magic Castle.*** This castle creation is open to members only (they have to have some serious or professional connection with the magical arts and be voted in by other members—but these standards, too, have relaxed over the years, and now you just have to know "somebody"), who must say the secret password before the wood-paneled walls of the library-looking lobby will part. At Yamashiro's you don't even need a reservation to sit in the bar overlooking the lights of L.A. with tall drinks served under low red lantern lights. The food, an overpriced Mom-meets-the-geisha menu, may not be worth the wait or the stay. The view, those red paper lanterns, and the lower Japanese gardens to walk while waiting for your car: perfect. Around the corner from the Hollywood Bowl at 1999 Sycamore Lane, (323) 466–5125.

Places to Stay in Hollywood

Luxe: $250 +
Deluxe: $150–$249
Good deal: $79–$149

Best Western Hollywood Hills Hotel
6141 Franklin Avenue, (323) 464–5181 or (800) 528–1234, www.bestwestern.com/hollywoodhillshotel.
Have a cappuccino by the pool in this 1930s Hollywood hotel in the shadow of the Hollywood sign. Good deal.

Hollywood Hills Magic Hotel
7075 Franklin Avenue, (323) 851–0800 or (800) 741–4915, www.magichotel.com.
Location and price make this a great bet for a night at the Bowl and a drink at Yamashiro; otherwise it's just another roadside hotel. Good deal.

Hollywood Orchid Suites Hotel
1753 North Orchid Avenue, (323) 874–9678 or (800) 537–3052.
This gem near the Chinese Theater includes kitchens in the rates. Good deal.

Renaissance Hollywood Hotel
1755 Highland Avenue, (323) 856–1200, www.renaissancehollywood.com.
Location is everything, and this hotel is in the center of it all. New and hip, it also has the necessary look and amenities. Perfect for families and business travelers. Deluxe.

Places to Eat in Hollywood

Expensive: $30.00 +
Reasonable: $15.00–$29.00
Bargain: $8.00–$14.00

Café des Artists
1534 North McCadden Place (off Sunset Boulevard), (323) 469–7300.
Country French in a California bungalow. Expensive.

Greenblatt's Deli
8017 Sunset Boulevard, (323) 656–0606.
Chicken soup, pastrami sandwiches, the New York works in its original 1950s attire. Bargain to reasonable.

Hollywood Canteen
1006 North Seward (at Santa Monica Boulevard), (323) 465–0961.
A mishmash menu of Hollywood eclectic, from chops and burgers to pasta and miso soup, in a 1930s retro setting with a back patio. Reasonable.

Off Vine
6263 Leland Way (off Sunset), (323) 962–1900.
California comfort food in a cute cottage. Find the patio and order the chocolate soufflè. Reasonable.

Pinot Hollywood
1448 North Gower (at Sunset), (323) 461–8800.
A swank power dining and cocktail spot for the studio mongers at nearby Paramount with California French cuisine created by Chef Joachim Splichal. Expensive.

Sharkey's Mexican Grill
1716 North Cahuenga Avenue (at Hollywood Boulevard), (323) 461–7881.
The best Baja cuisine in the neighborhood. Short on space and price, but long on taste. Bargain.

West Hollywood

West Hollywood is a dot on the sidewalk in the scope of L.A.'s sprawl, but it packs 1.9 miles of style into its wedge between Hollywood and Beverly Hills. Its borders seem to be everywhere—across the street over there, up to the wall over here, up to that traffic light but not beyond it, up to that curb, but not to that house. As a general guideline, though, it runs from La Brea Avenue to Doheny Drive along Santa Monica, Sunset, and Beverly Boulevards and Melrose Avenue, with lots of cuts from Hollywood and L.A. zigging and zagging through. The telltale signs of West Hollywood are the sudden plethora of blue-painted police photo boxes ready to nab your license plate at the first flash of yellow, the roving teams of parking cops ready to throw you a ticket at the first hint of transgression, and the marked increase in wonderful restaurants, boutiques, and galleries to draw you into these traps. The good news, however, is that West Hollywood is eminently walkable, very compact, and full of movieland's hippest ambience—as long as you don't drive through it.

The city of West Hollywood prides itself most on gay pride. The blocks are lined with clubs and restaurants serving the city's 36,000 residents, of whom a third are gay, 75 percent nonfamily and renters, all mixed in with hefty immigrant populations from Russia and Iran. The frenzy of focus on fashion, design, and fronting world trends rivals Paris and Milan. Hotels, restaurants, clubs, stores, boutiques, and services all cater to the gay clientele in this city that wants the world to know gays and lesbians are more than welcomed.

And with that comfort comes a smorgasbord of fabulous browsing, whether you're exploring the lumbering glass spread of the Pacific Design Center, the one-of-a-kind couture shops catering to Oscar-bearing stars, or the ambient gardens where you can sip any kind of tea. Celeb spotters, this is your territory. The ***West Hollywood Convention and Visitors Bureau*** **(CVB)**, located in the Pacific Design Center, is only too gracious and can make the visit worthwhile with maps, discount coupons, and information as well as a toll-free number, (800) 368–6020,

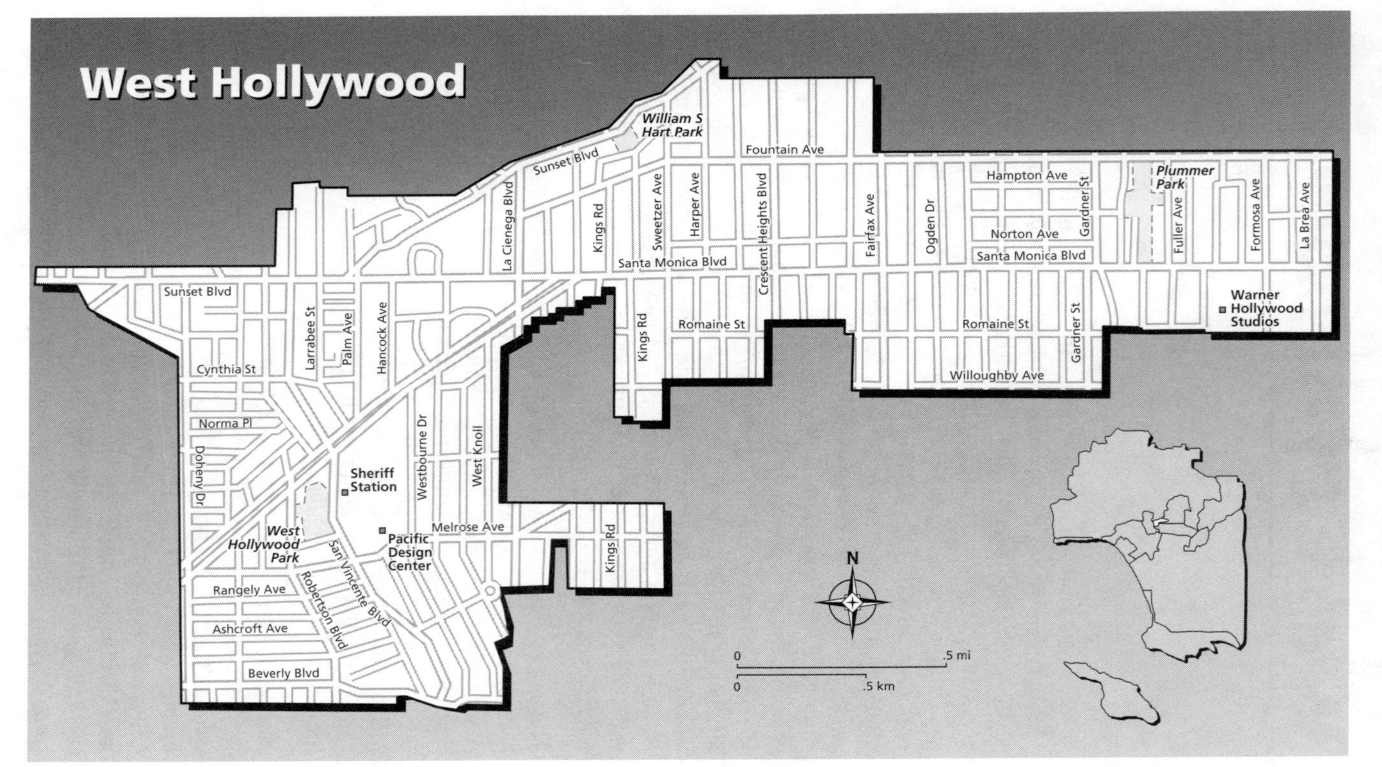
West Hollywood
William S Hart Park
Sunset Blvd
Fountain Ave
Plummer Park
Hampton Ave
Norton Ave
Santa Monica Blvd
La Cienega Blvd
Kings Rd
Sweetzer Ave
Harper Ave
Crescent Heights Blvd
Fairfax Ave
Ogden Dr
Gardner St
Fuller Ave
Formosa Ave
La Brea Ave
Warner Hollywood Studios
Romaine St
Willoughby Ave
Larrabee St
Palm Ave
Hancock Ave
Cynthia St
Norma Pl
Doheny Dr
Sheriff Station
Westbourne Dr
West Knoll
Melrose Ave
Pacific Design Center
West Hollywood Park
San Vincente Blvd
Robertson Blvd
Rangely Ave
Ashcroft Ave
Beverly Blvd
N
0
.5 mi
0
.5 km

and a Web site: www.visitwesthollywood.com.

Author's Top Picks in West Hollywood

Pacific Design Center and MOCA

Elixir Tonics and Teas

Paper Bag Princess

Just about everything in this tiny, tony, and tattered hip city is off the beaten path, if not off the beam. Start with the 1975 Cesar Pelli–designed ***Pacific Design Center.*** Locally tagged The Blue Whale (a new big red one may be in the works), it's a bit of a landmark in these parts—the round glass containment gives the city a sort of lapis lazuli shimmer, and the cavernous interiors are filled with showrooms catering to the world's top interior designers with furniture, carpets, and accessories. In recent years most showrooms have started opening their wares to the public, and clearance sales once or twice a year return the $10 entrance fee with hours of pickings and deals. These events and other promotional Design Center happenings can be tracked online at www.pacificdesign center.com or by calling (310) 657–0800. 8687 Melrose, at La Cienega.

The L.A. Museum of Contemporary Art has a branch here, although at press time the site was revamping with a garden component and closed. Famed steak-house gourmand Charlie Palmer has a restaurant on the top floor called ***Astra,*** open for lunch only. You'll find here a reasonably priced menu of finely crafted salads, sandwiches, and pastas; a rooftop dining terrace overlooking the city; and dining furniture that models some of the designs showcased in the building. Contact (310) 652–3003 or www.charliepalmer.com.

Since West Hollywood or WeHo is rather spread out in odd-shaped areas of interest, consider the area around the Whale to be design and fashion, the strip along Santa Monica Boulevard to be sophisticated, grunge, and gay, and the Sunset Boulevard passage to be 1960s-chic-meets-rock-and-roll-heaven-meets-the-far-side-of-hip. Confused? Don't judge it. Just do it.

You're in fashionland, now officially coined the ***Avenues of Art and Design*** by the CVB here, so head toward sedate and precious Robertson Boulevard and prepare to sniff around. A drive down this whitewashed street of sharp window displays and hidden courtyards reveals a few places of interest. Among them: ***Armani Casa,*** 6,800 square feet of sleek lines and tamed hues to shelter what the Italian designer likes to cushion himself with at Milan prices. The boutique is one of two Armani Casas in the States. A bricked-in recess next to ***Jordan's Enchanted Cottage*** at 409 North Robertson Boulevard provides a shaded respite from your sidewalk travels with a bird fountain and cement garden bench squeezed into this corner enclave inhabited by tea roses. Across the street at 454 North Robertson Boulevard, the ***Earl McGrath Gallery*** provides a private front courtyard that belongs in Mexico City. Plaster seating areas in bright orange and red support a forest of bamboo, a pungent orange tree, and assorted cacti, while bursts of bougainvillea complement the oddly placed bronze sculptures.

Continue south, passing at least eight fine-arts galleries along your way toward Beverly Boulevard and Third Street beyond. Stop at ***Petrossian Paris*** at 321 North Robertson for a spot of Caspian caviar with your foie gras and truffles in a quiet sidewalk shop with just a few tables. If you're looking for a show—as in people watching parade—check out ***The Abbey*** nearby at 692 North Robertson Boulevard. The setting is Gothic, the food American and affordable and rich (don't stint yourself on the overfrosted desserts), and the scene is colorful, melodramatic, and, well, très gay. Patio seating is preferred.

For a good breakfast, usually a celebrity or two, and no pretense, go to ***Ed's*** at 460 North Robertson, local diner of choice for over thirty years. Meat loaf, omelettes, and a vegetable platter are among Ed's favorites, but the meal depends on what Ed is in the mood to cook and when Ed feels like coming to work. When he does, it's breakfast and lunch only.

Beverly Boulevard lines up in a neat row of gorgeous furniture, carpet and antiques shops in warehouse-sized dimensions. Stop at ***Antiquarius,*** 8840 Beverly Boulevard, where some thirty established antiques and jewelry vendors roll out the estate goods, some for a steal, most for their Sotheby's-worthy price tag. What makes this stop nice is the convenience of one-stop shopping—or at least intensive browsing. Stop at ***Celestino's*** next door at 8908 Beverly Boulevard for pasta and insalata with a precious fileto. Eavesdrop on the tables around you, too, where eager screenwriters and agents frequently do lunch to determine what new pictures may be in the works. Call (310) 858–5777.

Move north along Robertson to get back to the WeHo wonders to be found on Melrose Avenue. Check out ***Elixir Tonics and Teas*** and let practiced herbalists create a custom blend for your immediate needs and desires. The off-the-shelf tonics here will also keep your depth recharged, your brain in gear, and your karma aligned if you use them right. The spot is back from the street a bit, but the distance seems like miles when you step into the peaceful and airy interiors leading to a shady and quiet backyard meditation garden, usually peopled by scribblers. You can have your tea here and savor it without disturbance until enlightenment comes to call. 8612 Melrose Avenue.

Walk down Melrose, past more odd collectibles shops and comely cafes, to the ***Bodhi Tree Bookstore*** at 8585 Melrose Avenue. The store is housed as it has been for nearly forty years in a little white house with wooden floors and secret corners and aisles of wisdom on New Age and old sage matters. A recent add-on is the seminar room where authors give presentations and lectures—and of course everything smells like sandalwood incense. For less up-to-date tomes, cross the street to the ***Heritage Book Shop*** at 8540 Melrose Avenue, where ghostly books of vintage value are housed in a former funeral home. Wander the display cases for first editions, artful bindery, and original manuscripts but don't overlook the medieval collection. One preserved volume from the fourteenth century is on sale here for a mere $400,000.

Just two blocks east is the ***Urth Café,*** with the usual assortment of organic coffees and too-sweet snacks, but the crowd here is A list—mostly models and actors and hopelessly aspiring types lounging the day away on the dual-level outdoor terrace flanking the sidewalk.

Moving north on LaCienega Boulevard to Santa Monica Boulevard, coffee shops—whether Buzz, Starbucks, or a personal statement on the industry—are the order of the day. The sidewalks fill with mostly men running between cafes, as well as a mélange of retail activity. Look for

Heritage Book Shop

hardware stores, a twenty-four-hour fitness club, and the ***Different Light*** gay bookstore, which offers all the theme-based titles you wouldn't find in conventional bookstores plus nearly nightly literary events by the authors who created them. Find them at 8853 Santa Monica Boulevard, www.adlbooks.com. The boulevard is also L.A.'s extension of Route 66 if you get lost and need to find your way to St. Louis. Notable along this road is ***The Troubadour,*** where legends like Arlo Guthrie, Joan Baez, and Bob Dylan got their starts in the early 1960s, and where every musician en route to greatness must play, often accompanied by famous drop-ins. The place still keeps the crowds coming with popular artists in rock and indie funk. 9081 Santa Monica Boulevard; contact (310) 276–6168 or www.troubadour.com for a current schedule.

Where some legends and a lot of regular folks get their designer duds is the ***Paper Bag Princess.*** The store maintains 3,000 square feet of vintage couture and designer resales. Owned by a noted expert in vintage couture collecting, the store is actually three separate boutiques. The front store houses the women's vintage and vintage couture clothing as well as contemporary garments and a large range of accessories. The other two shops, The Paper Bag Princess For The Palace and The Annex, are located directly behind and house the men's department, as well as the antique and vintage furnishings departments. Basically the Bag is bursting at the seams with the largest collection in the world of vintage

Play Dates

There are three events that must be heeded in the laws of West Hollywood living: Halloween, West Week at the PDC, and Gay Pride. Halloween is now called ***Carnaval*** *and hosts a costume couture awards event: 400,000 people descend into the streets of this 1.9-mile city and turn it into a writhing snakeskin of glamorous, ghoulish drag. The entertainment, the awards, and the cameras make it* the *place to be for trick-or-treat. No charge, but costumes are recommended.*

West Week *at the Pacific Design Center happens the last weekend in March and brings out the best of design showroom paraphernalia this side of New York. From odd wearable accessories to hand-sewn sheets to floor upon floor of wacko and well-heeled room furnishings, the event brings in the crowds and the bargains. Contact (310) 657–0800 or www.pacificdesigncenter.com.*

Then ***Christopher Street West,*** *on the third weekend in June, brings one of the biggest gay and lesbian pride parades in the world. Contact (323) 969–8302 or www.lapride.com.*

Emilio Pucci clothing and accessories, not to mention other sought-after vintage designs by Chanel, Hermes, Gucci, Cardin, Dior, Gernreich, Balenciaga, Yves Saint Laurent, and many others. Prices are not cheap, but the dress-up opportunities are divine. 8700 Santa Monica Boulevard, (310) 358–1985.

Moving east, find the third oldest restaurant in Los Angeles, ***Barney's Beanery.*** The chili and south-of-the-border meat loaf menu has been bringing them in since 1920 but came into itself during the depression as a roadside bean house along Route 66. It's still a favored hangout for rock musicians. Janis Joplin supposedly "beaned" Jim Morrison over the head here with a bottle of her favorite bourbon, and the story sticks that the Beanery was the last place she was seen alive. 8447 Santa Monica Boulevard, (323) 654–2287.

Animal Instincts

Animals rule in West Hollywood. The city council voted recently to ban the business of declawing cats, which is seen as cruel; local vets who perform onychectomies are cited. The city had previously ruled that the term pet owner *is not allowed in these parts. All human companions of animals are now considered pet guardians. The city has a "no-kill" policy at pet shelters, and renters are assured of their pet guardianship rights.*

Belly, at 7929 Santa Monica Boulevard, is worth checking out—although the entrance is hidden and you have to look for the relic One Hour Photo stand in the parking lot. Inside is retro-television ambience—*I Dream of Jeannie* to be exact, with a selection of tapas and Cal-Spanish foods and cocktails like classic martinis and sangrias.

Thunder Road Classic Cycles & Coffee Shop is a strange combo of turbocharged coffee and combustion. This is where you go to buy new and classic Harleys, or have your muffin and coffee—or both. You'll find cycles and umbrella tables on the sidewalk here, and a new breed of polite hog to help you with your order. 7253 Santa Monica Boulevard.

On the eastern edge of the great West Hollywood divide lies the ***Formosa Café,*** a favorite three-martini dive for glamour stars working the Warner Bros. Hollywood lot. (It's supposed to be haunted by a star, of course, but no one knows just which star that would be.) It's still intact down to its 1940s red vinyl seats and caboose lounge. A new outdoor terrace was recently added, but the real deal is inside, in the low-ceilinged, slightly rancid and clammy room dating to 1925 where all the stars eventually wound up. Many left their signed photos, which still crowd the walls. It's possible to get waited on by someone who served cocktails to Lana. The Formosa was the real backdrop for the 1997 film noir *L.A.Confidential,* in which a detective mistakes a hooker for the real Lana Turner. Actually, Lana Turner and her gangster beau, Johnny

Stompanato, were regulars at the Formosa back in the 1950s, before her daughter stabbed Stompanato to death.

Johnny's associates, Mickey Cohen and Bugsy Siegel, were also regulars at the cafe. Cohen hid his gambling winnings in a secret floor safe here; these days the money is long gone, but the safe is still there. The Formosa's "Star Dining Car," a former railroad car, once served as the center of a thriving bookmaking operation. Today the cafe is under threat but so far has stood its ground—although the ground next to it is now a gargantuan pit in the process of becoming a mega chain shopping center. 7156 Santa Monica Boulevard, (323) 850–9050.

For all the fun we've had so far, Sunset Boulevard—parallel to Santa Monica, mostly, and a few blocks north—is where the real action is in these parts. This area, called ***the Strip,*** is probably the mother of all Strips and made famous during the 1960s with the *77 Sunset Strip* series. It continues to corner the market on hip and cool. With the advent of the House of Blues in the mid-1990s and designer retail blocks between La Cienega and Fairfax, the Strip returned to its former glory days, minus the bands of Hell's Angels that once owned the road here.

We'll start at the western edge—Sunset from Doheny to Palm. This area packs the loud stuff—the legendary clubs like the ***Roxy, Rainbow,*** and ***Whiskey a Go Go,*** where the first go-go girl surfaced. With the opening of the Whiskey in 1964, the discotheque was born. The owners, who had seen Paree, found that mod made more sense than the slow-dancing, high-dressing club scene still at large. During a break from the club's first act—Johnny Rivers, to be exact—a mini-skirted, white-booted babe spinning discs in a cage above the dance floor started to boogie to the tunes she was spinning. Suddenly she had a wildly enthusiastic audience screaming for more. It doesn't take much to become a star in L.A., and this girl's fifteen minutes launched a movement.

The ***Key Club*** shores up the western frontier of Sunset's club row; others, such as the ***Viper Room*** and the ***Cat Club,*** dot the spots in between. One soft spot on the landscape is ***Hustler Hollywood*** at 8920 Sunset near San Vicente. The clothing and lingerie line here is the work of *Hustler* publisher Larry Flynt's daughter—'nuff said. Still, other items such as soaps, crèmes, and candles are cozy and comforting, and you can have your coffee and fresh-squeezed vegetable juice while reading the latest in the newsstand bookstore area.

Along the 8500 and 8600 blocks of Sunset is Designer Row at ***Sunset Plaza*** with signature stores by Nicole Miller, Dolce & Gabana, Herve Leger,

Bond, Jim Bond

*The **Spy Agency** is not as secretive a place as you might think. The company has been in business for twenty years selling hidden gun holsters, eavesdropping equipment, cameras the size of pearls, and all manner of ID-camouflage tools. The owner, a former actor and detective, now makes his fortune by designing security systems for the rich and famous, but his store is a Disneyland of odd barrier-busting equipment, including camera ties, infallible lock-picking devices, and answering machines that tell designated incoming callers that you've packed up and moved to China. 8519–8521 Sunset Boulevard, (310) 657–6333.*

Club Monaco, Traci Ross, and Anna Sui. Outdoor cafes keep a Mediterranean effect going, and the views on this hill complement the effort.

A favorite spot for casual meals with a book and a view or coffee and a paper and a view is ***Book Soup*** at 8818 Sunset. Readings by authors, great bulletin boards, a healthy inventory of periodicals and poetry collections, and a hip, edgy atmosphere make this a good stop. Tables overlook the wandering crowds on the sidewalk as well as lower West Hollywood.

Celebrity seekers will want to grab coffee at ***The Coffee House*** at 8226 Sunset Boulevard. Owned by Christian Slater, it's a cozy drop-in spot and one preferred by ambling notables who live in the neighborhood. ***Il Sole*** at 8741 Sunset Boulevard is a favorite local trough as well. Steve Martin dines here every day for lunch.

But the best dining terrace for people-watching and romance is the ***Plaza del Sol*** at 8439 West Sunset Boulevard, where Sushi Roku has cast another gem in Japanese cuisine at ***Katana.*** The southern Mediterranean terrace warmed by heat lamps and hot sake is something out of a movie set, and it all comes together with the sushi.

The Comedy Store at 8433 Sunset still packs the crowds in search of a chortle. Since it opened in 1972, it's showcased the talents of Robin Williams, Richard Pryor, Richard Lewis . . . the list is long. Even in its previous incarnation, Ciro's, it was the Rat Pack holdout that put Sammy Davis Jr. on the talent roster.

Across the street, ***the Grafton Hotel on Sunset*** blends South Beach, Hollywood, and a serious application of feng shui in its rooms, its organic bath products, and the quiet Mediterranean pool garden in the back. Meanwhile, its ***Balboa Restaurant & Lounge*** rocks. 8462 Sunset Boulevard, (323) 654–4600, www.graftononsunset.com.

Next door, the ***Mondrian*** is still getting the ink and the buzz with its sleek white-lined interiors and its ***Sky Bar,*** a patio deck and lounge scene that features the famous Rande Gerber opium beds. The view is kind, and the sky, interrupted by twinkle lights on the decorative ficus trees, is romantic. Still, the too-hip-to-be-here list is a little . . . selective. To get in, you have to know someone, be a guest of the hotel, be very pretty, or be a star. And the $10 tariff for a glass of Chardonnay is absurd. 8440 Sunset Boulevard, (323) 650–8999, www.ianschragerhotels.com.

A few doors down at the ***Argyle,*** life gets a bit tamer. The 1929 ode to Art Deco is a glorious landmark; over the years it's housed Howard Hughes, Billie Burke, John Wayne, Zasu Pitts, and Bugsy Siegel, among other legends. It sits in the background of many a past and recent film noir production and remains a hit with hipsters for its preserved suites and its restaurant, ***Fenix,*** which becomes a twenty-something nightclub on weekends—to anyone who will pay the $20 cover, no names needed. 8358 Sunset Boulevard, (323) 654–7100, www.argylehotel.com.

Steps eastward on the same side of the street is ***The Standard,*** the current flavor of the time for scenesters and worth the look. The converted apartment building is the brainchild of Andre Balazs, owner of Hollywood's legendary Chateau Marmont (see below), the Mercer in SoHo, and, more recently, the New Standard in Downtown L.A. A drop into the lobby is enough: simple furniture, simple shapes, and a performance artist behind the front desk, of course. Most nights this show consists of some young model reading a magazine in a display case on the wall. A lobby diner serves well-hyped comfort food twenty-four hours a day. The pool and view area with white cushy patio props and tea lights is a good place to party or sit alone and doesn't require an intro to do it. The rattan, egg-shaped chairs in the lounge, however, require a varying cover charge on weekends. 8300 Sunset Boulevard, (323) 650–9090.

At the eastern end of the city on a hill and hidden by trees like a castle on the hill is the Gothic presence of a long-standing L.A. icon, ***Chateau Marmont.*** The place was made even more famous in 1982 when John Belushi met his maker in Bungalow 2, but it had been catering to the troubled and famous long before Belushi found it. Built in 1927, it has been home to such privacy seekers as Garbo and Monroe, De Niro, Paul Newman and Joanne Woodward, and Sam Shepherd and Jessica Lange. Those star-studded bungalows remain a preference with the celebrity crowd and accommodations are pricey, but the ***Bar Marmont*** is an affordable way to get a piece of the action, or simply take in some amusing decor. The walls are of horsehide, while the flooring is Parisian; look to turn-of-the-twentieth-century Dutch fac-

The Argyle

tories for the lighting and to vintage Fairfax Avenue for the bricks. 8221 Sunset Boulevard, (323) 656–1010.

Take a few steps over to ***Saddle Ranch.*** The bull's the thing at this rowdy chophouse, and mounting it might win you a beer. Or sit back and let the country-western ambience entertain you with open-fire pits, fake horses

Schindler's Shack

The home at 835 North Kings Road is an homage to Viennese modernist Rudolph Schindler, a disciple of Frank Lloyd Wright and master of the modernist design movement in architecture, which you'll spot in dribs and drabs throughout Los Angeles. In the 1920s and 1930s, the house was considered a salon for leading thinkers of the time, including Theodore Dreiser and John Cage. In 1925 Richard Neutra—a fellow Viennese architect and further inspiration of modernism—moved in with Schindler. The home combines Wright's Craftsman elements with modernist twists such as sparse spaces and furnishings. Schindler lived here until 1953; and following a poorly considered renovation or two by subsequent owners, the house was finally restored to its original design and intent and is now used as a headquarters for architectural art and design information. Hours to tour the house are Wednesday through Sunday, 11:00 A.M. to 6:00 P.M., with docents available on the weekends. The cost is $5.00. 835 North Kings Road, (323) 651–1510, www.mancenter.com.

and hay bales. 8371 Sunset Boulevard, (323) 656–2007.

To end this West Hollywood tour back where we began, check out ***Tail o' the Pup*** at 329 North San Vicente Boulevard near the Pacific Design Center. This vintage-1945 stand comes in the shape of a hot dog and bun, with a striped awning in the middle. The kitsch kitchen makes it into a lot of movies and has a few fans of its own, including Billy Crystal, Richard Dreyfuss, Lily Tomlin, Magic Johnson, Whoopi Goldberg, Robert Culp, and Jenny McCarthy. But the stand is usually quiet except for a few construction workers and designers not on expense accounts that day—although in West Hollywood they're most likely actors as well.

Places to Stay in West Hollywood

Luxe: $250+
Deluxe: $150–$249
Good deal: $79–$149

Best Western Sunset Plaza
8400 Sunset Boulevard, (323) 654–0750, www.bestwesternsunsetplazahotel.com.
Great rooms, a pool view, and breakfast thrown in, all at Best Western prices. One of West Hollywood's best-kept bargains. Good deal.

Hyatt West Hollywood
8401 Sunset Boulevard, (323) 656–1234, www.westhollywood.hyatt.com.
Still the pick of hard-rock stars ever since Jim Morrison stayed here. Good location, so-so rooms. Good deal.

Le Montrose Suite Hotel
900 Hammond Street, (310) 855–1115, www.lemontrose.com.
Quiet suites with kitchens in a neighborhood close enough to the clubs but not in them. Good deal.

Le Parc Suite Hotel
733 North West Knoll Drive, (310) 855–8888, www.leparcsuites.com.
A European-style boutique hotel convenient to Melrose and the PDC that has a great pool. Good deal.

Ramada West Hollywood
8585 Santa Monica Boulevard, (310) 652–6400, www.ramada-wh.com.
One of *the* places to stay if you're gay and love pancakes. Fabulous accommodations for this chain, and look for a health club onsite as well as a Jamba Juice, a Starbucks, and Du-Par's (known for its pancakes) only other location. Good deal.

Sunset Marquis Hotel and Villas
1200 North Alta Loma Road, (310) 657–1333 or (800) 858–9758.
Lush gardens and lavish pool privacy in a three-and-a-half-acre property are key features here. Upscale rooms and private bungalows make it a favorite of famous rock stars. A recording studio and scene bar add to the appeal. Luxe.

Wyndham Bel Age Hotel
1020 North San Vicente Boulevard, (310) 854–1111 or (800) 996–3426, www.wyndham.com.
The quiet pool, the restaurant Diaghilev, the beauty salon that's well frequented by locals, and the jazz concerts on weekends put this hotel on the map for those who appreciate culture but don't want an in-your-face, required-to-be-hip experience. Deluxe.

Places to Eat in West Hollywood

Expensive: $25.00+
Reasonable: $15.00–$24.00
Bargain: $8.00–$14.00

Basix Café
8333 Santa Monica Boulevard, (323) 848–2460.
Friendly and tasty Italian. Bargain.

Confete
7953 Santa Monica Boulevard, (323) 848–7700.
A marriage of Mexico and France, with a little South America mixed in. Reasonable.

Dan Tana
9071 Santa Monica Boulevard, (310) 275–9444.
Old-style Italian with a Godfather feel. Expensive.

Jozu
8360 Melrose Avenue, (323) 655–5600.
Serious fish on a masterful menu of Pacific Rim creations. Expensive.

Koi Restaurant
730 North Cienega Boulevard, (310) 659–9449. Fusion Japanese. Expensive.

La Boheme
8400 Santa Monica Boulevard, (323) 848–2360. Pan-Asian and French in a hip, gay, Gothic environment. Expensive.

Lola
945 North Fairfax Avenue, (323) 736–5652. French, Thai, Mexican, and burgers with killer martinis in a hip, casual setting. Expensive.

Noura
8479 Melrose Avenue, (323) 651–4581. Middle Eastern–style dollops and dishes in a warm and casual Mediterranean cafe. Bargain.

Author's Favorite Places to Eat in West Hollywood

Formosa Café
7156 Santa Monica Boulevard
(323) 850–9050
(see page 69 for more information)

Il Sole
8741 Sunset Boulevard
(310) 657–1182
(see page 71 for more information)

Katana
8439 West Sunset Boulevard
(323) 650–8585
(see page 71 for more information)

Beverly Hills

Beverly Hills sits squarely in the middle of the muddle of L.A., in a spot that was once a swamp but is now home to the wealthiest zip code in the United States. The 5.7 square miles of manicured lawns, oceans of swimming pools, and stacked chateaus makes no apologies for its values. This is the place to have it all, show it all, and do it all. Forget about the price tag, just wrap it up, Jack.

While roving swatches of tourists crowd the sidewalks of what is appropriately tabbed the Golden Triangle—bounded by Wilshire Boulevard, Canon Drive, and Little Santa Monica—it's no trumped-up urban legend that you will see any number of film celebrities shopping, dining at sidewalk cafes, or standing on street corners in intense cell phone conversation. A star-centered Disneyland for some, the neighborhood coffee stop and errand hub for others, Beverly Hills is twenty blocks of beyond-style, cutting-edge showpieces. And for the Off the Beaten Path wanderer, it's a bounty of celebrity moments and over-the-top oddness.

On the historical side, Beverly Hills started as an oil investment gone bad. But the site, where the water in the mountains above what is now Sunset Boulevard collected into cascades that fell into the Los Angeles basin, became a prime target for land speculators. They named the area for Beverly Farms, Massachusetts, a favorite vacation spot of President Taft.

By 1920 the population of this hilly grove of bean farms and ranches had mushroomed to more than 600, and the settlement caught the eye of Hollywood privacy seekers looking to escape the scandal and mayhem in the Hollywood Hills to the east. Douglas Fairbanks Sr. bought a rustic hunting lodge in the heights behind what is now

Broadway Beverly Hills

In a city where everyone's an actor, there has to be a stage somewhere. The ***Canon Theater*** *runs star-studded versions of* The Vagina Monologues *as well as big and little theater productions, all with at least one household name. 205 North Canon, (310) 859–2830.*

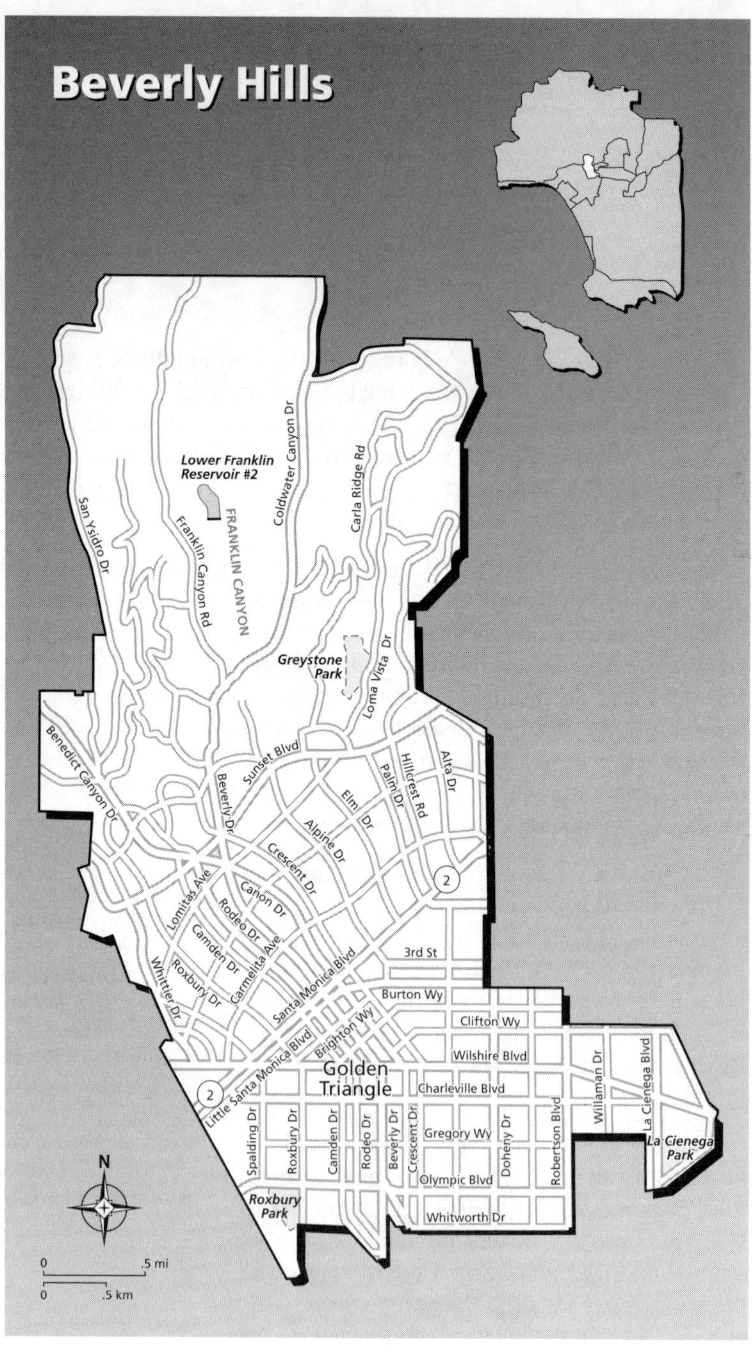
Beverly Hills
Lower Franklin Reservoir #2
FRANKLIN CANYON
Coldwater Canyon Dr
Carla Ridge Rd
San Ysidro Dr
Franklin Canyon Rd
Greystone Park
Loma Vista Dr
Benedict Canyon Dr
Sunset Blvd
Beverly Dr
Hillcrest Rd
Palm Dr
Alta Dr
Elm Dr
Alpine Dr
Crescent Dr
Canon Dr
Lomitas Ave
Rodeo Dr
Camden Dr
Carmelita Ave
Whittier Dr
Roxbury Dr
Santa Monica Blvd
3rd St
Burton Wy
Clifton Wy
Brighton Wy
Little Santa Monica Blvd
Wilshire Blvd
Golden Triangle
Charleville Blvd
Gregory Wy
Spalding Dr
Roxbury Dr
Camden Dr
Rodeo Dr
Beverly Dr
Crescent Dr
Doheny Dr
Robertson Blvd
Willaman Dr
La Cienega Blvd
La Cienega Park
Olympic Blvd
Whitworth Dr
Roxbury Park
2
2
N
0
.5 mi
0
.5 km

the Beverly Hills Hotel. He remodeled the lodge into a lavish lair for his bride, Mary Pickford, and named the fourteen-acre Tudor-style estate ***Pickfair.*** Charlie Chaplin, Gloria Swanson, Will Rogers, and an A list of studio escapees were soon to follow, and by 1930 the population had exploded to more than 17,000—enough to incorporate into its own little town and stay out of the reach of conservative Los Angeles politicians.

Author's Top Picks in Beverly Hills

Brighton Coffee Shop
Greystone Manor grounds
Franklin Canyon
The Witch's House
Beverly Hills Hotel

Beverly Hills has remained an independent enclave and prides itself on its own rules: Smoking in restaurants was banned here long before it became law in California, for instance, and fast-food restaurants are verboten. What the casual wanderer will find, however, is that not all streets are Rodeo Drive and not everything is about shopping in these miles of style. There are bargains to be found, streets to be walked, and parks to be enjoyed no matter what your wallet dictates.

Start with ***Two Rodeo Drive*** on the corner of Wilshire Boulevard and Rodeo. This $200 million Disney-style Spanish Steps homage is home to a cobbled pedestrian walk lined with diamond-dripping designer showrooms. The Roman arches, columns, solid bronze doorways, sculpted fountains, and Italian glass street lamps are welcomed touches given the somewhat squat and square 1960s building designs forming the rest of the neighborhood. Tiffany, Cartier, Charles, and Gianni Versace all have spots here. The ***Piazza Rodeo*** at the end of the cobblestone promenade is a great place to stop and people-watch while having lunch at an outdoor bistro. For a dinner that will satisfy the dangerous eater in you—and set you back more than a few hundred clams per person—have a sushi event at ***Ginza Sushi-Ko,*** camouflaged between the lavish doorways along Via Rodeo. There's no menu here; you eat what the chef gives you, and chances are at least one of the items will be fugu, or blowfish. But this is one of the only places in the United States where you might want to sample the poisonous treat, prepared by the expert hands of chef and owner Masa Takayama. Dinner only is served, and expect to see some household names among the tables. 218 North Rodeo, (310) 247–8939.

Parking Tips

On-street parking may be slim and valet parking may be pricey, but Beverly Hills is loaded with free and cheap spots to leave your vehicle. From Two Rodeo (with a 600-space underground garage) to tower structures on Brighton, Camden, and Bedford, parking is free for the first hour or two and then charged out at $2.00 an hour after. No validations necessary.

Pit Stop, Beverly Hills—Style

If you're driving, check out the ***Union 76*** *gas station on Little Santa Monica Boulevard where it becomes Burton Way on the eastern edge of the commercial district. The station is one of the only full-service operations in the city (with the most expensive gas to match) but preserves the fanciful sloping and angled elements of the Googie movement in California design so popular in the early 1960s.*

A quick run-through of the stores encountered along ***Rodeo Drive*** includes Valentino his and hers, Frette linens, Bang & Olufson, Ralph Lauren, La Perla, Bulgari, Dolce & Gabana, Chanel . . . Every shop has its thing: ***Harry Winston,*** where the stars line up to borrow their diamond neckware on Oscar night; ***Fleur de Lis,*** where Barbra, Whoopi, and Faith Hill buy their dried flower bouquets; ***Donatella Versace,*** where J.Lo buys her barely dresses dresses; ***Judith Ripka,*** where the Clintons go for their jewelry when they're in town . . . the list is daunting, and when you're just an average face in sneakers, even entering a shop can be intimidating. The low-wage-plus-commission sales staff might stare you down and ignore you otherwise, but show some serious interest and you could have a good time. Do pay attention to who might be in the dressing room next to yours, and note that most of these shops have private hidden entrances in the back alley or a subterranean garage that are employed by celebrities but also open to anyone who wants to use them.

Just to the east of Rodeo Drive is ***Beverly Drive,*** which operates as a sort of "off-Rodeo" complement. Stores like Ann Taylor, Anthropologie, Williams Sonoma, and other upscale emporiums here mix with rarefied shoe and accessory shops. The items are more off the rack than Rodeo, but prices are at chain levels and bargains can be had. Similarly, even Rodeo Drive has clearance sales during the usual post-Christmas and midsummer seasons, among other times. That Valentino blazer you saw for $1,800 might cost $800 now.

Along the side streets of ***Brighton Way*** and ***Dayton Way*** and the minor throughway of ***Little Santa Monica Boulevard,*** look for a number of independent boutiques where up-and-coming designers try to make a statement of their own. Stores with names like Kitty B, Jill Roberts, Laila, Selfish, Laurence, and Votre Nom make wonderful segues from the usual Rodeo listings, and they tend to be a lot more welcoming.

The off-off-Rodeo store of the hour these days is ***Lily et Cie,*** where all those designer-name custom couture creations get a second chance. This is not your mother's thrift shop. The classy vintage-clothing store at Burtan Way and Doheny Avenue is the boutique of choice for Renée Zellweger, Winona Ryder, Demi Moore, and Chloë Sevigny—it's an inside secret among stars. On the racks are signature American pieces such as sequined cocktail creations by Norell; the collections of Yves Saint Laurent, Givenchy, Chanel, Balenciaga, and Cassini; and American designers like Trigere and the futurist Gernreich. Check the handbag collection: Hermés, Chanel, and Judith Lieber, in addition to jewelry from the 1940s through the 1970s by Miriam Haskell, William De Lillo, and Kenneth Jay Lane. All items are in mint condition. The stock is the culmination of twenty years of scouring and collecting by proprietress Rita Watnick. Although the prices aren't St. Vincent's, they're not Sotheby's either. 9044 Burton Way, (310) 724–5757.

Ambassador of Hospitality

The Regent Beverly Wilshire has had its own ambassador for twenty-six years. Ron Howard (no relation to the child-star-turned-director) has been welcoming heads of state with mariachi bands or with the Boston Pops; he's also had to hail Prince Charles with a gangplank and a boatswain's mate, procure elephants for some partying Republicans and a cheetah for a fashion shoot, and make sure guests are happy as honeymooners on their way to Hawaii through it all.

While many of the restaurants along these gilded sidewalks tend to be chic, pricey, and loaded with attitude, there are still a number of down-to-earth cafes where the food is fine and the atmosphere runs the gamut from casual to casual. Celebrities tend to prefer these corners, often on first-name terms with the cooks or counter help and basking in the lack of attention afforded them in a neighborhood setting. ***Nate 'n Al's*** is one such place. Serving pastrami to the stars since 1943, it's *the* place to go in Beverly Hills for a good bagel and a great bowl of matzo ball soup. Not much has changed here since Doris Day used to wander by in her bathrobe to get her coffee and smeared toasted bagel. Rita Hayworth and Ava Gardner were regulars, as were the Sinatras (pre-Mia), Lew Wasserman, and James Garner. Today the dark corners tended by matronly waitresses keep the coffee brewing for Lakers players, rock stars, and a few of the old guard in search of a good breakfast. 414 North Beverly Drive.

Another spot, favored by *Seinfeld* creator Larry David and featured regularly in his HBO comedy series *Curb Your Enthusiasm,* is the ***Brighton Coffee Shop.*** Club sandwiches, hamburgers, a tall Diet Coke with homemade potato salad—this is the kind of lunch place every small town has. Prices fit the food, and the place is buzzing at lunch with agents, actors, construction crews, and office workers. 9600 Brighton Way.

On the other side of the refreshment spectrum are the afternoon high teas run at the ***Regent Beverly Wilshire*** (9500 Wilshire Boulevard; 310–275–5200) and ***Peninsula Beverly Hills*** (9882 South Santa Monica Boulevard; 310–551–2888), where menus of precious green and black tea infusions are presented with finger sandwiches, petits fours, and the requisite selection of scones with crème fraîche and jellies, all served by handsome white-gloved waiters with accents.

Beverly Hills counts no fewer than a hundred beauty salons and spas among its compact streets and avenues. Many of these establishments are household names now, thanks to daytime television: ***Jose Eber, Juan Juan, Georgette Klinger, Frederic Fekkai, Joseph Martin,*** and ***Christophe.*** Every one of them boasts an A-list clientele, often seen sitting in quiet corners dripping in foil wraps. A date with the artist of name is a privilege open to anyone who will pay the tariff, however. Day spas, too, come with cachet and top-of-the-line products—the latest from Paris, Milan, or Sydney, brow lines by the artists who invented them, and facials delivered in back gardens amid fountains and props of greenery.

Although Beverly Hills is largely about shopping, dining, pampering, and more shopping, it does have its share of museums and attractions, as well. ***The Museum of Television and Radio,*** for instance, archives several hundred thousand hours of broadcast programming, from Franklin Roosevelt's fireside chats to classic episodes of *The Lucy Show,* and makes them available to visitors in listening and viewing rooms. The 150-seat theater runs regular programs on rare television footage, usually with expert discussions afterward. The lobby runs regular exhibits such as Star Trek costumes and drawings for Peanuts holiday specials. 465 North Beverly Drive (at Little Santa Monica Boulevard), (310) 786–1000, www.mtr.org.

Though not a museum, the ***Academy of Motion Picture Arts and Sciences*** at 8949 Wilshire Boulevard is a magnet for film study and events, including screenings and lectures at the Samuel Goldwyn Auditorium and other area theaters. The lobby often posts photographic Oscar moment displays. The nearby ***Margaret Herrick Library of the Academy of Motion Picture Arts and Sciences*** houses one of the world's most extensive and comprehensive research and reference collections on film, including more than 20,000 books; 1,400 periodical titles; 60,000 screenplays; 200,000 clipping files; 15,000 posters; lobby cards, pressbooks, and other advertising ephemera; more than 6 million photographs; over 300 manuscript and other special collections relating to prominent industry individuals, studios, and organizations; sheet music, musical scores, and sound recordings; production and costume sketches; artifacts; and oral histories. All of this is open to the public on a noncirculating basis in a Spanish Revival–style complex that was once a water treatment plant. 333 South La Cienega Boulevard, (310) 247–3020.

The Museum of Television and Radio

The residential side of Beverly Hills brings a bit of history, a lot of fantasy, and some unexpected tides of beauty to an L.A. exploration. The ***Virginia Robinson Estate*** presents a rare chance for wanderers to check out a real live Beverly Hills mansion. Built in 1911, this spot doesn't offer much in the way of scandal and fancy. It belonged to Virginia Robinson (of Robinsons-May department store fame), who was known as the "First Lady of Beverly Hills." She had a green thumb and transformed her hilly, fifteen-acre estate into a lushly landscaped, tropical oasis, inviting the likes of Fred Astaire, Charles Boyer, Maurice Chevalier, and Ronnie Reagan to her grand parties. She died just before her hundredth birthday and willed the lot to the county. The gardens are modeled after the great gardens of Europe, and the grand 6,000-square-foot (modest by Beverly Hills standards) Beaux-Arts residence is fitted with mirrored walls to reflect the gardens and Palladian poolhouse on the grassy front terrace. Docent-led tours of the house and gardens run ninety minutes by appointment Tuesday through Friday (calling a week in advance is suggested), and cost $7.00. 1008 Elden Way, above Sunset and behind the Beverly Hills Hotel, (310) 276–5367.

For the spontaneous ambler, a trek to Greystone Park and Mansion is in order. Located above Sunset Boulevard, this spread is loaded with history and scandal and with grounds that are open daily and free to wander. The largest home ever built in Beverly Hills, the fifty-five-room ***Greystone Manor*** was the work of Edward Doheny, who made the first oil strike in the city and purchased and developed the 415-acre plot for his only son. Nearly $5 million went into this project—and that was 1927!

Although Doheny was in the middle of indictments at the time for his role in the Teapot Dome scandal, the home was built and son Ned moved in with wife and five kids. Ned hadn't lived here for even a year, however, before his body was found—along with that of his male secretary—in his bedroom in what was believed a murder-suicide.

The mansion later served as home to such owners as George Hamilton before being sold off piece by piece; eventually what was left was given to the city of Beverly Hills. Although you cannot go into the massive Tudor mansion (unless it's hosting a movie production or special event), the sixteen acres of eucalyptus-shaded grounds, lavish green meadows, and peaceful courtyards are here for your enjoyment. A peek through the smudged windows of the mansion will reveal vast marble halls and grand parquet ballrooms, crystal chandeliers, massive marble fireplaces, and sweeping stone archways. The grounds are maintained and nearly always uncrowded, but they do show their age with dried-up water features, cracked cement structures and missing tiles here and there. 905 Loma Vista, (310) 550–4796.

Continuing northward and up the canyons of Beverly Hills, a look at ***Franklin Canyon,*** a nature track also owned by the Dohenys until 1977, provides good hiking and great views. It is one of the most accessible areas of the Santa Monica Mountains National Recreation Area, with more than one hundred acres of hiking, picnicking, and marked trails. A pond in the upper canyons is left as a preserve for wild fauna; a nature center offers interpretive displays and lectures. The best way to find the area is to follow Beverly Drive above Sunset Boulevard to 2600 Franklin Canyon Drive, or call (310) 858–3090.

Rent a 'Vette

You, too, can drive a Ferrari, and it will only cost you $200—for the day. The best way to test-drive your dream ride is to rent one, and ***Budget Car Rental*** *in Beverly Hills runs a line of exotic and luxury sports cars that will help you fit in with the occasion. 9815 Wilshire Boulevard, (310) 274–9173 or (800) 227–7117.*

Meanderings around the neighborhoods in the vicinity offer their own share of amusement and history. The ***O'Neill House*** at 507 North Rodeo is an architectural beauty built in the style called Gaudí-esque Art Nouveau or Art Nouveau Fantasy, inspired by Spanish architect

Take It to the Tailor

When in Beverly Hills, do as the natives do—and what the style-focused natives here do when stocking their wardrobes is go to ***Amir****, designer to the stars as well as to royalty, at the Beverly Hills Hotel. Cary Grant made him famous, and since the 1970s his clients have included President Clinton, Larry King (Amir gave him the suspender touch), Prince Charles, Mikhail Gorbachev, King Juan Carlos, and, well, a few locals like Kevin Costner and Tony Bennett. A custom shirt will set you back only five or six C-notes. But you get the stories for free.*

Antonio Gaudí. All the rooms are round or oval to celebrate the organic forms of nature. Mushrooms and dancing girls sprout from the colorful tiled roof of the guest house in the rear and the tile work, done by six different craftsmen, bears each signature in the tile designs. At 516 North Walden (at Carmelita), you'll find what is known as ***The Witch's House,*** built in 1921 when the fairy-tale design so ubiquitous in L.A. was the thing. The house leans and dips in irregular shapes with a steep shingled roof and a scary angled gable over the entrance. The house is a residence, and no nefarious activity around the grounds has been reported.

The clean geometric lines of lower Beverly Hills and the curving canyons above Sunset are full of celebrity and scandal that any number of mind-numbing bus tours might illuminate. Among them: ***Lana Turner's home*** at 730 North Bedford Drive, where her daughter stabbed Mom's lover Johnny Stompanato to death in the kitchen (it was later deemed "justifiable homicide"); ***Jimmy Stewart's*** former home at 918 Roxbury; and ***Lucille Ball***'s nearby at 1000 Roxbury. Then, at 1011 Beverly Drive, find the former home of ***Marion Davies*** and the spot where William Randolph Hearst died in 1951.

Another requisite piece of Beverly Hills landscape and history is the ***Beverly Hills Hotel,*** also known as the Pink Palace, sitting at the corner of Sunset Boulevard and Beverly Drive. The grande dame of Beverly Hills is eighty-three years old and—following a three-year, $100 million face lift in the mid-1990s—restored to her former glory. This is where you have that lunch in the Polo Lounge and make sure you get publicly paged as often as possible. Although now importance is measured in cell phone activity, the place is still a valued spot for getting noticed. The history here involves affairs between stars such as Marilyn Monroe and Yves Montand in the private bungalows by the pool. The same bungalows were also employed by such names as Elizabeth Taylor, Walter Annenberg, Howard Hughes, and Jean Peters over the years. 9641 Sunset Boulevard, (310) 276–2251 or (800) 283–8885, www.thebeverlyhillshotel.com.

The big secret at the Beverly Hills Hotel is the ***Fountain Coffee Shop*** in the downstairs area, which remains true to every inch of its 1949 splendor. Open from 7:00 A.M. to 7:00 P.M. daily with informal breakfast, lunch, and light dinner menus, it also serves homemade natural ice creams, fresh fruit smoothies, and fresh-baked pastries, pies, and cakes. The soda fountain offers a large selection of the specialties from the 1950s—sodas, floats, malts, and shakes—to customers sitting on the twenty pink bar stools that originally surrounded the classic curved soda fountain counter.

An easy way to do Beverly Hills without reading maps and addresses is to take one of several trolley tours offered by the city in the warm seasons. Regular forty-minute docent-led tours use an open-air San Francisco cable car departing from the Trolley Stop at Rodeo Drive and Dayton Way to local spots of interest, pointing out the architecture, street art, and celebrity trivia.

An ***Art and Architecture Trolley Tour*** is a fifty-minute option that visits the Gagosian Gallery, Creative Artists Agency, and the Museum of Television and Radio. You'll also hear about the City Hall building and the Civic Center Complex, designed by Charles Moore, one of the architect founders of the postmodernist movement. Tours cost $5.00 and run hourly from noon to 4:00 P.M. on Saturday from May to November and Tuesday through Saturday until 5:00 P.M. July 5 through Labor Day. Call (310) 285–2438 for added information.

On Sunday the ***Beverly Hills Farmer's Market*** gets under way with bins of fresh California-grown and -made fruits and vegetables, juices, breads, and specialty items in what amounts to a festive outdoor block party on North Canon Drive. The market runs 9:00 A.M. to 1:00 P.M., rain or shine.

The ***Beverly Hills Conference and Visitors Bureau*** runs a pretty tight ship of visitor services, with maps and materials and a comprehensive Web site at www.beverlyhillscvb.com. Call (800) 345–2210.

Places to Stay in Beverly Hills

Luxe: $250+
Deluxe: $150–$249
Good deal: $79–$149

Avalon Hotel
9400 Olympic Boulevard, (310) 277–5221 or (800) 535–4715, www.avalonbeverlyhills.com. Midcentury modern for the new millennium, this hotel boasts lava lamps and bar cabanas around a figure-eight pool. Featured in the film *Catch Me if You Can*, it's still a party and meeting hotel for area media and trend followers. Deluxe.

Beverly Crescent
403 North Crescent Drive, (310) 247–0505. Cute, comfortable rooms in a great location a stone's throw from Rodeo Drive. This small hotel leans toward the European tradition of hospitality, with continental breakfast included. Good deal.

Beverly Hills Inn
125 Spaulding Drive, (310) 278–0303 or (800) 463–4466, www.innatbeverlyhills.com. Now part of a chain called Mosiac Hotels, this hip, forty-six-room boutique hotel packs all the amenities: fitness room, sauna, business center, bar, American breakfast, and turndown service. Good deal.

Beverly Reeves Hotel
120 South Reeves Drive, (310) 271–3006, www.bhreeves.com. This cozy, boutique forty-room property in a residential neighborhood is a bargain and a find. The Euro-provincial rooms aren't fancy but can be had for as little as $45. Good deal.

Four Seasons Los Angeles
300 South Doheny Drive, (310) 273–2222 or (800) 332–3442, www.fourseasons.com. This 285-room (a third of them balcony suites) luxury abode at the eastern edge of Beverly Hills is a favorite for privacy-seeking celebs, film and music industry execs, and anyone else who values calm, beauty, and service. Complimentary limousine transfers to Rodeo Drive add a nice touch. Luxe.

Luxe Hotel Rodeo Drive
360 North Rodeo Drive, (310) 273–0300 or (800) 468–3541, www.luxehotels.com. This is the only hotel right smack dab in the heart of Rodeo Drive. The eighty-eight airy, pastel-colored rooms all look out over the ritzy shopping district or the lush inner courtyard. Reasonably priced for the location and level of style. Deluxe.

Maison 140
140 South Lasky Drive, (310) 281–4000 or (800) 432–5444, www.maison140beverlyhills.com. This forty-five-room boutique hotel in a house once owned by Lillian Gish is awash in ultrahip ambience played out in Euro-Asian accents running from the tasteful to the neobordello. Room services and fitness amenities are dependent on its sister property, Avalon, but rates for the ambience and location remain reasonable. Deluxe.

Suite Dreams

*The **Regent Beverly Wilshire** rents out its Pretty Woman Suite (known for its use in the movie where Roberts and Gere had their fairy-tale tryst) to those who will pay the price. In real life it's the Presidential Suite. Nightly rack rates start at $5,500. 9500 Wilshire Boulevard, (310) 275–5200.*

Merv Griffin's Beverly Hilton
9876 Wilshire Boulevard, (310) 274–7777 or (800) 922–5432, www.merv.com.
This hotel, home of the Golden Globe Awards, was a favorite of the Reagans and the Sinatras long before Merv bought it. The 1970s talk-show celebrity brought it back to its former glory with extensive renovations and upgrading and the jewel in the crown: the Coconut Club at Trader Vic's, featuring mai tais, big-band sounds, salsa, and disco—depending on the night—and a swinging crowd to match. Deluxe.

Peninsula Beverly Hills
9882 Little Santa Monica Boulevard, (310) 551–2888 or (800) 462–7899, www.peninsula.com.
Still a favorite of the name-brand A-list crowd, this is a place where staff greet you by name. The very comfortable rooms have high-thread-count bedding, silk cushion coverings, and balconies overlooking trellised gardens; many have a fireplace. The rooftop pool and spa add spice to any moment, and the Belvedere dining room is the favored power-lunch spot for producers, agents, and their actor clients. Luxe.

Radisson Beverly Pavilion
9360 Wilshire Boulevard, (310) 273–1400 or (800) 333–3333, www.radissonbeverlyhills.com.
You'll find 110 recently renovated rooms here, along with a rooftop pool, views of the city, a fitness center, and an excellent restaurant–coffee shop—all for rates under $200. Deluxe.

Raffles L'Ermitage
9291 Burton Way, (310) 278–3344 or (800) 800–2113, www.lermitagehotel.com.
This is where the Saudi sheikhs come to stay and spend money in Los Angeles. Rooms wax Japanese in style and are stacked with high-tech, big-screen everything, while the minimalist design of the public areas offers a sense of serenity in a complex world. Luxe.

Places to Eat in Beverly Hills

Expensive: $25.00+
Reasonable: $15.00–$24.00
Bargain: $8.00–$14.00

Crustacean
9646 Little Santa Monica Boulevard, (310) 205–8990.
This cavernous homage to French, Vietnamese, and Chinese cuisine does not disappoint. The spiced crabs are a must, and all the dishes deserve a focused moment to indulge in the piquant tastes. The menu is a pricey one, although quite reasonable for Beverly Hills. Expensive.

Author's Favorite Places to Stay in Beverly Hills

Peninsula Beverly Hills
9882 South Santa Monica Boulevard
(310) 551–2888
(see page 81 for more information)

Regent Beverly Wilshire
9500 Wilshire Boulevard
(310) 275–5200
(see page 81 for more information)

Luxe Hotel Rodeo Drive
360 North Rodeo Drive
(310) 273–0300 or (800) 468–3541
www.luxehotels.com

Il Cielo
9018 Burton Way,
(310) 276–9990,
www.ilcielo.com.
Il Cielo is all about the sky and the garden and remains one of the most romantic places to dine in L.A. Candles on the tables, twinkle lights on the trees—all is shadow and low lights enjoyed in the open air with a classic Italian menu. Expensive.

Kate Mantilini
9101 Wilshire Boulevard,
(310) 278–3699.
An ode to classic American cooking in a contemporary white-linen setting. Steak sandwiches, meat loaf, and mashed potatoes are the fare and a hit with the industry moguls who eat here. Reasonable.

Maple Drive
345 North Maple Drive,
(310) 274–9800, www.mapledriverestaurant.com.
Maple Drive is the spot for haute gourmet comfort food, avant-garde meat loaf, prime ten-ounce Culotte top sirloin, chicken in the pot, and what's well known in these parts as "Kick-Ass" Chili. Great jazz quartet on weekends. Expensive.

Nouveau Café Blanc
9777 Little Santa Monica Boulevard,
(310) 888–0108.
Creative and pricey French-Asian fusion in an upscale bistro setting near Rodeo Drive. Try the foie gras, soft-shell crab, rack of lamb, and mango tart. Expensive.

Spago
76 North Canon Drive,
(310) 385–0880,
www.wolfgangpuck.com.
Wolfgang Puck's original and still a landmark for good eating. You're bound to see a star or three at lunchtime. The vegetable soup with goat cheese and basil is irresistible even to the rich and famous. Expensive.

Author's Favorite Places to Eat in Beverly Hills

The Fountain Coffee Shop at the Beverly Hills Hotel
9641 Sunset Boulevard
(310) 276–2251
(see page 86 for more information)

Brighton Coffee Shop
9600 Brighton Way
(310) 276–7732
(see page 81 for more information)

Nate 'n Al's
414 North Beverly Drive
(310) 724–0101
(see page 81 for more information)

Crustacean
9646 Little Santa Monica Boulevard
(310) 205–8990

West Los Angeles

West Los Angeles makes Beverly Hills look like a hiccup. The term is used to describe anything that isn't nailed down to another city and lies south of the Santa Monica Mountain ridge, north of L.A. International Airport, and just east of the ocean. For our purposes it means ***Westwood, Culver City, Brentwood, Bel Air,*** and the ***Pacific Palisades***—and be prepared to load up at the gas station and go nowhere in the traffic.

Still, navigated at the right times of day—usually between 10:00 A.M. and 2:00 P.M.—the streets will be friendly enough and the finds will be worthwhile.

The sprawl that is West Los Angeles got started in the 1920s with the opening of the University of California Los Angeles in 1919. Westwood, the anchoring village, remains today a precious Spanish Revival enclave of quads and courtyards with motley cafes, theaters, and retail shops to wander. Between Beverly Hills and Westwood lies a 1970s experiment in Naked City architecture in Century City, a personalityless pimple of corporate glass-and-steel high-rises with the gray suits to match inside and an outdoor shopping mall to service all the worker bees in this ultraplanned community. South of Westwood and Century City is Culver City at the spine, cushioned by an ethnic and chain mix of retail in what is called West Los Angeles. To the north of Century City and Westwood is the manse parade of Bel Air. West of Bel Air is eclectic but mostly residential Brentwood, followed by sweeping views of the ocean offered by Pacific Palisades.

Enter ***Culver City*** along Venice Boulevard, a broad street that runs from Downtown to the beach. Just west of Fairfax Avenue, the ***Helms Bakery*** complex will be your first stop. This five-acre campus of furniture warehouses and interior design showrooms would not be worth mentioning except that the architects and planners of this imposing city block did it right. The site is the old Helms Bakery, a landmark Art Deco building that was the source of smothering bread smells since 1930 when it dis-

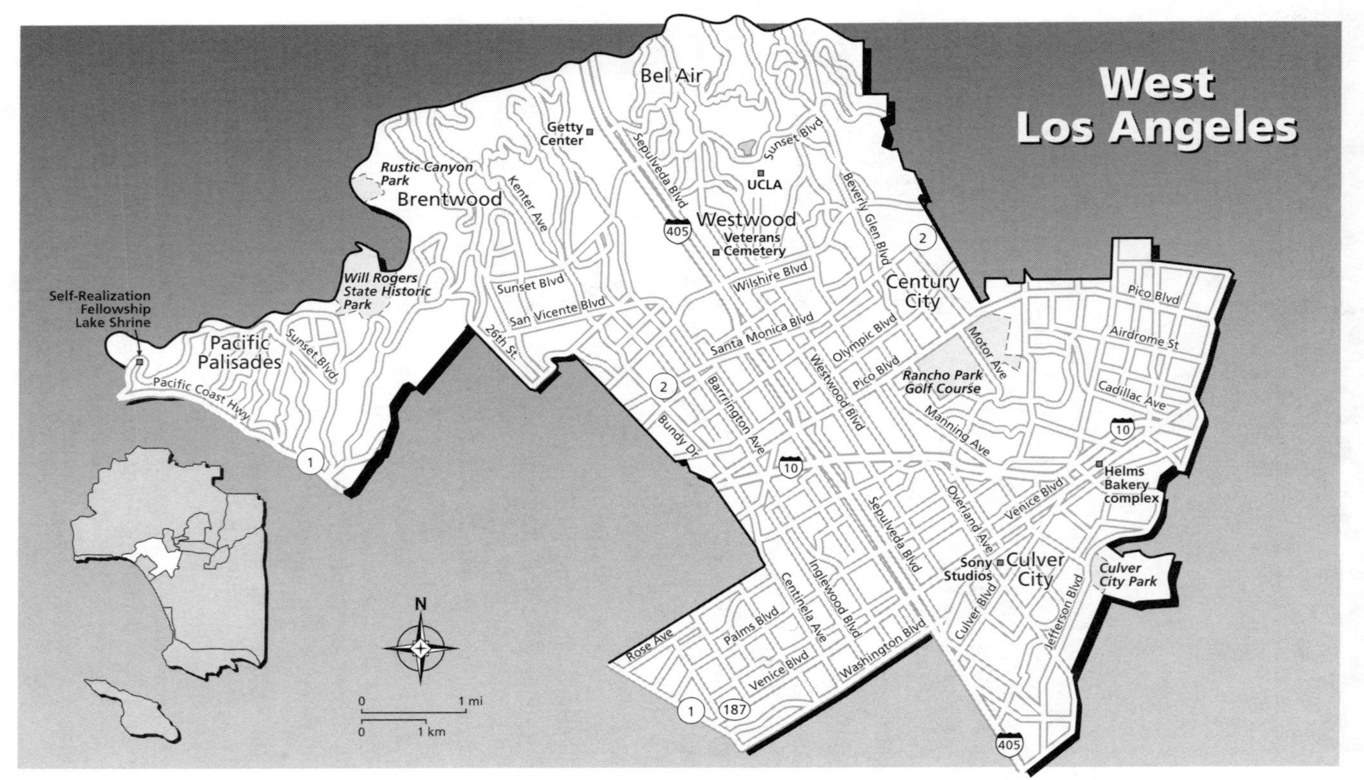
West
Los Angeles
Bel Air
Getty Center
Sepulveda Blvd
Sunset Blvd
UCLA
Rustic Canyon Park
Brentwood
Kenter Ave
405
Westwood
Veterans Cemetery
Beverly Glen Blvd
2
Will Rogers State Historic Park
Sunset Blvd
Wilshire Blvd
Century City
Self-Realization Fellowship Lake Shrine
San Vicente Blvd
Pico Blvd
Pacific Palisades
Sunset Blvd
26th St.
Santa Monica Blvd
Olympic Blvd
Motor Ave
Airdrome St
Pacific Coast Hwy
2
Barrrington Ave
Westwood Blvd
Pico Blvd
Rancho Park Golf Course
Cadillac Ave
Bundy Dr
Manning Ave
10
1
10
Helms Bakery complex
Venice Blvd
Sepulveda Blvd
Overland Ave
Sony Studios
Culver City
Culver City Park
Centinela Ave
Inglewood Blvd
N
Palms Blvd
Culver Blvd
Jefferson Blvd
Rose Ave
Washington Blvd
Venice Blvd
0
1 mi
0
1 km
1
187
405

patched loaves of fresh, wholesome white bread to the city in mustard-yellow trolley trucks that wandered the vast neighborhoods along with milk trucks, ice cream trucks, and vegetable sellers.

Though the bakery shut down in 1969, the landmark and lore live on through the conversion of the spaces to stores, galleries, stages, and the obscure ***Helms Bakery Museum,*** located on the ***Antiques Guild*** floor.

AUTHOR'S TOP PICKS IN WEST L. A.

Helms Bakery

Museum of Jurassic Technology

Westwood Memorial Park

Dutton's Books

Self-Realization Fellowship Shrine

Among the spots to note within the complex of showroom floors of antiques, carpets, Danish design, and contemporary home furnishing is a store called ***Pacific Green,*** which features home accessories all made from Fijian palmwood carved by cottage industry woodworkers in that island nation.

A theater called ***Play 7,*** tucked away in the old bakery corridors, features independent stage productions from a number of local theater companies and can be reached for times and schedules by contacting (323) 960–7772 or www.play7.com.

The Jazz Bakery lives at the Helms, at 3233 Helms Avenue, and brings world-class musicians and live big-band sounds to a coffeehouse-club setting. The club operates year-round and every night as a nonprofit jazz venue that runs the gamut in audience from hipsters to effete musicologists. The Web site, www.jazzbakery.org, tells all; or call (310) 271–9039.

Naturally, all that browsing and nosing around will give you an appetite. ***La Dijonaise*** is a quaint indoor-outdoor cafe and boulangerie on the southeast side of the bakery offering a menu of French-inspired sand-

Culver Query

Who was Culver, anyway? The thirty-year-old Nebraska native named Harry Culver might be considered this studio neighborhood's first PR man. In the years 1910 through 1915, Culver bought up the barley fields around Washington Boulevard and decided to create a city. To get attention he installed an 80,000-watt searchlight on his office roof, staged polo matches with Fords (no, the SUV commercial was not an original idea), promoted marathons that ran from Downtown L.A. to his office in Culver City and ran Most Beautiful Baby contests. In 1915 he convinced Thomas Ince to move his Inceville studios to 10202 Washington Boulevard. As they built, the studios came.

wiches, pâtés, soups, salads, and serious entrees. 87-3 Washington Boulevard, (310) 287–2770.

Across from the bakery on its southern Washington Boulevard side are some cafes and boutiques that add to the casual, funky flavor of the area, which is projected to be L.A.'s next great neighborhood to take off in design and retail statements. Advertisement and architecture agencies are already making a presence in the converted gray-box warehouse buildings that seem to characterize Culver City. Moving west on Washington a block or two toward Bagley Avenue, outdoor bistros, odd boutiques, and thrift and hardware stores cut the broad, nondescript boulevard with some needed character. This is the center of Culver City, where the Culver Hotel and Culver Studios shore up the village with history and color.

The Culver Hotel is a bit of a landmark—it was built in 1924 and hosted such stars as Clark Gable, Greta Garbo, Joan Crawford, Red Skelton, Buster Keaton, Ronald Reagan, and 120 Munchkins when, in 1938, they filmed *The Wizard of Oz* at the Culver Studios next door; it was owned for a time by John Wayne. Reborn in 1998, the hotel still makes celebrity appearances *(The Last Action Hero* and TV's *Party of Five)* but mostly serves as a forty-six-room hotel, each space with its own special style and theme. A campy pink indoor-outdoor bistro-like cafe called The Scarlet Restaurant serves coffee shop food from 7:00 A.M. to 10:00 P.M. every day. 9400 Culver Boulevard, (888) 3–CULVER, www.culverhotel.com.

Just walking by ***Culver Studios*** next door will recall sensations of Atlanta burning. The exterior facade is a close copy of George Washington's Mount Vernon, fronted by sweeping green lawns, sculpted hedges, flowering rosebushes, and the plantation, bringing only a glimpse of what lies behind the white walls. Movie classics filmed on these backstreets include *Gone with the Wind, Duel in the Sun, Wizard of Oz, Citizen Kane,* the original *King Kong* with Fay Wray (1933), Alfred Hitchcock's first American film, *Rebecca* (1940), and such television classics as *Lassie, Andy of Mayberry, Batman,* and, more recently, *Mad About You.*

The sets are still there—from Tara to narrow New York street scenes—but public access is out unless you attend a taping. For that, contact Audiences Unlimited (818–753–3470, www.seeing-stars.com) for schedules and times. All tapings are free.

In the Line of Fire

When the studios that Thomas Ince built became Selznick International Studios and Gone with the Wind *was in production, the fire started to re-create the burning of Atlanta ended up burning up all the sets from the 1933 production of* King Kong.

Down the block at ***Sony Studios,*** you can pay your Andrew J. and take a solid two-hour guided walking tour into the inner workings of movie magic. Reservations are required. This look into the studio's past (as venerable M-G-M) and present includes exposure to soundstages where *Wizard of Oz* was filmed, the commissary where Clark Gable and Carole Lombard dined daily at their favorite table, idle television sets from *Party of Five, Jeopardy,* and *Wheel of Fortune,* and hot sets from current film projects. Celebrity sightings are common but not guaranteed. Naturally, there's a mini museum near the ticket office hosting a small number of exhibits from current and past films. Some fast-food snack areas will help you calorie up for the walk. 10202 West Washington Boulevard, (323) 520–TOUR.

Back on Venice Boulevard and Bagley Avenue, the ***Museum of Jurassic Technology*** would fit nicely into an A. S. Byatt novel. Honoring the nexus between art and science, this museum celebrates the unseen, paradox, and conundrum. Check out the mice-on-toast exhibit—two dead mice on burned bread are presented as an elixir for bed-wetting—next to the mouse pie facsimile that was used to cure childhood stammering. You'll also find a woman's skull with a horn growing from it, a diagram explaining the habits of a Cameroon stink ant, and a small white rodent from South America known as the piercing devil bat, which can fly through solid objects. Some presentations are more philosophical, such as a scientific theorem proving that memory is an illusion.

The gift shop presents T-shirts with strange messages on them; a View-Master reel with seven three-dimensional vistas detailing the life and work of micro miniaturist Hagop Sandaljian, whose inside-the-

The Rail Thing

Leave it to a neighborhood of movie production houses to harbor the world's largest model train store. ***Allied Model Trains*** *offers a scale replica of L.A.'s own Union Station and plenty of model railcars to drive through detailed village reproductions and landscaping. The store has provided model train and rail components for a number of films, including* Star Trek *and* Stuart Little, *and sells to train buffs all over, many of them celebrities. These are not necessarily your coveted childhood toys; many handcrafted locomotives cost more than $2,000. 4411 Sepulveda Boulevard, Culver City, (310) 313–9353.*

needle's-eye sculpture is featured in the museum; and Phantogram stereoscopic sets.

Entering the museum is as mysterious as wandering it. The unmarked door on the street displays the address only, patrons must ring a bell and be escorted inside. It's open four days a week: Thursday from 2:00 to 8:00 P.M., and Friday, Saturday, and Sunday from noon to 6:00 P.M. Suggested donations of $4.00 for adults are appreciated. The Web site adds an entertaining sideshow. 9341 Venice Boulevard, (310) 836–6131, www.mjt.org.

Next door to the museum resides one of the best Thai restaurants in the city. ***Emerald*** (9315 West Venice Boulevard, 310–836–6860) is an unassuming hole in the wall but serves a sublime BBQ chicken signature dish that will wake up every sense in your body. On the other side of the museum and across the street is an Indian grocery called ***India Sweet*** that offers inexpensive home-cooked curries-to-go, to be enjoyed under an awning on outdoor tables overlooking the street. 9409 Venice Boulevard.

Make your way northward on Motor Avenue and find yourself in ***Century City,*** a 1970s vision of corporate splendor in steel and glass built on 178 acres, every inch preplanned. It was created by architect Welton Becket. There's not much to see here unless you want to marvel over the outdoor ***Westfield Century City Mall*** between Constellation Avenue and Little Santa Monica Boulevard. Bloomingdale's and Macy's serve as anchors for myriad chain stores and an eight-theater movie house. The mall has a 10,000-car parking garage that offers three free hours, no validation necessary. For those with appointments or errands in the surrounding office high-rises, this lot can make a great alternative to the $6.00-per-hour fees charged at other parking structures.

Die Hard Again

Seen Die Hard, *the first of the Bruce Willis series? Relive the excitement at 2121 Avenue of the Stars in Century City. The steel, glass, and granite structure overlooking the Fox Plaza was taken over by terrorists and blown up in more than a few places in the film.*

Across Constellation Boulevard, abutting Avenue of the Stars, is the ***Westin Century Plaza*** with its signature ***Spa Mystique.*** This is one of the few resort spas geared to accommodate both day-spa-goers and walk-ins. The Zen interiors allow you to take tea and relax on overstuffed chaises overlooking the bustle of Century City, a bustle far from your current inner space. The ***Yamaguchi Salon*** at the spa brings feng shui hair consultations by the world's foremost expert in such matters and a hair change that is destined to bring good fortune. 2025 Avenue of the Stars, (310) 551–3251 or (877) 544–2256, www.spamystique.com.

In the mileage surrounding this once futuristic eruption on the West L.A. landscape, there are a few spots of interest to consider. East of Century City sits the ***Beit HaShoa Museum of Tolerance,*** an extraordinary interactive journey through some of the darkest periods in human history. The theme here is really intolerance, and the museum presents a comprehensive look inside the Holocaust experience in Germany as its prime example. While the dioramas, the story sets, and the computer resources are impressive in their own rights, the museum also brings in survivors to tell their stories to the patrons—and the effect is chilling. The facility is not open on Saturday and closes early on Friday. Admission is $8.00. 9786 Pico Boulevard, (310) 553–8403, www.museumoftolerance.com.

A different kind of experience can be found at ***Rancho Park Golf Course.*** Perfect weather, cheap holes—what could be more pleasing for a duffer with an iron to swing? Just south of Century City, Rancho Park Golf Course is a decent eighteen-hole, par-seventy-one deal and costs only $20 to $25 per round. Reserve early or get there early. 10460 West Pico Boulevard, between Motor and Patricia Avenues, (310) 838–7373.

Continuing west on Pico to Overland, you'll come to the ***Westside Pavilions,*** a light, almost carnival-like setting for an indoor mall. There's a Nordstrom here, a very sizable Barnes & Noble, and a multiplex cinema, of course, tucked in a corner away from the multitude of chain stores. But what's really notable about the Westside Pavilions is that author Ray Bradbury (*Martian Chronicles, Fahrenheit 451*) helped design it.

The other spot of note might require a calling. The ***Mormon Temple*** is the largest Church of the Latter Day Saints facilities outside Salt Lake City and sits on a hill like a giant depression-era mausoleum fronted by a perfectly coiffed massive lawn. The angel Moroni presides in a spire of solid gold. The temple is for Mormons only, but non-Mormons can check out the side-entrance visitor center, where you can marvel at a 12-foot Jesus and submit to some missionary zeal. 10777 Santa Monica Boulevard at Overland Boulevard.

Westwood is the destination now. Drive West on Santa Monica Boulevard and North on Westwood to Wilshire Boulevard. ***Westwood Village*** is all charm, distinctly 1920s Mediterranean in design, and full of fun restaurants, fine film houses, and office supply stores. In the 1960s and 1970s, Westwood was *the* spot for browsing, ambling, cruising, gathering, happening. The sidewalks filled up on weekend nights with college kids from UCLA running the clubs and bars; there were bookstores on every corner. Shabbier these days, Westwood's bookstores are gone and the college kids go elsewhere for their social necessities. Still, it's a village,

The W Touch

*The **W Los Angeles** hired set designer Dayna Lee to create its edgy touches and special effects. Lee, whose film credits include* Dances with Wolves, *created a shimmering fiber-optic effect at the entrance that gives you the sensation of walking on water. The beds at the W are well known for their extreme comfort and can be purchased upon checkout. 930 Hilgard Avenue, (310) 208–8765 or (877) WHOTELS.*

user-friendly and walkable with lots of cheap noodle shops and a gourmet coffee counter on every corner.

A severe glass building at the edge of Westwood and Wilshire belongs to Occidental Petroleum—one of the companies that had a heavy role in ripping out all the trolley lines and ran an efficient citywide public transportation system until the middle of the last century. It's now making up for its past with an acclaimed art museum in its interior. The ***Armand Hammer Museum*** presents an eclectic range of work, from its permanent collections of French nineteenth-century master painters to temporary exhibitions that include Daumier, the precious porcelains of Erick Swenson, and the junk-laden room-sized installations of Tomoko Takahashi. The museum hosts New American Writing discussions with contemporary authors every Sunday at 5:00 P.M., poetry readings by authors on varied weeknights at 7:00 P.M., and lunchtime art talks with curators on Wednesday at 12:30 P.M. Admission is $5.00 and parking, beneath the museum, is $2.75. 10899 Wilshire Boulevard, (310) 443–7094, www.hammer.ucla.edu.

The village hugs the campus of the ***University of California Los Angeles,*** once a safety school for local rich kids and now a veritable Harvard West. The campus is a study in northern Italian Romanesque design, with lots of sienna-colored brick along rolling greens shaded by seventy-five-year-old eucalyptus stands. Once you have settled your $7.00 bill to park on campus (you can get two hours free with a store validation in the village at the Ralph's Supermarket and Best Buy lot if you want to walk), there are gardens to explore and more museums to visit.

Start with the ***Mildred E. Mathias Botanical Garden*** on the southeast edge of the campus, flanking Le Conte Avenue and Hilgard Avenue right off the village. This is an unexpected area of peace, free for the walking, with plenty of sitting spots to stop and stare at some of the 5,000 species of flora.

The ***Franklin D. Murphy Sculpture Garden*** at UCLA qualifies as one of the most distinguished outdoor sculpture collections in the country. It spans more than five acres in UCLA's North Campus and features over seventy sculptures by artists such as Jean Arp, Alexander Calder, Claire Falkenstein, Barbara Hepworth, Gaston Lachaise, Jacques Lipchitz, Henri Matisse, Henry Moore, Isamu Noguchi, Auguste Rodin, David Smith, and Francisco Zuñiga.

Amid the sculptures and gardens can be found the ***Fowler Museum of Cultural History*** along Bruin Walk at Westwood Plaza on the campus, dedicated to the range of multicultural art expression and political works and emphasizing such unusual collections as the rare textiles from Madagascar or folk art from Polynesia. On Thursday from 6:00 to 8:00 P.M., the museum runs special educational symposia that include performances by singers, dancers, artists, musicians, and writers. All is free. For information, contact (310) 825–4361 or www.fmch.ucla.edu.

Off campus and toward Bel Air is the ***UCLA Hannah Carter Japanese Garden.*** Bellagio Road, found traveling west along Sunset Boulevard about a mile up and on your right, winds through a fairyland of mansions where the only cars you will see are spit-shine-new luxury models or broken-down gardeners' trucks. Inspired by gardens in Kyoto, the modeled land was donated to the university in 1965 by Edward West Carter, then chairman of the regents of the University of California. Nagao Sakurai, a leading architect, was engaged to design the garden; structures from the main gate to the teahouse, the bridges, and the shrine were built in Japan and reassembled stateside by Japanese artisans. Key symbolic rocks were shipped from Japan, and antique stone carvings and water basins imported. Except for the old native coast live oaks, which predate the garden, nearly all the trees and plants are species grown in Japan. The 400 tons of lichen-covered dark brown stone here, however, were imported from Ventura County. Visiting hours are few: Tuesday, Wednesday, and Friday, 10:00 A.M. to 3:00 P.M. Reservations are required, although admission is free. Reservations are made for the top of the hour, and visitors are given fifty-five minutes to tour the garden. 10619 Bellagio Road, (310) 825–4574, gardens@support.ucla.edu.

Television and film buffs will want to check out the ***UCLA Film and Television Archives,*** with its special screening events at the James Bridges Theater on campus. The closest entrance is on Wyton Drive and Hilgard Avenue, and there's plenty of street parking after 6:00 P.M. Screenings run almost daily at 7:30 P.M. and range in theme from Chinese martial arts collections to the films of W. C. Fields, often with guest speakers. Screenings cost $7.00. A calendar can be accessed online at www.cinema.ucla.edu or by calling (310) 206–8013.

On Thursday, another fun distraction awaits at the ***Westwood Farmer's Market.*** Blocks along Weyburn and Glendon Avenues become pedestrian-only zones from 2:00 to 7:00 P.M. and host close to a hundred stalls selling all manner of fresh produce, notions, and prepared delicacies, with live jazz in the offing.

A ghostly side trip on a Westwood journey might be to 1218 Glendon Avenue, home of ***Westwood Memorial Park*** and more than its fair share of young actresses who met with an untimely death. Most notable in this bunch is Marilyn Monroe, who has a crypt here that never suffers from lack of a bloom brought by a fan on pilgrimage. Nearby are the burial sites of other tragic divas: Playmate Dorothy Stratton, Natalie Wood, singer Minnie Riperton (who died of throat cancer at thirty-one), Heather O'Rourke (who played the lost child of the *Poltergeist* movies and died at age thirteen), and Dominique Dunne, who played O'Rourke's older sister in the film and was strangled by her boyfriend.

The Dish

*The Hotel Bel Air hosts **Table One** in a private dining room off the hotel kitchen, where Chef Douglas Dodd will feed you from his private stock. Reservations are hard to come by—this dining option is the flavor of the week for L.A. glitterati. Lunch is $75 and Dinner $115 per person with a minimum of six for lunch and eight for dinner. A credit card reservation and two-week cancellation policy applies. Call (310) 472–5234, (800) 648–4097, or (310) 472–1211, or visit www.hotelbelair.com.*

Head north to Sunset Boulevard and the road now traveled leads to Bel Air and Brentwood, residential enclaves of celebrity mansions and winding mountain roads. Among the ivy and marble you'll find the homes of Humphrey Bogart and Lauren Bacall (232 South Mapleton Drive); Joan Crawford in her *Mommy Dearest* abode (426 North Bristol Avenue), where she lived from 1929 to 1959; Shirley Temple's nearby childhood home (231 North Rockingham Road); the real *Beverly Hillbillies* home (750 Bel Air Road); and Judy Garland's home, built in 1940 (1231 Stone Canyon Road).

Just at the entrance to Bel Air a block north of Sunset is ***Hotel Bel Air***, a ninety-two-cottage, 1920s Mission Revival hideaway tucked into a lush, overgrown canyon. This is where celebs go to get away from their hairdressers and personal assistants (star sightings are virtually guaranteed), and there's little the staff won't accommodate (including pets, yay!). A pond that feeds into a stream running through the property with swans and waterfalls gives a fairy-tale touch to this property, and it's easy to get hooked on the provincial cottage setup with private gar-

Welcome to Bel Air

den entrances, a fireplace, French doors, Queen Anne furnishings and in-room massage offerings until 10:00 P.M. 701 Stone Canyon Road, (310) 472–1211 or (800) 648–4097, www.hotelbelair.com.

Brentwood, south of Bel Air, brings a bit of a village feel to the mostly residential environs. The hills to the north of Sunset Boulevard boast a number of signature residential designs, with homes by Frank Lloyd Wright (Sturges House, 449 Skyewiay Road); son Lloyd Wright (Evans House, 12036 Benmore Terrace); Richard Neutra (Nesbitt House, 414 Avondale Avenue); Frank Gehry (Schnabel House, 526 North Carmelina Drive) and Cliff May (Mandalay, 220 Old Ranch Road).

Below Sunset, Brentwood becomes denser in housing and population,

High Noon for Brentwood

Brentwood Village's first honorary mayor was Gary Cooper, who took the title in 1949.

with a nice mix of restaurants, cafes, and shopping. Follow Barrington Avenue to San Vicente Avenue to come to the ***Village of Brentwood,*** where a number of chain stores mix with older independent outlets. Find here places like California Pizza Kitchen, Daily Grill, Gaucho Grill, and Chin Chin's. But you'll also come across health food sandwich spots, quaint Italian kitchens, and plenty of casual sushi counters. A Votre Sante has a sister location here at 13016 San Vicente Boulevard, where the organic and health food cuisine never disappoints and serves the appetites of the multitudes who like to dine here after a good workout with the private trainer.

A posh designer mini mall here at 11677 San Vicente called ***Brentwood Gardens*** keeps the local ingénues in *du jour* duds. Still, the best spot on the block is ***Dutton's,*** a campus of new and used-book and music stores with a peaceful courtyard connecting them where you can sit as long as you want and read on the benches or rummage through boxes of free used books. Regular readings and book signings happen here, and unusual gifts also take some space. Overall it's a centering and meditative way to spend an hour, whether browsing, reading, or listening. 11975 San Vicente Boulevard, (310) 476–6263.

The neighborhood also has its sordid side. This is the area where Nicole Brown Simpson and friend Ron Goldman were murdered in front of 875 North Bundy Drive. ***O.J. Simpson*** lived around the corner with roomy dude Brian "Kato" Kaelin at 360 North Rockingham. The neighborhood was so crowded with lookyloos during the criminal trial that police issued tickets to cars that slowed down to 10 miles per hour. The neighborhood also marks the spot where Marilyn Monroe died, in a nondescript bungalow at 12305 Fifth Helena Drive.

East Coast Air

A little New York, a little bit of Boston, and a lot of down-home California cooking is the message at ***Zax****, a Brentwood neighborhood restaurant where a good flatiron steak with french fries and dandelion greens is always in season, served in a welcoming room of exposed brick and high ceilings that's popular with neighborhood diners. It's a comfortable blend of California casual and enough elegance to impress—with a wine list to match. 11604 San Vicente Boulevard, (310) 571–3800, www.zaxrestaurant.com.*

Brentwood divides from Bel Air at an area known as the ***Sepulveda Pass.*** The pass follows the often overcrowded 405 freeway from the Los Angeles International Airport to Van Nuys along a route that hugs the curves of the Santa Monica Mountains and passes the Getty Center and Skirball Museum as it goes.

While much has been written about the ***Getty Center,*** the $1 billion dollar monument from the classics to the nineteenth century, European artworks it's quite emphatically the richest museum in the world and one worth swinging by if you have a moment. After you pay the $5.00 parking fee (call to reserve a space ahead of time, especially on the weekends), the admission is free, the views of the Palisades and Pacific are priceless, and the six pavilions designed by Pritzker Prize–winning architect Richard Meier of travertine stone and natural lighting contain much more than the masterworks of civilization. Tours of the museum grounds, and interpretive talks about new and permanent exhibitions led by docents, and seminars on period painting techniques or the prominent painters of an era are delivered almost daily in different sections by acclaimed artists and experts in their fields. Kids get some hands-on time in ***The Family Room***—a place where they can investigate clues that artists use to make a painting, try on costumes and pose for a post-Renaissance portrait, mess around in the book corner, or see what Getty has in store on their interactive computers.

The center presents book signings and lunch with prominent authors on crafts and cooking as well as concerts by purveyors of world music. A user-friendly calendar is available on the Web site. Contact (310) 440–7300 or www.getty.edu.

Swinging Suites

For a real retro experience, check into a themed suite at the ***Luxe Summit Hotel Bel Air.*** *This establishment, adjacent to the Getty Center, is a throwback to the 1960s with a private branch of rooms and suites in the upper quadrangle, many offering balconies and garden terraces. But the cool in these accommodations comes mostly from the themed suites. Try the New York Suite, aglow in black and gold lamé textiles and Art Deco details; the leopardskin-filled Africa Suite; the Japanese Suite in muted Asian tones and tasteful floral designs; the French Provincial Suite, with a country-fresh Pierre Deux ambience; and the Rock Suite, which has* Indiana Jones *written all over it. 11461 Sunset Boulevard, off the San Diego Freeway, West L.A.; (866) 589–3411 or (310) 344–0309, www.luxehotels.com.*

The ***Skirball Cultural Center and Museum,*** north of the Getty Museum by a good mile or two, keeps as its focus American Judaica, with galleries that present—through paintings, photographs, and artifacts—the story of Jewish life from ancient Israel to the Diaspora, immigration and struggle in American life, and Jewish ritual and meaning in modern American daily life. The museum serves as a magnet for intercultural lectures and discussions, with prominent commentators and scholars presenting special programming on a regular basis, usually for a significant seating charge. You'll also find themed film fests, dance and music concerts, and prolific productions by L.A. Theaterworks in which local actors (in this case *local* means "international celebrities") read plays in front of an audience for National Public Radio specials. General admission is $8.00; docent-led tours are available by reservation. 2701 North Sepulveda Boulevard, (310) 440–4564.

It's time to head west on Sunset Boulevard toward the ***Pacific Palisades,*** where 27,000 well-heeled residents call themselves Paladians. There's not much to wander by way of retail sites, but plenty to explore among natural wonders of the place. Stay on Sunset Boulevard past Brentwood, then make a fast right at Capri Drive and follow it through curve and bend all the way to the top, where a short street at the top called Casale is your spot for a left turn. When you realize you can't go any farther, that's where you want to be. Park somewhere that won't land your car in an impoundment property and start walking the dirt road ahead. This is ***Lower Rustic Canyon,*** a trail at the convergence of six canyons in the Santa Monica Mountains and full of natural and historic splendor. There are two trail sets here to choose from. One is the fire road that leads to Camp Josepho, a Boy Scout camp; the other is in the valley below, a wild and overgrown paradise of creeks and creepers and ruins of days gone by. Don't be dismayed by the skeletons of trucks and cars that met their dooms over the edge. You're on foot here, and there are several entrances with wooden steps to the trail below that will give your hams a workout. The area has a history. It wasn't always full of wild and woolly hiker secrets; it was actually a retreat at various times for cowboy philosopher and socialist Will Rogers and friends—among them Anatol Josepho (for whom the camp is named, and who is credited with inventing the pay phone), and artists, writers, and even Nazi sympathizers. A 1978 fire wiped out most of the cabins in the hidden valley, but the curious hiker gets to ponder the remains. A forest of mountain mahogany, chamise, manzanita, toyon, sumac, sycamore, and buckwheat has reclaimed the region, but you can still see the shell bunkers of what was called "Murphy's Ranch." Once protected by a high fence and armed guards, a small cult of spies and lovers of the Third Reich found refuge here, as well as sending radio transmissions to Germany. The hike into the forest can connect with the trail at Rustic Canyon. Above lies part of a soon-to-be-seamless trail system called the ***Backbone Trail*** of the Santa Monica Mountains, which crisscrosses and hopscotches through backyard chaparrals, remote canyons, and cliffs on 70 miles of footways that overlook the Pacific at most points.

Venturing onward through the Palisades, come to ***Will Rogers State Historic Park,*** a favorite for polo players and watchers, horse lovers, and picnickers. The depression-era ranch was the home of Will Rogers, who died in 1935 in a plane crash but made his fame coining such phrases as "I never met a man I didn't like," "All I know is what I read in the papers," "Spring has sprung," "Everyone is ignorant, only on different subjects," and "A man who doesn't love a horse . . . there's something wrong with him."

The spread bought by these sentiments is a lush 200 acres of bridlepaths, meadows, horse stalls (well used by area celebrities to board their horses), and a little Will Rogers museum filled with cowboy gear, ropes and lariats, and sculptures by Frederick Remington. A 2-mile trail leads from the house to Inspiration Point, where views of the Pacific and the city are easy to access and worth the time to get there. Farther on, the trail hooks up to the Rustic Canyon Trail and later to the Backbone Trail. Puttering around the grounds and museum is free, but parking is $5.00 unless you park in other parts of the neighborhood. Polo matches still run on occasion and are free for the watching. 14243 Sunset Boulevard, just before the Pacific Coast Highway.

Another gem along this Palisades path is the ***Self-Realization Fellowship Lake Shrine.*** The sight at first is incongruent; you might think it's an illusion from too many hours looking at taillights and bumpers. But the sixteenth-century windmill facsimile and gilded lotus shrine you glimpse out of the corner of your eye are real. The shrine was dedicated by Paramahansa Yogananda in 1950 and enjoys a ten-acre site with gardens and a natural spring-fed lake, swans, ducks, koi, and lotus flowers. Meditating is what this place is all about . . . and this is a spot outside four walls where you don't have to fight barking dogs, in-your-face smokers, talky post-teenyboppers, schizophrenic loiterers, road-rage-aholics, and ubiquitous con artists to do it. The grounds include a Court of Religions honoring the five principal religions of the world; the Mahatma Gandhi World Peace Memorial, where a portion of Gandhi's ashes are enshrined; a small museum with exhibits on Paramahansa Yogananda's work; and a gift shop with arts and crafts from India.

But . . . why the windmill, you ask?

In the 1920s the spot was a setting for Inceville movie productions. It was sold in 1927 to a real estate developer, who dug a big hole and then ran out of money. The hole soon filled with water from the abundant springs in the area, but the land stayed idle until 1940 when a 20th Century Fox executive saw it, bought it, and started to create his dream spread. A man of the movies, the new owner, one Everette McElroy, brought in his houseboat and moored it on a spot overlooking the dream house he was building that was crowned by a Dutch windmill, no price too high, no set too outrageous in a city built on celluloid fantasies.

In the hands of Paramahansa Yogananda now, the site is open to the public every day but Monday and holidays. It offers lectures, services, energy exercises, and meditation workouts on Thursday, Friday, and Sunday free of charge. 17190 Sunset Boulevard, slightly inland from the coast; (310) 454–4114, www.yogananda-srf.org.

Places to Stay in West L.A.

Luxe: $250+
Deluxe: $150–$249
Good deal: $79–$149

Century City

Park Hyatt
2151 Avenue of the Stars, (310) 277–1234 or (800) 778–7477, www.parkhyatt.com.
Luxury accommodations within walking distance of shopping and corporate industry, the Park Hyatt also offers complimentary limousine services to Beverly Hills and shopping. There are lots of suites, several with large sundeck. Luxe.

St. Regis
2055 Avenue of the Stars, (310) 277–6111 or (877) 787–3452, www.stregis.com.
An elegant vertical hotel with a stylish New York–style lobby bar and spa that is gaining buzz all over the city. Twenty-four-hour butler service is available for an extra C-note or two per night. Complimentary limo transport within 5 miles. One of Nancy Reagan's favorite hotels. Luxe.

Westin Century Plaza
2025 Avenue of the Stars, (310) 277–2000 or (888) 625–5144, www.centuryplazala.com.
The hottest hotel in its day (1970s), it used to be the choice of Sinatra as well as its share of U.S. presidents coming to town. A recent redo puts it back on track, especially with a sensational Asian-themed spa. Sunday brunches at Breeze are a known secret among foodies looking for good deals. Located directly across from the Westfield Century City Mall. Deluxe.

Westwood

Beverly Hills Plaza Hotel
10300 Wilshire Boulevard, (310) 275–5575.
This is an all-suites hotel, and many of those quarters come with kitchens. Charming European-style quality in an urban location that's convenient to Beverly Hills, Century City, Westwood, and Santa Monica. Deluxe.

Century Wilshire Hotel
10776 Wilshire Boulevard, (310) 474–4506 or (800) 421–7223, www.centurywilshire hotel.com.
A cozy boutique property converted from residential use includes complimentary continental breakfast, parking, around the clock, complimentary coffee and tea service, and five European languages. Deluxe.

Hilgard House
927 Hilgard Avenue, (310) 208–3945 or (800) 826–3934, www.hilgardhouse.com.
A quaint Euro-style boutique property with pleasant rooms, good prices, and a great residential location near Westwood Village and UCLA. Good deal.

Hotel Del Capri
10587 Wilshire Boulevard, (310) 474–3511 or (800) 444–6835, www.hoteldelcapri.com.
Here's a charming and affordable Euro-style property from the 1950s five blocks from UCLA. The beautiful courtyard—with a fountain—is a find in these parts. Continental breakfast is served poolside or in your room. Good deal.

Westwood Doubletree
10740 Wilshire Boulevard, (310) 475–8711 or (800) 472–8556, www.losangeleswest wood.doubletree.com.
In a good location near Westwood Village, this hotel has all the amenities from twenty-four-hour room service to an in-house cafe and concierge desk, as well as rooms with good views on the upper floors. Deluxe.

Brentwood

Holiday Inn Brentwood
170 North Church Lane, (310) 476–6411 or (800) HOLIDAY.
This hotel has two great things to offer. The first is location—it's right at the confluence of Sunset Boulevard and the 405 freeway. And then there's shape—the round, seventeen-story tower that is this hotel is a bit of a curiosity when you're passing on the freeway. The rooms are claustrophobic, however, and the path to them, dizzying—and if that won't get you, the leftover cigarette smoke will. Still, location can be everything. Bargain.

Pacific Palisades

Channel Road Inn Bed & Breakfast
219 West Channel Road, (310) 459–1920, www.channelroadinn.com.
You'll find fourteen rooms here, each with a different personality and all above a large, comfortable beach-house living room with fireplace and views to the ocean. A secret escape for romancing Angelenos. Breakfast is served in your room or on the patio; after-

Author's Favorite Places to Stay in West L. A.

W Los Angeles
930 Hilgard Avenue
(310) 208–8765
(see page 98 for more information)

Hotel Bel Air
701 Stone Canyon Road
(310) 472–1211
(see page 100 for more information)

Hilgard House
927 Hilgard Avenue
(310) 208–3945

Channel Road Inn
219 West Channel Road
(310) 459–1920

noon cookies and tea. Bikes can be borrowed for the beach three blocks down. Deluxe.

Places to Eat in West L.A.

Expensive: $25.00+
Reasonable: $15.00–$24.00
Bargain: $8.00–$14.00

Culver City

Café Brasil
10831 Venice Boulevard, (310) 837–8957.
Hot salsa and garlic in a kitsch, yard sale setting with lots of Brazilian music and casual confusion. Bargain.

El Sazon Oaxaqueno
12131 Washington Place, (310) 391–4721.
Oaxacan specialties and pan-Mexican fare. Bargain.

La Dijonaise
87-3 Washington Boulevard, (310) 287–2770.
Good deal. See page 93 for more information.

Zabumba
10717 Venice Boulevard, (310) 841–6525.
Shrimp pizzas, passion fruit juice, and jungle fish stews in a funky Bahian food shack. Bargain.

Westwood

Apple Pan
10801 West Pico Boulevard, (310) 475–3585.
Heavenly hamburgers are served fat, charred, and juicy with Tillamook cheddar around a U-shaped counter in a diner that has been a favorite lunch spot with locals since the 1940s. Bargain.

Eurochow
1099 Westwood Boulevard, (310) 209–0066.
It's white-on-white decor in this hot spot for glam Italo-Chinese cuisine. Expensive.

John O'Groats
10516 West Pico Boulevard, (310) 204–0692.
The best big American breakfasts in town, and served all day. Bargain.

Shahrezad Flame
1422 Westwood Boulevard, (310) 470–9131.
Farsi fare, slick and edgy interiors, and every manner of eggplant on the menu. Bargain.

Brentwood

Berty's
11712 San Vicente Boulevard, (310) 207–6169.
Consistent and accountable continental and American cuisine in unpretentious surroundings. Bargain.

Bel Air

Four Oaks
2181 Beverly Glen Boulevard, (310) 470–2265.
Upscale, rustic, and woodsy elegance with exquisite French cuisine—this is a great date or celebration spot. Expensive.

Mulholland Grill
2932 Beverly Glen Circle, (310) 470–6223.
Home-style Italian cooking with home-style American prices in a casual, comfortable setting. Reasonable.

Pacific Palisades

Gladstones 4 Fish
17300 Pacific Coast Highway, (310) 573–0212.
Big portions of surf-and-turf served right over the water. This is a casual sunset-and-fried-calamari kind of place if you get here before the crowds arrive. Reasonable.

Venice, Santa Monica, and Malibu

L.A. may be a great big freeway—but if you gotta ride, do it on the PCH. The Pacific Coast Highway runs for 74 miles between Malibu and Long Beach, hugging the coastline through most of this stretch and passing some of the city's trendiest neighborhoods. Still, if you really want to see the beach, you have to get off the road. The cool waters and aggressive surf of the Pacific Ocean in these parts are here to be savored whenever you're ready to take a break from your urban explorations and segue into the bohemian beach life of Venice and Santa Monica while chancing the gilded cliffways of Malibu.

You might want to listen to your mother when you wander these coastal towns and bring a sweater. It can be broiling at Mid-Wilshire but the beach will bring on a chill. Always breezy, the shore can run twenty degrees cooler than inland areas, and the morning fog may not burn off until past noon. Summer temperatures run a heavenly seventy-five to eighty degrees most days, and bladers in hot pants think that's just perfect.

Venice, Santa Monica, and Malibu got their starts as resort villages—escape realms for studio refugees, big-eyed developers, and artists in search of a community on the edge. Today they're the crowded, overpriced playlands they were intended to become, where every dreamer has a place and no recreational need goes unsatisfied.

Venice, on the southern end of this stretch, might weigh in on this outing with the most colorful history. The city started out as an ocean outback that one visionary decided to transform into the Coney Island of the Pacific. The year was 1905. Abbot Kinney, a tobacco mogul caught in the Hollywood land rush, saw a chance to bring Venice to America, creating a premier spot to visit and live. He started an elaborate project of digging canals and byways and filling them with houses, gardens, and gondolas, all capped with an amusement pier at Windward Avenue. The style was Venetian Renaissance, and the electric trolley brought in the crowds. By the end of the year, construction of the Ship Cafe and Auditorium (located on the Abbot Kinney Pier), the Venice Canals, and the St. Mark's Hotel on Windward were well under way.

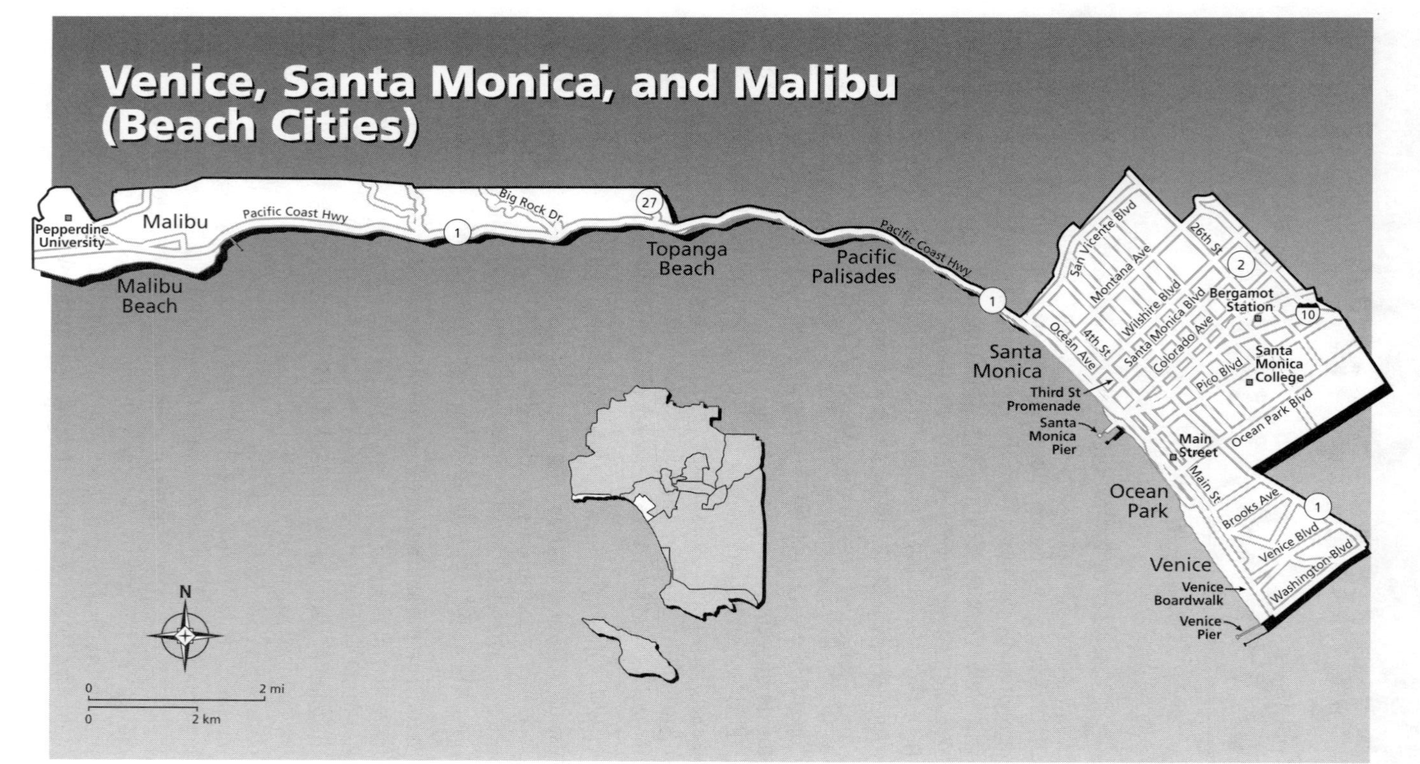
Venice, Santa Monica, and Malibu
(Beach Cities)
Pepperdine University
Malibu
Pacific Coast Hwy
Big Rock Dr.
27
1
Malibu Beach
Topanga Beach
Pacific Palisades
Pacific Coast Hwy
1
San Vicente Blvd
Montana Ave
26th St
2
Wishire Blvd
Santa Monica Blvd
Bergamot Station
10
Ocean Ave
4th St
Colorado Ave
Santa Monica College
Pico Blvd
Santa Monica
Third St Promenade
Santa Monica Pier
Ocean Park Blvd
Main Street
Main St
Ocean Park
Brooks Ave
1
Venice Blvd
Venice
Washington Blvd
Venice Boardwalk
Venice Pier
N
0
2 mi
0
2 km

Author's Favorite Attractions in the Beach Cities

Venice Canals
Venice Boardwalk
Main Street
Bergamot Station
Serra Retreat
Leo Carrillo State Beach

With the canal network near completion and the adjacent residential lots sold, Venice's population swelled. Imported gondolas and a miniature railroad made it a magnet for out-of-town sideshows and amusements. Roller skating became the rage, and a skating rink went up along with a huge dance hall on the pier. The Ocean Park Pier, just 0.75 mile north of the Kinney Pier, also had its own share of the spotlight with a $150,000 heated indoor saltwater plunge. By 1909 an aquarium opened on the pier, followed by a scenic railroad ride with a tunnel, a carousel, a Ferris wheel, a rapids ride, a Japanese tea house, and the Ocean Inn Restaurant.

Another pier nearby, Fraser's Million Dollar Amusement Pier, soon opened, claiming to be the largest in the world at 1,250 feet long and 300 feet wide. The pier housed a dance hall, two carousels, a crooked fun house, the Grand Electric Railroad, the Starland Vaudeville Theater, Breaker's Restaurant, and a Panama Canal model exhibit.

The area quickly became a beacon for the speakeasy crowd. Secret tunnels to waterfront supply loading areas were built from the basements of area businesses. But hard luck and several fires eventually took Venice Beach into hard times. The honky-tonk town was annexed by Los Angeles, which dismantled a number of the rides and attractions, filled in half of the fourteen canals, and left the area to the sailors and fun seekers who came for the rides and midway at Pacific Ocean Park (which managed to stay intact until 1967). Kinney died of lung cancer in 1920, before most of the fires and deterioration. But his ghost still gets ink now and then—a specter along a canal path in a top hat and high black leather boots who seems to have places to go and people to see.

Now the last six canals have been cleaned out, lined, and landscaped. The ducks have come back, and among the haute design homes that line these waterways, connected by Venetian-style bridges, a certain calm and natural spirit can be found on the paths near Venice Beach.

The canals and a network of traffic-free "walking streets" have breathed new life into the Venice scene in the recent decades of redevelopment. Once a magnet for hippies and flower children soaking up the rays and the vibes along the beachfront, Venice is still the last bastion for anything-goes behavior in L.A.; here the rites of commercial development have maintained a soft touch, and the real attraction is the human element. Any amble down ***Ocean Front Walk,*** or ***the Board-***

walk, is the place to start a Venice exploration. The Boardwalk stretches for 2 miles along between Ozone Avenue and Washington Street where you'll find the ***Venice Pier.*** The canals are just a block or two away, bordered by Washington Street to the south, Venice Boulevard to the north, and Pacific and Ocean Avenues to the west and east.

Back on the Boardwalk, however, the scene is anything but calm and natural. Mimes will follow and mimic you; apocalypse prophets will preach to you; fortune-tellers by the dozens will read for you; masseuses and aura tuners will heal you; skating guitarists will play for you; snake charmers and parrot tamers will pose for you; portrait artists will have you pose for them; political activists will talk to you; drugged-up artists will paint for you; body painters will design for you; used-book collectors will sell to you; and, if you're lucky, the crowds will part for you. Inline skaters will dart in and out of your path, and tattoo parlors, army-surplus stores, skateboard shops, and leather boutiques will all beckon from the city side of the strand.

While most of the commercial spots along the Boardwalk are honky-tonk stands and don't merit mention, a few landmarks do stand out. ***Muscle Beach,*** just north of the pier, really is the place to get pumped up. The outdoor gym between the Boardwalk and the beach features bench presses and weights and usually a number of less-than-savory-looking characters using them. Basketball courts nearby have games going most hours—but don't enter unless you're trying out for the NBA. Rather, try the ***Graffiti Skate Park,*** part of a recent $6.5 million face-lift to the area that presents a fun spot to work your spray-paint magic or get your in-line skills down before taking off on the bike path.

Windward Avenue is the heart of venice and of Abbot Kinney's vision to turn a few blocks on the Pacific Coast into the famous Italian Renaiisance city. Running from the beach to the once flourishing canal system, the street is still a reminder of its former self, with an arcade lined in columns and two- and three-story buildings that house cute French cafes, smoke shops, and used-clothing stores. Continuing onward down the Boardwalk, pass Frank Gehry's ***Norton House*** at 2509, an unusual box in Gehry style with sawtoothed window frames and whimsical metalwork in the facade; the Art Deco ***Yacht House*** at 3900; and the Jewish Center marked by a Chagall-inspired mural at 201 that has been standing for nearly eighty years.

Along the Boardwalk and the streets just off this area are funky shops, mostly of the vintage-clothing sort or honky-tonk stands at the beach selling burgers and one-size-fits-all beach pants. A good place to end up is the ***Figtree Café,*** at the north end of Ocean Front Walk at 429. The cafe offers patio dining with tables overlooking the Boardwalk scene and the beach. Dogs are welcomed—they even get a bowl of water—and while the entertainment is priceless, the breakfasts are superb at diner prices. Try the tofu scramble with homemade cornbread, or the fusion-style entrées made from organic ingredients and herbs grown in a local Venice garden.

Dramatic and artistically significant wall murals are part of the visual Venice experience. Among the more famous of these works is Rip Cronk's *Venice Reconstituted,* a parody of Botticelli, and his *Morning Shot* depicting the Doors' Jim Morrison.

Venice is a beacon for artists, the more successful of them able to afford home and galleries near the beach. The ***Venice Art Walk*** in May opens up these galleries once a year in a self-guided amble that's a benefit for the Venice Family Clinic.

The artist's mind is also the focus of ***Beyond Baroque,*** a bookstore center for literary arts in Venice located in the Old City Hall building. Fiction, nonfiction, poetry, and performance art are the media here. The Beyond Baroque bookstore brings in writers from around L.A. with limited-edition works and rare literary finds. Call for a reading events schedule. 681 Venice Boulevard, (310) 822–3006.

Moving northward between Venice and ***Santa Monica,*** a renaissance on ***Main Street*** has given new life to the early-twentieth-century commercial structures that were sliding down skid row before the economic flash of the 1990s. Now the fourteen blocks between Pico Boulevard and Rose Avenue are a little Greenwich Village, a little Worth Avenue, and a little Union Square, with upscale chains and chic boutiques making the scene for wandering beachgoers. The area has not yet been discovered, even by Angelenos, and makes its way by catering to the well-heeled crowds of the west side who want to stay on the west side. The result is a flow of funky coffeehouses and used-book stores next to Armani clothing outlets and high-fashion furniture stores. Off-street parking and inexpensive municipal lots are still available, and the efficient and ubiquitous Santa Monica bus system called the ***Big Blue Bus*** transports passengers from as far east as Westwood Boulevard and certainly from nearby Santa Monica Promenade, which

Before You Go

For information about Santa Monica, write to the ***Santa Monica Convention & Visitors Bureau,*** *520 Broadway, Suite 250, Santa Monica, CA 90401-2428; telephone (310) 319–6263; or visit www.santamonica.com.*

Car Smart

The ***Tide Shuttle*** *is a nonpolluting electric bus in Santa Monica that serves a loop of eighteen stops, including four major hotels, the downtown shopping district, the beach, Main Street, and the pier. Buses run every fifteen minutes seven days a week. The fare is 25 cents.*

is just out of reach for walkers. The No. 14 bus is a go for the Getty Center, dropping off passengers at a stop near the museum tram.

Several stops along the way bear mentioning. First, the Santa Monica ***Heritage Museum*** is a good anchor for the area with an attached parking lot; it's a fun place to check out. It's housed in an original 1894 building that was once the residence of the son of Santa Monica's founder, Nevada senator John Percival Jones. The style marks the transition from the elaborate Victorian Queen Anne Revival to the simpler American Colonial or Georgian Revival style, with turn-of-the-twentieth-century furnishings to match. The $3.00 entrance free is a bargain for the two floors of historical California detail and the bookstore and notions shop, housed in what was no doubt a closet a century ago. 2612 Main Street, (310) 392–8537.

The museum shares a driveway with ***The Victorian,*** an "Age of Innocence" catering and events venue that offers a fabulous array of baked goods and coffee on Saturday and Sunday mornings when the Main Street Farmer's Market is under way.

Across from the museum is the best bargain in town: the ***Sea Shore Motel*** (2637 Main Street, 310–392–2787, www.seashoremotel.com). These quaint, nonsmoking, pet-friendly rooms rent for $75 and up a night and offer a private suntanning deck, in-room refrigerator, and goodies from ***Amelia's,*** the attached coffee bistro. Amelia's is a fun hang on Sundays when poets and opera divas perform their latest wares.

Continuing along Main Street the skinny sidewalks are lined with all manner of aromatherapy feel-good stores, bikini and beach wear, romantic finery at ***Paris 1900,*** Pakistani carpets at ***Moonlight Rugs & Art,*** a store selling Eames furniture designs and art, plenty of French bakery-cafes, ***Joe's Diner*** for blue-plate specials with a healthy twist, and even a Gap to keep the *main* in Main Street. A sweet side street is ***Pier Avenue,*** where the aged brick buildings with their aromatherapy shops, used-book stores, and health food stores create a local East Coast feeling that can be enjoyed with coffee and newspaper at comfortable tables along the block.

Along the way catch the ***Edgemar Building.*** Built by Frank Gehry on the site of an old dairy and egg farm, the mixed-use building that went up in 1988 is a hard-edged sculpture blending high-tech, Streamline, and minimalist styles around an open courtyard. 2415 Main Street.

Santa Monica is the happening place in Los Angeles, if indeed Los Angeles has one premier happening place. Its transformation from a down-and-out neighborhood of drunks and homeless where the principal attraction was a Woolworth's on Third Street was a dramatic one that took the city by storm. ***Third Street Promenade*** started it all in 1989, and the effects of development are still under way. Third Street Promenade is a pedestrian-only outdoor pavilion of shops, cinemas, bookstores, cafes, restaurants, and offices that runs from Wilshire Boulevard for three blocks to Broadway and packs in an ongoing circus of quality outdoor performance art along the way. Peruvian flautists, silver-draped mime mannequins, string quartets, dueling banjos—every 20 feet is another show on weekend nights, and there's enough space in the streets for crowds to amass and watch. The streets are lined with outdoor cafes of dubious culinary repute but perfect for a glass of wine, a cup of coffee, and all the people-watching you can handle.

Borders and Barnes & Noble share the promenade, but the area is a holdout for some independent bookstores as well. ***Hennessey & Ingalls*** is the largest art and architecture bookstore on the West Coast, while ***Arcana,*** across the walk, is filled with specialty art and photography volumes. A favorite here is ***Midnight Special,*** with hardwood floors, floor-to-ceiling stacks, lots of specialty press revolutionary manifestos, and an area in the back where well-known authors speak to serious readers about life and times. A Starbucks next door with tables abutting the sidewalk crowds is the perfect place to relax with a purchase.

Unlike Main Street, chain stores have found Third Street, but their presence brings in the shoppers. Find here such stores as Z Gallery, Pottery Barn, Urban Outfitters, Brookstone (surprisingly, lingerie here stays local—no Victoria's Secret so far), Swatch, Guess, Tommy Hilfiger, Fred Segal, Abercrombie, and Banana Republic, among others. The chain effect ends at ***Santa Monica Place,*** an indoor mall on Broadway and Third designed by Frank Gehry with more than 140 stores, including a Macy's and Robinsons-May. Parking is free here for three hours. Otherwise, it's off to the municipal lots, which charge a $3.00 flat rate on weekends. Street parking is not recommended: The Santa Monica parking enforcers operate like magpies on a mosquito mission.

The streets around Third Street Promenade benefit from the bustle, with coffeehouses, restaurants, clubs, and specialty shops. Fourth Street is a fun place where you can dine at the original ***Border Grill*** for splashy Mexican fare and take in a show across the street at ***Magicopolis,*** which

Skate Date

*A regular event for the bodybuilding in-line crowd is the **Friday Night Skate.** A group starts out near the Santa Monica Pier on skates and takes a guided tour that turns into a party on wheels through the streets with music. The free event is held the first and third Friday of every month, starting at 8:00 P.M. and running until around 11:00 P.M.*

hosts regular shows on weekends often enjoyed by celebrities in the audience. 1418 Fourth Street, (310) 451–2241, www.magicopolis.com.

For some reason Santa Monica is a central meeting spot for all things British. A number of English-style pubs here put a pint in its place, and darts rule. ***Ye Olde King's Head*** at 116 Santa Monica Boulevard is one such spot, and ***The Tudor House*** at 1403 Santa Monica Boulevard is another. Antiques shops sell tea china.

A stop at ***Angel's Attic*** is a must for tea and cakes and more. Indeed, this shop is a strange find in this city of belly-button charms, tattoos, and lava lamps. It's a restored Victorian home in a town full of late-1960s apartment complexes, and it's dedicated to collecting dollhouses and miniatures and putting them on display. More than four dozen such treasures, from a simple two-floor house to a mini Versailles and a toppling-from-the-shelves Lilliputian antiques shop fill the bottom floor; collections of elegantly robed antique dolls fill the second. A white trellised gazebo garden in the back offers a certain sanctuary, while the front-porch solarium features afternoon tea on white rattan chairs and Irish tatted tablecloths. Hours are Thursday through Sunday, 12:30 to 4:30 P.M. 516 Colorado Avenue, (310) 394–8331.

The inland side of Santa Monica holds a few spots of interest, especially for art lovers. ***Bergamot Station*** is Santa Monica's SoHo of sorts. Named for a trolley stop on the Pacific Car line, the industrial complex proves that looks can be deceiving. Inside the corrugated-steel-and-aluminum warehouses are more than two dozen galleries, a cafe, unusual jewelry and crafts stores, framing and fine-arts paper boutiques, design and film studios and the ***Santa Monica Museum of Art.*** Openings, fundraisers, and auctions happen here regularly. 2525 Michigan Avenue, www.bergamotstation.com or www.smmoa.org.

Those who are starstruck on their visit to L.A. might consider the Friday-night star show at the ***John Drescher Planetarium*** at Santa Monica College. A 7:00 P.M. show presents an interactive discussion of the current night sky in crystal Digitstar II projection, followed by a feature discussion by an expert from UCLA, Cal Tech, or the Jet Propulsion Laboratory on such topics as Astronomy in Iran, Stars Over the Nile, and Black Holes in Globular Clusters. The $8.00 ticket will get you into both shows. 1900 Pico Boulevard, (310) 434–4223.

Back at the beach, the 1,620-foot-long ***Santa Monica Pier*** lights up at night with a midway-style amusement park with pay-as-you-go thrill rides over the ocean. A solar-powered nine-story Ferris wheel that gets a fair amount of Hollywood studio attention, a 1916 carousel seen in *The Sting* and other classics, a mild roller-coaster ride, and a few more stomach wrenchers keep the kids screaming and the crowds coming to this beach area. For some reason the pier attracts a lot of day fishers, but the fish are not destined for the kitchen here. A wide-planked wooden deck with benches away from the action provides a romantic spot for lovers, dealers, meditators, and thinkers to watch the waves and the occasional schools of dolphins that swim by. During the summer the city runs the Thursday-night ***Twilight Concert Series*** on the pier with name-brand rock and roll—it's a cool place to boogie. ***The Lobster,*** a fine-dining seafood restaurant at the entrance to the pier, is a good place to watch the waves with wine in hand and lobster at the ready.

Santa Monica Pier Ferris Wheel

Air from Chairs

The free concerts on the Santa Monica Pier (Thursday from July through September, and Sunday from February through April) aren't the only complimentary musical performances you'll find in Santa Monica. Check out the "Singing Beach Chairs" at the beach just south of the pier. The 14-foot-high outdoor furnishings are harmonically tuned to whistle while they work, and the sounds can be quite haunting on a windy day.

The entrance to the Santa Monica Pier also marks the start of a glorious walking path called ***Palisades Park.*** The cliff walk looking over the Pacific from whitewashed wooden fencing is no doubt a familiar sight—it's a good, cheap background for film and television projects. Benches line the well-worn paths under gnarly overgrown bonsai and towering palms. Modern sculptures mix with bronzed-over cannon aimed at Japanese attackers from the Pacific and a strange find in these parts–a gadget called ***Camera Obscura,*** obscured in a closet of the Santa Monica Senior Center. Enter the 1940s Moderne building and ask the desk clerk for a key to the camera. You'll head to a dark room with a large crystal in the middle, something that Merlin might have invented for himself. Moving the cranks this way and that, images of the outside world appear in the crystal and suddenly you are looking out at, well, Palisades Park. Only you're in a dark closet in a senior center.

That done, continue your walk along the path that parallels the traffic on Ocean Avenue. Benches offer varying vantages of the sea and are occupied by ambling seniors, perky dog walkers, lovers, lonelies, families, readers, knitters, and coffee sippers. The park runs ten blocks along an idyllic spot that used to be a haven for the city's homeless. Santa Monica, once considered the People's Republic of California for its stiff rent-control laws and liberal social policies, still tries to keep the people in mind. The twenty-five-acre park offers clean bathrooms, fountains, and clean places to picnic and play cards along the way, as well as artful landscaping and respectful patrons.

Fun Down Under

*U**nder the Carousel** on the Santa Monica Pier is another world of wonders at the UCLA Ocean Discovery Center. The admission is $3.00, but the expressions you'll see on your child's face are (as they say) priceless. There are interactive touch tanks, wall displays, shark tanks, natural tide pools, and windows onto more than fifty forms of jellyfish. It's open to the public on weekends and from Tuesday through Sunday during the summer. Call (310) 393–6149. Afterward, grab your pole or rent one for $3.00 at the bait shop; Santa Monica Pier is one of the only places you can fish without a license.*

A number of hotels and gathering spots along this ocean quay cater to a young and hip crowd. ***Casa Del Mar*** (1910 Ocean Front Walk) offers the best sunset spotting in town with an elegant white rattan tea lounge to enjoy a glass of wine and a book or conversation behind a panoramic window overlooking the ocean. Built as a private club in 1926—and frequented by the likes of Douglas Fairbanks Sr., Mary Pickford, and Charlie Chaplin—it eventually fell on hard times and in recent years was a "longevity center." A recent renovation reinstated the 1920s feel to the hotel. ***Shutters on the Beach*** (1 Pico Boulevard) is right across the way and is the only hotel in Los Angeles that offers rooms right on the beach. ***Hotel Le Merigot*** a few doors down has a spa of note that offers exotic stone massage therapies, and ***Loew's Hotel*** next door has a jazz and blues lounge on weekend nights that moves the blood for the cost of a cocktail.

Peoples' Music

__McCabe's Guitar Shop__ (3101 Pico Boulevard, 310–828–4497) stages casual, coffeehouse-style concerts in its back-room theater. Meanwhile, __Harvelle's__ (1432 Fourth Street) offers punch-packed blues performances and plenty of room to dance in an unpretentious bar scene for nominal covers.

About six blocks north of Wilshire is another Santa Monica gem: ***Montana Avenue.*** The fun starts around Sixth Street and runs east to Seventeenth Street, with shops, cafes, trendy boutiques, designer clothing, furniture stores, and costume jewelry shops, most named for their wealthy owners, although a few knowns like Chico's and David Dart can be counted. Montana might be considered a poor man's Rodeo Drive—it exudes cachet but calls in a younger, hipper, more casual crowd. Celebrities from the Palisades and Malibu frequent these shops with their one-of-a-kind designs in furnishings and clothing accessories. But the main thing here is coffee. There seems to be a connoisseur's coffee spot on every corner, between the homemade pasta bars, gelato stands, and boulangeries.

Cosmetics and hair care companies like Kiehl and Jurlique have signature stores on Montana Avenue, too, where soap and aromatherapy boutiques have a pretty strong presence. The walking is good, and the stretch from the cliff walk at Palisades Park to the tail of the shopping district is a satisfying and entertaining amble almost guaranteed to net you a few purchases along the way.

Naturally, the beach at Santa Monica is a wide-open playground of sand, in-line skaters, beach walkers, and people-watchers. The safety of the water is still questionable despite the good efforts of Heal the Bay to curb urban runoff. A smooth bike path that parallels the water in the sand is a lot less crowded in these parts than it is in Venice, even though

Steps from Heaven

Dare to try some of the lofty stairways to be found between Santa Monica and Malibu. They're good for the rear and good for the eyes—and the view from the top is worth the trouble. The ***Castellammare Stairways*** *are reached from Sunset Boulevard via a segue through Castellammare Drive that leads to hefty-priced homes overlooking the grand Pacific. Other step hikes include the stairway off Posetano Road to Revello Drive, a series of steps from Breve Way to Porto Marina, and the ultimate stairway in its class, the* ***Adelaide Stairway,*** *which runs 200 steps at Fourth Street and Adelaide Drive to East Channel Road.*

it's used by skaters, bikers, and walkers. ***Perry's Beach Cafe*** is a good place to find rentals, be they bikes, skates, boogie boards or beach umbrellas. There's a BBQ stand, too—and the food isn't bad. Contact (310) 246–1418 or www.perryscafe.com.

A good place to dine alfresco in the sand is at ***Back on the Beach Café,*** right on the bike path in Santa Monica. The sandwiches and pasta dishes are reasonably priced, and the setting is clean and sublime. 445 Pacific Coast Highway, (310) 393–8282.

If you're in the right skates, you can roll right on through to ***Malibu,*** but for the rest of us, the drive—which runs 10 miles north on the Pacific Coast Highway—is just as scenic and fun. A good place to stop for calories is the ***Reel Inn,*** where cracked crab and lobster in the rough are always in season. Order at one window, pick up at another; grab napkins and forks along the way, bring the beers, and pick a picnic table on the back patio. 18661 Pacific Coast Highway, (310) 456–8221.

The water and beaches en route to the celebrity-studded beach community are clean, and parking is easy along the side of the road. Alcohol is a problem—you could get a ticket if you're caught red-handed with a glass of Chardonnay—but most of the time the cops stay off the sand.

The beaches in this area are the choice for professional surfers. ***Surfrider Beach,*** known for its perfect swells during the summer months, was the scene of countless Frankie and Annette movies and the Gidget series of the mid-1960s. The pier here, a 700-foot landing area that has seen many demolitions and resurrections over the last century, had its last inauguration in 1945 and remains largely a fishing stage with little attraction or fanfare other than the occasional use as a setting in a Walter Mosley mystery.

An interesting landmark that still haunts these hills is ***Thelma Todd's Sidewalk Café.*** When it opened in 1934, it was *the* place to go in your chauffeur-driven Rolls to have a cocktail and be seen by all your friends. Owned by the comedienne who could hold her own with Groucho and was known as "Hot Toddy," the actress fell in with Chicago money. When she wouldn't submit to opening a gambling joint in a cafe storage area, she met her fate in the front seat of her Lincoln wearing her fur and $20,000 in diamonds. The cafe has gone mostly empty through the years, although the Paulist Fathers recently seized on the property for use as a video production center. 17531 Posetano Road, abutting the Pacific Coast Highway.

Nearby up the coast is the ***Serra Retreat Center,*** run by Franciscan friars and available for use by anyone interested in building a relationship with God and view. The retreat rooms are simple, as are the meals, and silence is appreciated. The grounds once belonged to Malibu socialite May Rindge, who spent much of her life fending off the progress of the Pacific Coast Highway and building a forty-room Mediterranean-style mansion on top of her castle grounds. She eventually ran out of money and sold to the friars, who salvaged what they could following a 1960s wildfire. The retreat at 3401 Serra Road can be accessed and reserved by contacting (310) 456–6631 or www.sbfranciscans.org.

The hefty twelve-bedroom, seven-bathroom villa at 23200 Pacific Coast Highway is a testimonial to what money can buy, and a tasteful one at that. ***The Adamson House***—along with the grounds that come attached to the ***Malibu Lagoon Museum*** for those interested in the ancient-to-modern record of Malibu—was designed by Stiles O. Clements in 1929 for Rhoda Rindge Adamson and her husband, Merritt Huntley Adamson, the last owners of the Malibu Spanish Land Grant. For the most part this is a celebration of tile in its myriad uses, from the pool to the bathhouse, kitchen, and living room, all leading up to the most exquisite opus to the earthen arts—an entire corridor floor covered in the design of a Persian carpet runner made entirely out of tile and laid into the floor.

The lavish use of ornate ceramic tile, produced by Malibu Potteries (1926–1932), clearly enhanced the Moorish architecture of the house. The company used the red and buff burning clays that existed in the Malibu area, as well as abundant water from a spring in Sweetwater Canyon, to establish the Malibu Potteries and begin a tradition of brilliant tiles seen in residences throughout southern California. Tours run Wednesday through Sunday, 11:00 A.M. to 3:00 P.M. 23200 Pacific Coast Highway, (310) 456–8432, www.adamsonhouse.com.

A mountainside eye-catcher to consider along this oceanside ride moving north is the ***Malibu Castle,*** a mammoth thirteenth-century Scottish castle on top of a hill near Civic Center Way, with arched windows and a stone turret and innumerable ramparts for fighting off invaders and tourists.

Also check out ***Pepperdine University,*** awash in a rolling green meadow that runs from the hill to the highway. There isn't much to see here if you're not a student, but the Pepperdine steps are some of the best in the business when it comes to exercising obscure muscles in your derrière. As at the supermarkets, video rental stores, and gas stations in these parts, don't be surprised if you see a celebrity on your path. Chances are you won't recognize him or her without makeup and script anyway, but if you do, the rule is not to care.

The beaches in this area are often private-club turf, but several excellent public beach spots are just as nice. ***Paradise Cove,*** for one, is a secluded spot just east of ***Zuma Beach,*** with the ***Paradise Cove Restaurant*** right on the beach. A hefty parking charge can be levied to leave your vehicle here, but this can be waived with a meal in the restaurant. You will likely have to share the beach with a film crew, though. The beach remains a popular backdrop for any movie involving California and the beach.

Just over the rocks next door is ***Pirate's Cove,*** a nudist beach most of the time and a good place to catch the spectacle of whales in migration from November through March. The northern tip of Malibu is marked by ***Leo Carrillo State Beach,*** a long sandy quay with few people most of the year. A system of boulders and bluffs creates an underwater cave and tunnel you can traverse at low tide. The beach is the only one in L.A. that allows dogs.

An expensive last stop might be ***Ramirez Canyon Park.*** The former residence of Barbra Streisand is now a feature of the Santa Monica Conservancy, with twenty-two acres of gardens and houses that once provided shelter and privacy for the perfectionist diva who lived there. The wandering paths of sycamores and firs, roses, foxgloves, asters, sweet peas, and camellias are part of a two-hour tour that includes the Peach House, the Barn, the Deco House, and the Barwood. Each building is a piece of art in its own right. The Peach House, named for its color, is a Mediterranean-style villa that was converted from a one-story stable. An upper level, designed as a screening room with automatic blackout curtains and dropdown screen, is accessible only by an exterior winding brick staircase. The whimsical Barn building was Streisand's favorite and is covered inside and out in "aged" wood carved by craftsmen and toy makers. Then there's the Art Deco temple with stainless-steel panels from L.A.'s Atlantic Richfield building, and the Barwood—Streisand's production company—built around existing sycamore trees with Douglas fir framing for that tree-house effect. For $30 you get tea and scones at the end. But unless you pay the toll, this Malibu hideaway will remain hidden away. Reservations are required: (310) 589–2850, ext. 301. 5750 Ramirez Canyon Road.

Places to Stay in the Beach Cities

Luxe: $250+
Deluxe: $150–$249
Good deal: $79–$149

Venice

Venice Beach House
15 39th Avenue, (310) 823–1966, www.venicebeachhouse.com. This nine-room bed-and-breakfast makes good use of an old California Craftsman-style beach-house and marks its place on the National Register of Historic Places. For basement rates, request the Tramp's Quarters—or else splurge with the Pier Suite offering a fireplace and a sitting room. It's a block away from the beach but a good hike from everything else. Good deal.

Santa Monica

Casa Del Mar
1910 Ocean Front Walk, (310) 581–5533 or (800) 898–6999, www.hotelcasadelmar.com. This 1920s neo-Renaissance dowager just underwent an expensive two-year redo that's turned it back into the jewel of yore. Most of the 129 Mediterranean-style rooms face the ocean, and you can stroll just a few steps out to the beach, or to the Santa Monica Pier or Promenade. Luxe. See page 119 for more information.

The Fairmont Miramar
101 Wilshire Boulevard, (310) 576–7777 or (800) 325–3535, www.fairmont.com. The Fairmont Miramar makes great use of a one-time private mansion and playground to the stars and has kept the imposing wrought-iron gates and 123-year-old fig tree at center stage. You'll find Miami Beach–style rooms here, many with views of the ocean. For a touch of romance, book one of the jungle bungalows, once a favorite of Garbo and Davis. Luxe.

Hotel Oceana
849 Ocean Avenue, (310) 393–0486 or (800) 777–0758, www.hoteloceana.com. This chic apartment-buildings-turned-beach-hotel is a bit off the beaten path, across from the Santa Monica cliff walk and several blocks from the popular Third Street Promenade. Stocked kitchenettes and ocean breezes in artfully designed rooms. Deluxe.

Shutters on the Beach
1 Pico Boulevard, (310) 458–0030 or (800) 334–9000, www.shuttersonthebeach.com. More Cape Cod than SoCal, the 198 rooms here come in odd shapes; the place is sort of like a sprawling summer beach compound that's been in the family forever. Two fine-dining rooms and public areas adorned with original art by Hockney and Lichtenstein complete the picture, and the location is just a stone's toss from Santa Monica Promenade. Luxe. See page 119 for more information.

New Rooms

Santa Monica is home to more than 3,300 hotel rooms, including L.A.'s newest (at least at press time!). ***The Ambrose*** *opened in spring 2003 as a boutique Craftsman-style hotel dedicated to calm in crazy times, with a library and fireplace, an Asian garden, and Elixir teas for the soul. The seventy-seven rooms start at $169. 1255 Twentieth Street, (310) 315–1555, www.ambrosehotel.com.*

Malibu

Malibu Beach Inn
22878 Pacific Coast Highway, (310) 456–6445 or (800) 4–MALIBU.
A pretty-in-pink, sunny Spanish Colonial setting with views to die for and a location near the Malibu Pier. In-room fireplaces add to the romance, as do the Spanish tile bathrooms and ocean-facing balconies. Luxe.

Places to Eat in the Beach Cities

Expensive: $25.00+
Reasonable: $15.00–$24.00
Bargain: $8.00–$14.00

Venice

Hydrant Cafe
1202 Abbot Kinney Boulevard,
(310) 401–2275.
Dogs love it here, and the hydrant is only the icing. While pups hang on the patio with their specialty bones and meaty ice cream, their masters enjoy homemade pastries and creative salads and sandwiches. Bargain.

On the Waterfront Café
205 Ocean Front Walk,
(310) 392–0322.
This charming, casual burger and seafood patio is right on the boardwalk. The focus is Swiss cuisine, with a menu of more than thirty types of beers. Bargain.

Rose Café
220 Rose Avenue,
(310) 399–0711.
This original Venice coffeehouse is a tradition in these parts for pastries, salads, and homemade specialties in a 1960s-type setting. Bargain.

Santa Monica

Cha Cha Chicken
1906 Ocean Avenue,
(310) 581–1684.
Caribbean cuisine, including Beard Award–winning Jerk Chicken Enchiladas served in a festive patio scene off the beach. Bargain.

Gagnier's Creole Kitchen
1622 Ocean Park Boulevard,
(310) 319–9981.
This casual Cajun joint is the mother ship for lovers of oyster loaves and peppery fried chicken. The gumbo and po' boys are pretty good, too. Reasonable.

Light House Buffet
201 Arizona Avenue,
(310) 451–2076.
All-you-can-eat sushi served seven days. There's something to be said for limitless sea eel and yellowtail by the boatloads. Reasonable.

Michael's
1147 Third Street,
(310) 451–0843.
Superb and pricey with plenty of expensive art on the walls, Michael's menu is more classic than trendy: slow-roasted monkfish, lavender-honey free-range chicken, and Colorado rack of lamb. The outdoor garden is still one of the most beautiful settings in California to dine in. Expensive.

Malibu

Allegria
22821 Pacific Coast Highway,
(310) 456–3132.
Considered a top-notch Italian roadhouse restaurant with great inside views of the outer ocean sunset, reasonable prices, and a pizza menu that gives Puck chase. Expensive.

Geoffrey's
27400 Pacific Coast Highway,
(310) 457–1519.
Come here for the view—in a garden overlooking the ocean with no obstructions. While the food is pricey and uneventful, the romantic environs more than make up for it. Expensive.

Neptune's Net
42505 Pacific Coast Highway,
(310) 457–3095.
This weathered roadside beach shack cafe on the edge of Malibu is the tradition in these parts for full-flavored dipping fish, great chowders, and cracked crab in the rough. Grab your order and a table outside and dine in the salt air. Bargain.

The South Coast

While the road to Malibu leads to riches, the beach route south is a mixed bag of industrial landmasses, lower-to-middle-income communities, and revitalized commercial zones mixed in with a few elements of charm. If you can ignore the 8-mile strip south of LAX that includes a Chevron Oil refinery and L.A.'s main sewage treatment plant, you may be on your way to some nook-and-cranny adventures in what lies beyond.

And that's Manhattan Beach, Hermosa Beach, and Palos Verdes, three beach city strands that keep a certain quality of fun alive around their piers. The northernmost of these is ***Manhattan Beach,*** home of the Beach Boys and an international surfing fest every August. Forget Frankie. Blame it on one George Freeth, who in 1907 became the man who could "walk on water." He was a Hawaiian import in a land promotion stunt by real estate magnate Henry Huntington. The sport of Polynesian kings soon took off once the boards—originally 8-foot, 200-pound monstrosities—took a tenable form.

Manhattan itself is a crowded semi-industrial town—except by the beach, where it becomes a crowded California beach town. The homes turn condo-like and cool, and the shops along Highland Avenue cater to this with health food stores and restaurants, funky jewelry shops, lots of Greek-style cafes, beachwear boutiques, and surf shops. In the summer it's wall-to-wall cars, possibly because it has a wide beach and popular pier. Meanwhile, if volleyball is your game, Manhattan Beach is Beach Volleyball Central, with lines of nets set up in the sand waiting for a game. The beach walk from Santa Monica—used by walkers, runners, skaters, sidewalk surfers, and every other version of low-tech mobility—runs through Manhattan, with shops and activities all around the strand.

For history buffs, Manhattan Beach wasn't born yesterday. A local museum tells you all about it with artifacts, art, and pottery, mostly from the depression and World War II. The ***Manhattan Beach Historical Society*** can be found in a cottage at 1601 Manhattan Beach Boulevard from noon to 3:00 P.M. on weekends. Call (310) 374–7575.

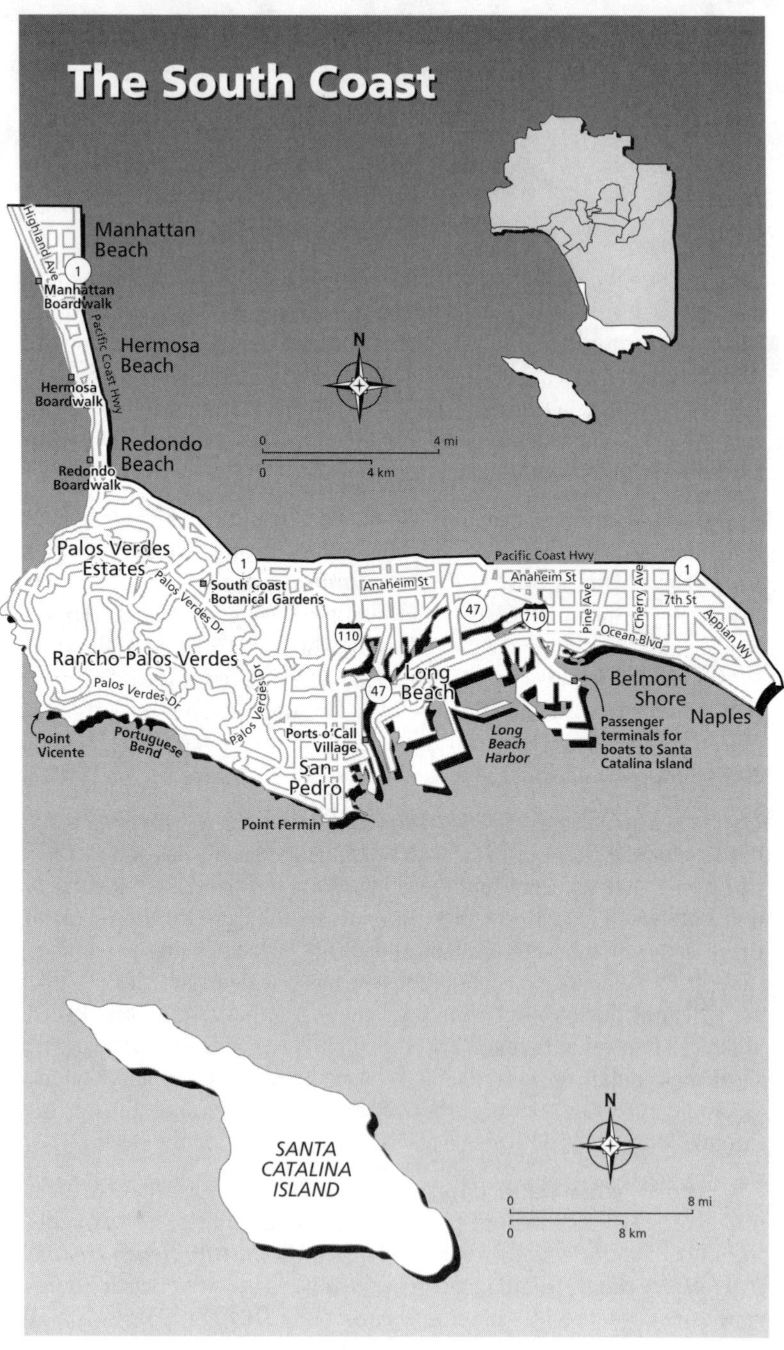

The South Coast
Manhattan Beach
Highland Ave
Manhattan Boardwalk
Pacific Coast Hwy
Hermosa Beach
Hermosa Boardwalk
Redondo Beach
Redondo Boardwalk
N
0
4 mi
0
4 km
Palos Verdes Estates
Palos Verdes Dr
South Coast Botanical Gardens
Rancho Palos Verdes
Palos Verdes Dr
Palos Verdes Dr
Point Vicente
Portuguese Bend
Ports o'Call Village
San Pedro
Point Fermin
Pacific Coast Hwy
Anaheim St
Anaheim St
Pine Ave
Cherry Ave
7th St
Ocean Blvd
Appian Wy
Long Beach
Long Beach Harbor
Belmont Shore
Naples
Passenger terminals for boats to Santa Catalina Island
1
1
1
47
47
110
710
SANTA CATALINA ISLAND
N
0
8 mi
0
8 km

THE SOUTH COAST

> **AUTHOR'S TOP PICKS IN THE SOUTH COAST**
>
> *Wayfarers Chapel*
>
> *Aquarium of the Pacific*
>
> *Museum of Latin American Art, Long Beach*
>
> *Catalina Island*

Just south of Manhattan, ***Hermosa Beach*** on a weekend is like Fort Lauderdale on spring break. The action along palm-lined Pier Avenue, extending from the beach and pier to Highland Avenue, is bursting with rock music, sports bars with sidewalk areas filled with blond babes of every gender and nationality, and shops selling everything from gifts and notions to liquor and cigarettes. One of the more notable spots is ***The Lighthouse*** at 30 Pier Avenue, a down-at-the-heels exposed-brick bar and bohemian coffeehouse in the 1950s where the greats in folk and jazz laid their chords. Today it's mostly a reggae club but still a popular spot on the promenade. The ***Comedy & Magic Club*** around the corner is a great spot for checking out the up-and-comers as well as the stars. The likes of Leno and Seinfeld are not strangers here and often drop by the club to try out new material. 1018 Hermosa Beach Avenue, (310) 372–1193, www.comedyandmagicclub.com.

To continue down to Redondo Beach might not be the best use of time or gas. Although the horseshoe-shaped pier at King's Harbor went through an uplift in the last ten years, its honky-tonk tenor is quite passé, and dining options are too lame and expensive to make this would-be retro tourist trap worth the trip.

A better bet is the scenic Pacific Coast Highway 1 down to ***Palos Verdes*** for a breathtaking drive around the peninsula to ***San Pedro.*** The peninsula that houses Worldport LA (where international cruise ships dock) shares the rock with beautiful Palos Verdes, where Rolling Hills marks the wealthiest neighborhood in America. The great green mound that is Palos Verdes is sparsely settled along its rugged coastline, and the route along Palos Verdes Drive reveals surf-swept remote crags that lead to hidden beaches (try nudist-loving ***Smuggler's Cove*** off Portuguese Bend) and natural attractions.

From the north you can drive around ***Palos Verdes Estates,*** founded in 1939 with faux Beaux-Arts mansions surrounded by elegant patches of green designed by John and Frederick Law Olmsted Jr., whose works in New York's Central Park and Boston's Public Gardens are landmarks. More than a third of this peninsula is preserved parkland; you may even see a peacock or two roaming freely through it. At the top of the hill is ***Malaga Cove Plaza,*** the only community in the area completed before the depression of the 1930s, thus escaping the ravages of suburban sprawl. It's built around a Spanish-style arcade completed in 1930 that

Pointing toward the Orient

*The **Hilton Hotel Palos Verdes** and the **Sheraton Hotel Palos Verdes** are both owned by a Malaysian company that's loyal to the Muslim faith—so much so that you will always know where Saudi Arabia is when you stay in one of its rooms. On the ceiling of each guest room is an arrow pointing toward Mecca to assist with prayers or help you figure out where the sun rises.*

has at its center the Neptune Fountain, a marble-and-plaster replica of a sixteenth-century bronze original in Bologna, Italy. With bougainvillea-covered bricks all around, the area retains the vision of a terraced Mediterranean village in harmony with the landscape. All roofs, as the local rules go, must be red tile.

Not far from this point, you'll find the ***South Coast Botanical Gardens.*** The eighty-seven-acre park is an ode to what you, too, can do with trash if you just set your mind (and money) to it. The former dump site held some three and a half million tons of trash in the 1950s until it was transformed into a California-style Garden of Eden in 1961 with more than 200,000 plants in 2,000 species divided into precious sections such as the Fuchsia Garden, Water-wise Garden, Herb Garden, English Rose Garden, and Garden of the Senses. The $5.00 admission comes with a map. 26300 Crenshaw Boulevard, (310) 544–6815.

The tour continues into ***Rancho Palos Verdes,*** the newest city on the peninsula, and ***Point Vicente,*** a cliff point with a historic landmark lighthouse. The lighthouse has operated since 1926 (interrupted by World War II), and was fully automated in 1971 complete with blaring foghorn.

Past Point Vicente, find the ***Wayfarers Chapel.*** Designed in 1951 by Lloyd Wright, Frank Lloyd's son, it's a true temple of glass and redwood. If you have time for only one stop along the cliff drive, this is it. The views are astounding, the interiors awe inspiring, and the venue popular with the wedding crowd. Don't come on a weekend unless you don't mind taking your place in the back of a long line of tuxedos and white satin, waiting for that winning photo of the chapel above Abalone Cove where the sunsets compete with those in Hawaii. 5755 Palos Verdes Drive.

Continue past Abalone Cove to ***Portuguese Bend,*** named for the nineteenth-century Portuguese whalers who made their living along what continues to be a cetacean freeway route, and slide into unpretentious San Pedro.

At the southern tip of the peninsula is ***Point Fermin,*** a landscaped park with a nineteenth-century lighthouse at the tip. Overlooking Point Fermin is Angel's Gate Park, with an odd addition: the ***Korean Friendship Bell,*** a replica of an eighth-century Korean bronze bell. Dedicated in 1976 as a gift from South Korea, it's rung by Korean dig-

Korean Friendship Bell

nitaries (using a painted wooden log) three times each year: on July 4, August 15, and New Year's Eve. More interesting is the encasing pavilion, with twelve red columns (representing the zodiac) supporting a pagoda-style roof from which the bell hangs, adorned with intricate carvings, patterns, and painted dragons.

San Pedro itself is not exactly a postcard kind of place. Located about 20 miles from downtown L.A., it's a place where rough-and-tumble work, labor strife, and serious populism have figured largely in its history as a fishing town and shipping port. But unlike other areas of Los Angeles, San Pedro wears no pretense and doesn't try to be hip, modern, or anything other than it is. And for all that, you get plenty of charm—the down-home kind, with businesses that have been serving up fried calamari and fresh sea bass right off the dock for sixty years or more. It's the sort of place where a British pub serves you a pint in small quarters that look like someone's living room, and where on the first Thursday of every month the locals come out to celebrate their town in arts and music along two blocks in the center of town.

And San Pedro offers some attractions, too. Military and maritime buffs will like the ***Fort MacArthur Military Museum*** in Point Fermin, where plenty of uniforms, photographs, deactivated bombs, mines, and missiles from twentieth-century wars can be perused. Contact (310) 548–2631. The ***Maritime Museum,*** in a 75,000-square-foot Streamline Moderne building, gives a fish's-eye view of the town's history from the salad days of fishing and whaling. But there are also nautical models, hundreds of them, from Columbus's galleons to Drake's *Golden Hinde* to midcentury steamships. The most haunting of these is an 18-foot encased replica of the *Titanic* in sliced side views full of exquisite interior and exterior details. Sampson Way and Sixth Street, (310) 548–7618.

My Big Fat Greek Dinner

*At **Papadakis Tavern** located at 301 West Sixth Street in San Pedro, handsome Pedro Papadakis greets you at the door, kisses you like family—no matter whose family you are—and sits you down personally. It isn't five minutes before the waiters come over with their choice cuts of today's steaks displayed on a tray. As the tavern fills up, so does the spirit when waiters break into a heady dance between courses. Call (310) 548–1186.*

The ***port area,*** part of **Worldport LA,** stands as the third largest commercial seaport in the world, right behind Singapore and Hong Kong. Cruise ships come in and out of the modern ports of call, bound mostly for Mexico and Hawaii, but occasionally Alaska and the Caribbean. And there's a ***Ports o' Call Village*** to cater to visitors just south of the terminal building, with lots of quick fish sushi and sandwich bars, tacky souvenir stores, and harbor tours that guarantee you'll see whales during the migratory season (December through April) or your money back. Check out ***L.A. Harbor Sportfishing,*** (310) 547–9916.

Kids might want to go to the ***Cabrillo Marine Aquarium*** in a Frank Gehry–designed building at 3720 Stephen White Drive. It's free and has more than three dozen saltwater tanks, plus a touch tank. (310) 548–7562.

As for local lore, San Pedro is the official eternal resting place for barfly poet Charles Bukowski. At the center of town is the ***Warner Theater,*** built in 1931 at 478 Sixth Street with all the intricate Art Deco trimmings. The ***Whale & Ale*** at 327 Seventh Street is the place to get your pint with fish-and-chips or steak-and-kidney pie if the urge gets you. Or you can hit ***Canetti's Seafood Grotto*** right at the docks, where Joe Canetti has been waking up at 3:30 A.M. each day to grab the catch that comes in at 4:00 A.M. and start cooking in his restaurant, which has been operating since 1949. He serves breakfast, lunch, and dinner with a chalkboard full of specials and a band that comes in on weekend nights. 309 East Twenty-second Street.

Moving south along Highway 1 or Seaside Boulevard, you'll end up in ***Long Beach,*** L.A.'s southernmost city and, with half a million resi-

Aquarium of the Pacific

dents, second largest. But for all its size it's mostly an industrial town, built on the pumping of more than 400 oil wells. The city is the outgrowth of the Long Beach Naval Station and shipyard, in use for the first half of the last century. The town provided amusement to all the sailors when they weren't aboard ship and attracted Angelenos near and far with its famed Pike Amusement Park, now long gone. Today it's very much a working-class town with some of its charm preserved in older homes, a charming sea walk, strands of greenery, the canals and yacht clubs of Belmont Shore, and the ongoing and hard-going revitalization of its gasping downtown area.

To augment the revitalization efforts with the $650 million Queensway redevelopment project, the city put a world-class aquarium along its bay shore and built a faux Cape Cod retail and dining village near it called Shoreline Village, where parking costs as much as a meal. The $100 million ***Aquarium of the Pacific*** models itself after the success of the Monterey Bay Aquarium. It features creative interpretations of the world's aquatic environments and 550 species of marine life, detailing seventeen major habitats and offering thirty-one focus exhibits. A stop here could possibly justify the $18.75 adult admission ticket. It's located just off Shoreline Drive at 100 Aquarium Way. Call (562) 590–3100 or visit www.aquariumofpacific.org.

While parked at the aquarium, stop at ***Shoreline Village*** for a taste of the town's heavy-handed tourism efforts and take a ride on the original 1911 Loofe carousel, a holdout from the Pike days.

From there, water taxis will ferry you to the ***RMS*** **Queen Mary** across the bay—the pride of Britain

Long Beach Location

Long Beach can look like any beach if you attach some celluloid to it. The city has served as a location for such films as Amistad, Pleasantville, Red Corner, Clear and Present Danger, Multiplicity, Batman and Robin, Stargate, Last Action Hero, The Cable Guy, Speed, Clueless, Mr. Bean, *and* The Muse.

that made her maiden voyage from Southampton in 1936 and came to rest in Long Beach in 1967 after more than 1,000 crossings. The 365 recently redone Art Deco staterooms have housed Winston Churchill, Marlene Dietrich, Greta Garbo, Fred Astaire, Bob Hope, and the duke and duchess of Windsor; most can be reserved for overnight use by visitors. The "faded" grandeur of the ship is kept intact, and with restaurants and clubs, a spa, coffee bar, and business center in full operation, the retro experience is a fun one. But overnighters may get the added benefit of the ghostly kind. The ship is said to be haunted; such specters as wet footprints near a dry indoor pool, voices in empty rooms and corridors, the apparition of a worker crushed in a huge metal door, floods, flashing lights, and other disturbances are not uncommon. Few areas today remain off-limits, and the ship is a floating museum of some of last century's most important moments. Fees for admission and a tour are steep unless you book a room: $19.95 for adult admission with a Web site discount plus parking. Call (562) 435–3511 or visit www.queenmary.com.

Here's the Skinny

The nation's skinniest house—skinny enough to get a listing in Ripley's Believe It or Not*—is located at 703 Gladys Avenue in Long Beach. The flat-faced home was built in 1932 by Nelson Raymond on a bet that an inhabitable residence could not be built on his lot, which measured 10 by 50 feet. A craftsman built the compact quarters and it stands today, three stories high.*

Nearby you'll find a tacky tourist-trap replica of a British coastal village and an odd juxtaposition: the Povodnaya Lodka B-427, aka *Scorpion*, commissioned in 1973 by the Soviets to spy on the West and launch nuclear torpedoes during the height of the Cold War. It was decommissioned in 1994 and acquired by Long Beach in 1998. Visitors get to sweat like the seventy-eight servicemen who operated it in cramped quarters using twenty-seven bunks and three bathrooms while examining the deadly torpedo bays and pretending they're in the film *Hunt for Red October.* Admission is $10, or $25 for a combo ticket with the *Queen Mary.* Call (562) 497–1102.

Home of the Dome

Adjacent to the Queen Mary *in Long Beach is the world's largest free-span aluminum geodesic dome. The 138,000-square-foot space was built to house the* Spruce Goose, *the giant flying boat developed by Howard Hughes. The* Goose *has since flown the coop, but the dome remains, now an ancillary soundstage for Warner Bros. Studios.*

Back on the city side of the bay, take a walk along the ***Shoreline Path,*** which leads from Shoreline Village to the beach of Long Beach. The pleasant grassy stroll offers views of the *Queen Mary,* the artfully disguised oil pumping islands farther out, and the active recreational boasting and shipping lanes. Across the street are the upscale homes of some of the landed gentry in the town, all leading to Belmont Shore. En route, pass the Gothic Revival original Villa Riviera and stop into the ***Long Beach Museum of Art,*** housed in a 1912 mansion. The collection is southern California contemporary, three floors of it, and includes photography and sculpture, a sculpture garden, and video art. 2300 East Ocean Boulevard, (562) 439–2119.

In ***Belmont Shore*** you'll notice you're not in Long Beach anymore. This is the upper-crust divider, with condo-like homes attached to yachts and a series of canals modeled ever so remotely after Naples, Italy. This district has a yuppie feel along tony Second Street, a fifteen-block walking district of cafes, entertainment, and designer clothing shops, complete with a fleet of Italian-style "loveboats" or gondolas to ferry people around the neighborhood. A fee of $55 per couple buys the bread, the cheese, the salami, and the singing.

Heading east from this area you'll want to check out the ***Rancho Los Alamitos adobe*** located (strangely enough) inside an upscale gated neighborhood. Once you find your way through the gates and get your pass (no invitation necessary; just tell them where you're headed), you'll find this adobe ranch a strange oasis of peace and nature inside a well-populated modern development. The ranch house was built around 1800 and eventually evolved into a lumbering, comfortable farmhouse and working ranch raising oversized shire horses and owned by Abel Sterns, once considered the richest man in California. The workhorses are still here and tended by on-site groundskeepers. Docents lead tours through the antiques-stocked house. Admission is free, and donations are accepted. The unsung gem of this ranch is the garden—four acres with a geranium walk, a rose garden and olive patio, a native garden, cactus garden, jacaranda walk, and friendly meditation garden. 6400 Bixby Hill Road, (562) 431–3541.

A second preserved adobe, ***Ranchos Los Cerritos*** is on the eastern edge of Long Beach. This two-story adobe was built in 1844 for Yankee cattle rancher and entrepreneur John Temple, who, it's reported, continues to haunt the adobe today. At one time the ranch raised some 30,000 sheep, and it's said that bells can still be heard in the haunted passageways. Temple has also been seen with two young girls, thought to be his daughters, who are buried on the property. Visiting the adobe is free and priceless if you have a sighting. 4600 Virginia Road, (562) 570–1755.

En route to or from Rancho Los Alamitos, stop by the ***Museum of Latin American Art.*** The vintage-1920 house, which was once a movie studio,

Hollywood South

Long Beach got its start in Hollywood before Hollywood. A studio was built in 1910 at Alamitos and Sixth in a spot that became Balboa Studios in 1916 and cranked out such silent classics as Little Mary Sunshine, St. Elmo, *and* The Awakening. *Both Groucho Marx and W. C. Fields had homes nearby. Now the studio is the home of the Museum of Latin American Art.*

presents the only museum in the western United States strictly focused on this genre. Located in what is considered the up-and-coming (though nowhere near there) ***East Village Arts District*** of Long Beach, the museum is spearheading the district with well-curated exhibitions of contemporary Latin American artists, and enhancing its programs with regular lectures and festival events. Admission is $5.00. A brown-bag lunch lecture at noon the last Friday of the month is free. The on-site restaurant, ***Viva***, serves hot and spicy selections from south of the border. 628 Los Alamitos Boulevard, (562) 437–1689, www.molaa.com.

Head back to Pine Avenue from Ocean Avenue to Seventh Street for a taste of Long Beach's developing restaurant, shopping, and club life. The Blue Line from Union Station stops right in the center of town, which is within walking distance of Shoreline Drive and Shoreline Village (described above). The 1920s architecture of the buildings downtown add to the focus on hipness here, and the streets are lined with trendy cafes. ***Alegria Cocina*** offers amazing Flamenco footwork with its tapas menu and turns into a hot salsa club when the serving stops. ***Blue Café*** brings in top blues artists in the area, and a sushi bar called ***Wasabi*** offers karaoke on Monday night. The area is compact, walkable, fun—and basically the only game in town for varied entertainment when the sun goes down.

Santa Catalina is a rare treat in the southern California landscape, for it is, among other things, a land without cars. The island lies some 22 miles across the Pacific from the Long Beach, but feels like someplace in the Mediterranean on warm days, which are always ten degrees cooler than urban L.A. Its history is ancient: 7,000 years have come and gone with Catalina Island playing a part. Various Native American tribes, such as the Gabrielinos and the Pimuguans, traded and fished and got on well, considering the island's abundance. Life was good . . . and then came Spanish conquerors and later the Mexicans, and Catalina became known as Smuggler's Cove. With Mexican rule in place up and down the California coast in the 1800s, tariffs became the government's main source of revenue, especially while taxing goods at 100 percent of their value. Catalina provided shelter for wayward merchants whose goods could be smuggled from the island onto the mainland. In 1864 Americans claimed it for Union barracks during the American Civil War. The barracks still stand.

Something to Chew On

Santa Catalina was named San Salvador by the Portuguese in 1542, renamed by the Spanish in 1602, and privately owned by Americans since 1811, mostly by chewing gum magnate William Wrigley, who lived in the gingerbread clifftop manner above Avalon that is now the Inn at Mt. Ada. He would ship out his baseball team, the Chicago Cubs, each year for spring training sessions in the island's interior.

Eventually vacationers claimed the island, as did Hollywood, whose celebrities flocked the two dozen miles across the ocean for fun in the 1920s to 1940s. Cameras found a perfect South Seas–looking backwater here to film *Mutiny on the Bounty* with Clark Gable along with a slew of other films, one that needed bison, which have remained here living happily and multiplying freely long after the cameras stopped rolling.

With 75 square miles of interior wilderness and cars restricted to a privileged few, Catalina replaces freeways with hiking trails.

As far as towns go, the island is flanked by Avalon on one end and Two Harbors on the other. Urban explorations may be limited to ***Avalon***, where over thirty hotels, notions shops, and restaurants fill the town's packed square mile and golf carts provide the wheels if needed.

Outside saltwater taffy shops and nautical souvenir stores, what's left to explore is Avalon's history, whose 1930s and 1940s heyday is preserved in the architecture and tiles. The ***Avalon Casino*** down the street from the main shopping district is worth a look. The round Deco building hosted live radio broadcastings of big-band concerts during the war years and movie screenings since its opening in 1925. It's a museum of its time and free for the looking.

But Catalina is mostly nature conservancy: 80 percent of the island belongs to a trust that requires its undisturbed preservation. If you take a tour into the interior, you're likely to see bison, waterfalls, even abandoned hunting lodges from days gone by amid Baja scrub and astonishing views of the Pacific Ocean washing against the cliffs.

The Catalina Nature Conservancy provides maps, permits, and advice on the hikes here, which range from a simple 3-mile amble to a week of backpacking from campsite to campsite in 9-mile stretches. Nearly everywhere you take your feet, the view is destined to be stunning. Catalina is a geography of cliffs and mountains that climb to 2,200 feet, with ocean expanses all around.

Bicyclists are restricted to nonconservancy lands but may take a paved and semipaved road from Avalon to Two Harbors along 18 miles of scenic touring.

Two Harbors is just that—an isthmus where the ocean pinches the island at its thinnest point and brings panoramic ocean views with two harbors. There isn't much to the commercial part of Two Harbors. Its one restaurant, single general store, and cute and quiet eleven-room bed-and-breakfast provide all the action. But people don't visit Two Harbors for its sensational nightlife. Rather, it's the private coves, camping, kayaking, scuba, snorkeling and quiet nature walks that attract visitors to this destination year-round.

Getting to Catalina is easy. The fastest way is in fourteen minutes by helicopter from San Pedro and Long Beach boat terminals via ***Island Express.*** Flights depart hourly until sunset and cost $80 one-way, $140 round-trip, for adults, kids, and seniors, including all taxes. Call (800) 2–AVALON. By boat there are several options. ***Catalina Express*** runs from Long Beach, San Pedro, and Dana Point and takes an hour to an hour and a half to cross. Rates start at $42 round-trip, with small discounts for seniors and children. Check-in is one hour before departure, and the company runs all year, with around thirty departures a day. Call (800) 618–5533. ***Catalina Explorer*** (877–432–6276) and ***Catalina Passenger Service*** (800–830–7744) also provide transport to Catalina from points along the southern California coast. Once there, diving, glass-bottomed boat excursions, kayaking tours, and safaris to the interior can be booked with different companies by contacting the ***Catalina Island Visitors Bureau*** at (310) 510–1520, www.catalina.com.

PLACES TO STAY IN THE SOUTH COAST

Luxe: $250+
Deluxe: $150–$249
Good deal: $79–$149

Barnabey's Hotel
3501 Sepulveda Boulevard, Manhattan Beach, (310) 545–8466 or (800) 552–5258, www.barnabeyshotel.com. A kitschy, Victorian-style property with 125 rooms decorated to the period and a warm, romantic restaurant that serves game. Located ten minutes from LAX with free shuttle transfers. Deluxe.

Hermosa Beach House
1300 The Strand, Hermosa Beach, (310) 374–3001 or (888) 895–4559, www.beach-house.com. This too-cool-to-be-true hotel is modern and sharp with big rooms that boast sitting spaces, ocean views, wood-burning fireplaces, wet bars, down comforters and pillows, and a location right on the beach. There's an on-site spa, too. Luxe.

Long Beach Hilton
701 West Ocean Boulevard, Long Beach, (562) 983–3400 or (800) HILTONS, www.longbeach.hilton.com. A premier leisure and business hotel close to downtown, Pine Avenue, the aquarium, and the convention center. Deluxe.

Lord Mayor's Bed & Breakfast
435 Cedar Avenue, Long Beach, (562) 436–0324, www.lordmayors.com. This cute home with cottages features antique fur-

nishings, claw-footed tubs, and wonderful home-baked breakfasts. Good deal.

Portofino Hotel & Yacht Club
260 Portofino Way, Redondo Beach, (310) 379–8481 or (800) 468–4292, www.hotelportofino.com. An intimate hotel with ocean-view rooms on a private stretch of King Harbor. Deluxe.

Sea Sprite Motel
1016 The Strand, Hermosa Beach, (310) 376–6933. The rooms here are noisy and nonfancy, but there are views of the ocean and you're right on the The Strand. Good deal.

PLACES TO EAT IN THE SOUTH COAST

Expensive: $25.00+
Reasonable: $15.00–$24.00
Bargain: $8.00–$14.00

Buster's Beach House and Longboard Bar
168 Marina Drive, Long Beach, (562) 598-9431, www.busterbeachhouse.com. Pork Luau, Macadamia Nut Chicken, and Mai Tais with pink umbrellas right on the water in Alamitos Bay. Reasonable.

Good Stuff
1286 The Strand, Hermosa Beach, (310) 374–2334. Burgers, teriyaki chicken sandwiches, fries, shakes, and breakfast until 5:00 P.M. are served in a casual, upstairs-downstairs, inside-outside spot on the beach. Bargain.

The Kettle
1138 Highland Avenue, Manhattan Beach, (310) 545–8511. Man-sized sandwiches, salads, and burgers are served here around the clock—and there's a cute patio over the main thoroughfare on which to enjoy them. Bargain.

Senfuku
380 West Sixth Street, San Pedro. Sushi is served at the bar or table with a catch of fish that's as fresh as it gets. Reasonable.

The Sky Room
40 South Locust, Long Beach, (562) 983–2703, www.theskyroom.com. Dinner and dancing the classic way in Long Beach's answer to New York's Rainbow Room, located in the penthouse of the historic Art Deco Breakers Building overlooking the water. Expensive.

Soleil
1142 Manhattan Avenue, Manhattan Beach, (310) 545–8654. An upscale experience in creative Mediterranean cuisine served in rustic, cathedral interiors with an inspired wine list. Reasonable.

Author's Favorite Places to Eat in the South Coast

Papadakis Taverna San Pedro
301 West Sixth Street
(310) 548–1186
(see page 130 for more information)

Barnabey's
3501 Sepulveda Boulevard
(310) 545–8466

The Sky Room
40 South Locust Street, Long Beach
(562) 983–2703

The San Fernando Valley

They call it "Valley of the Stars" for all the celebrities who, at some point in their lives, called the San Fernando Valley home—and for the plethora of film and production studios that still do. The former wheat and citrus groves of the early-twentieth century have turned to a 300-square-mile sprawl of cities and towns, from Glendale to Malibu, that is now just one endless neighborhood for its 1.6 million inhabitants. But the homogeneous flat cityscape may make sense in these parts. Earthquakes love the Valley. The Northridge neighborhood was the epicenter of a 1994 temblor that measured 6.7 in magnitude, collapsing apartment buildings and department stores in the area with equal vigor.

To outsiders stuck in the haze of making sense of it, at first glance there really doesn't seem to be any *there* there in the Valley—just a rolling carpet of cheesy strip malls, lower-to-upper-middle-class 1960s California ranch-style dwellings, and apartment buildings that look like nursing homes. But on second glance, a few shiny nuggets appear. Don't expect a windfall here. Still, though the pickings are few, some are real gems.

The San Fernando Valley is a valley because it's flanked by the Santa Monica Mountain ridge, which divides it from the rest of L.A. In 2002 residents felt this ridge was wide enough to merit secession from greater L.A., but the rest of the city voters did not agree and the Balkanization initiative failed. Getting to the Valley, then, is the first challenge. This is freeway land, and the 101 and 134 will do the job well enough in non-rush-hour moments. There's no real center of the Valley, and no way to negotiate it comfortably without a car. (The Red Line subway runs to North Hollywood, and at the Universal Studios exit a park shuttle bus takes you to the action of Universal Studios Theme Park and CityWalk, bypassing exorbitant parking garage fees—but that is about it.) Venerable Ventura Boulevard, runs through it. Once the cruising capital of California, it's now the one consistent street you can take from east to west, from Burbank to Van Nuys, with plenty of pockets for ritzy cafes and chic suburban boutiques. If the Valley has a center, this artery is it.

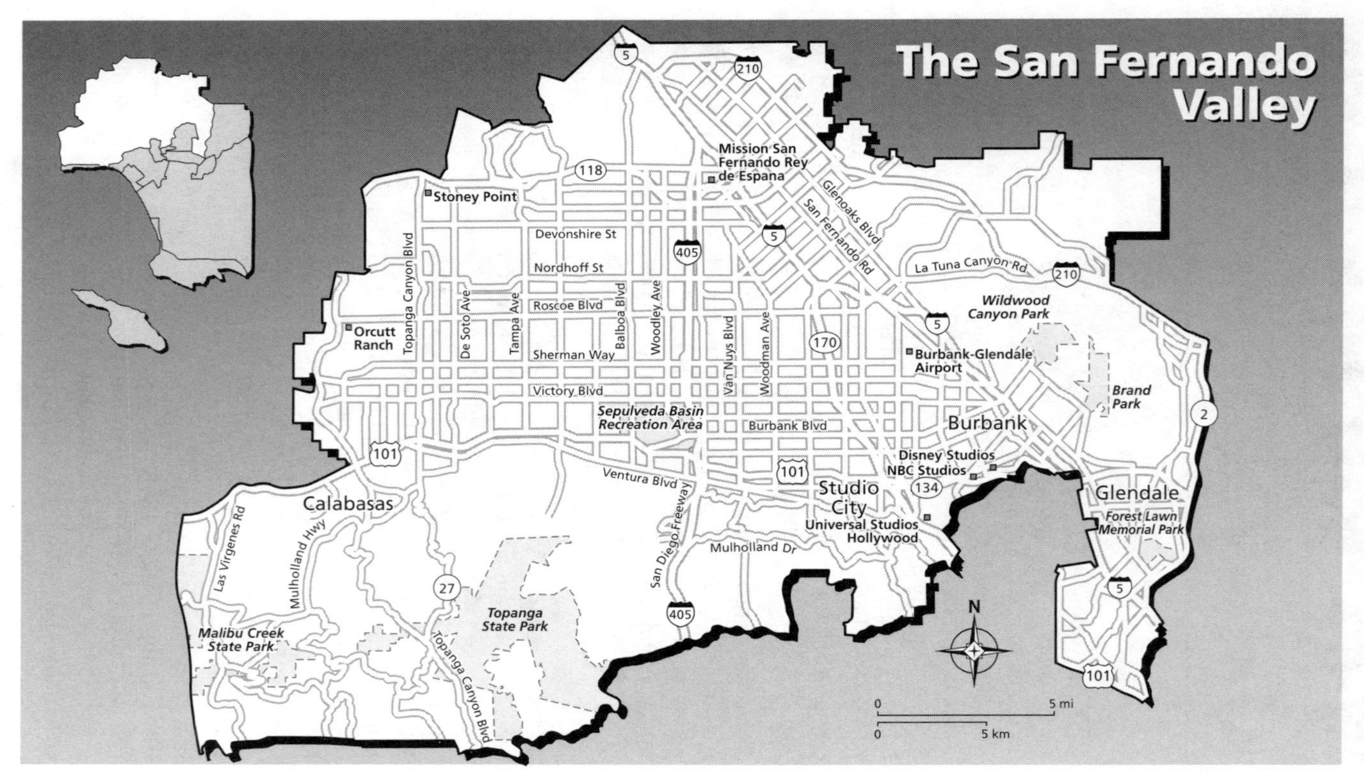
The San Fernando Valley
Mission San Fernando Rey de Espana
Stoney Point
Orcutt Ranch
Devonshire St
Nordhoff St
Roscoe Blvd
Sherman Way
Victory Blvd
Topanga Canyon Blvd
De Soto Ave
Tampa Ave
Balboa Blvd
Woodley Ave
Van Nuys Blvd
Woodman Ave
Glenoaks Blvd
San Fernando Rd
La Tuna Canyon Rd
Wildwood Canyon Park
Burbank-Glendale Airport
Brand Park
Sepulveda Basin Recreation Area
Burbank Blvd
Burbank
Disney Studios
NBC Studios
Studio City
Universal Studios Hollywood
Glendale
Forest Lawn Memorial Park
Ventura Blvd
San Diego Freeway
Mulholland Dr
Calabasas
Las Virgenes Rd
Mulholland Hwy
Malibu Creek State Park
Topanga State Park
Topanga Canyon Blvd
5
210
118
405
170
101
134
2
27
N
0
5 mi
0
5 km

THE SAN FERNANDO VALLEY

Although a tour of the Valley needn't start with Glendale at its easternmost flank, there is one spot here worthy of the traffic you have to fight to get there: ***Forest Lawn Memorial Park.***

Author's Top Picks in the San Fernando Valley

Forest Lawn Memorial Park Labyrinth

Paramount Ranch

Peter Strauss Ranch

Malibu Creek State Park

Inn of the Seventh Ray

Call it the mother of all L.A. cemeteries. Evelyn Waugh found it fodder enough for his book *The Loved One,* about the dark absurdities involved in the American way of death. This place is like a Valentine's Day card to the great beyond. In one afternoon, or even one hour, you can see Michelangelo's greatest works such as *David, Moses,* and *La Pietà;* Leonardo da Vinci's immortal *Last Supper* re-created in brilliant stained glass; the Crucifixion and the Resurrection; rare coins; thirteenth-century-style stained glass; Old World–style mausoleums—and much, much more. Winding roads take you through it like a Candy Land board game. It's a self-guided tour, though, and it can include ducks in a pond decorated with statuary or, my favorite, the labyrinth on top of the hill. In actuality the labyrinth is a find in these parts. A flat, granite surface overlooking Downtown L.A., the snaking circle can be contemplative, indeed. The location, near the intersection of the 101 and the 2 freeways, can be confusing without MapQuest. A self-guiding map is available at the entrance. 1712 South Glendale Avenue, (800) 204–3131, www.forestlawn.com.

As you head west on the 101, the studios start to pop into view—Disney with its cartoon facade, other whimsical animation studio buildings—and then you're in beautiful downtown Burbank, home of Warner Brothers, Universal, NBC, and countless independent studios.

Vision in a Chicken Ranch

Universal Studios started in 1915 as a chicken ranch founded by filmmaker-rancher Carl Laammle. While he built sets and filmed westerns, dramas, and comedies, he built bleachers for the public to watch and—in those days of silent films—cheer the good guy and boo the bad guy. At the exits he sold them fresh eggs.

Although the events of September 11 stopped the practice of public behind-the-scenes tours at most L.A.-area film studios, a few are back on track. ***Warner Bros. Studios*** in Burbank runs a two-hour walking tour weekdays that costs $32 and includes hot sets where possible. Call (818) 872–TOUR. ***Universal Studios Hollywood,*** home to *ER* and *Friends,* has a VIP Experience Tour that costs $125 and includes special theme-park privileges along with backlot and working-set tours. (818) 508–9600.

Eyes on the Fries

*Sure, the French started it, but the Belgians perfected it, and now **Benita's** brings it to the masses. Benita's Frites are Belgian fries made into a gastronomic art form with cones of medium-thick hot potato strands (not boiled in horsemeat fat here, though), seasoned and peppered and dipped in a menu of possibilities: malt vinegar, red wine vinegar, white wine vinegar, salt, pepper, cayenne, mustard, sauces from Thai to Spanish, and any combination of spices that can be mixed in with mayo and taste good. Positively addicting. Look for them at the Universal CityWalk promenade.*

NBC Studios has a seventy-minute, $7.50 tour that takes you into the sets of *The Tonight Show* and *Days of Our Lives* and adds some wardrobe, makeup, and sound-effect demos. If you have the legs for it, you can stand in line to score audience seats to Jay Leno. Call (818) 840–3537.

Swing by ***CityWalk*** for lunch. The movie and L.A.-themed facade promenade next to Universal Studios Hollywood is a hoot and not off-limits to celeb sightings. Restaurants like Gladstone's, Tu Tu Tango, Buca Di Beppo, Hard Rock Café, and Wolfgang Puck's Café cater to tourists as well as stars on set breaks and studio heads looking for a convenient place to meet. The ***Upstart Crow Bookshop*** is a surprising independent retail feature in this otherwise overcommercialized retail theme park and offers tables outside along the promenade, decent coffee, and great books to read while you watch.

Just north of Universal Studios is ***Burbank Airport,*** a small but sturdy gateway to the rest of the world and a convenient alternative to LAX. Here the curb cops don't hassle you and make you circle a dozen times before stopping, the parking rates are inexpensive, the traffic in and out is light, and the airport is served by Southwest Airlines, America West, American, Alaska, and United. What's even more amazing is that the airport is actually a stop on the Metrolink rail system, so it's possible to travel from Union Station to this hub without stepping into a car. Contact www.burbankairport.com for information.

Hamburger History

*The world's first double-decker hamburger was invented here, at **Bob's Big Boy.** And although the original 1938 diner in Glendale is long gone, the 1947 Streamline Moderne version at 4211 Riverside Drive in Burbank is quite happening and a habit with the local studio crowd. The chunky fiberglass statue of the happy boy chef with a plate full of burgers is right where he's been for years: in front of the diner. Inside, the same orange Naugahyde swivel counter seats and booth benches await.*

On the dividing line between Burbank and the rest of the Valley sprawl is ***North Hollywood***—NoHo, as the locals call it—an area that would like to consider itself up and coming with an array of cafes and a commercial strip on Lankershim Boulevard between Magnolia and Victory Boulevards fondly thought of as the ***NoHo Arts District.*** There find a Starbucks, a taquaria, a Color Me Mine pottery painting store, an arts space for local exhibitions, a couple of community theater stages, a few used-clothing stores, and a cool new and used-book shop called ***Iliad*** with a good bulletin board. These are all mixed in, of course, with attorneys' offices, appliance stores, a liquor store strip mall, and some small furniture stores. The district runs an arts festival every August with rock bands, theater productions, and lots of canvases.

Near the corner of Barham and Lankershim lies an odd monument: ***Campo de Cahuenga.*** Right next to the MTA station is what's considered the birthplace of California. An 1847 adobe marks the spot where the Capitulation of Cahuenga was signed on a rickety kitchen table to formalize the Treaty of Guadalupe Hidalgo, thus ending the final chapter in the war between Mexico and the United States. 3919 Lankershim.

The commercial district of Ventura Boulevard starts to get revved up right around here, in what's considered Studio City. The intersection of Laurel Canyon Boulevard and Ventura Boulevard is a crowded mass of chain stores like Bookstar and the Daily Grill, but it's still a good place to anchor and look around on foot. Except for a spattering of shopping malls, this is it for browsing in the Valley.

The way west, however reveals a rolling choice of gas stations, computer dealerships, bistro cafes, hotels, fast-food shops, office buildings, travel agencies, you name it, all the way to Topanga Canyon. A curious stop along the way is the ***Sportsmen's Lodge,*** a 1940s throwback; look for its meandering garden duck pond with bridges, gazebo, and waterfalls, along with 1960s-style rooms that overlook the Astroturf-and-potted-palm-lined pool area. The scene here was background to such TV classics as *Murder She Wrote, Baretta, Rockford Files,* and *Knight Rider* as well as films like *The Man with the X-ray Eyes,* starring Ray Milland. The hotel is considered *the* place to meet, greet, and dance away Saturday night for the over-fifty crowd. 12825 Ventura Boulevard, (818) 769–4700 or (800) 821–8511, www.sportsmenslodge.com.

Continuing westward, your next stop is ***Encino,*** a fairly uninteresting spread of homes. Still, the ***Tillman Reclamation Plant*** on the giant floodplain that is the Sepulveda Dam Recreation Area on Woodley Avenue has been made into a park of sorts, with a tree-shaded dog haven and picnic area, a jogging trail, and a golf course maintained by the treated water. An odd attraction here is the six-and-a-half-acre Tillman Japanese Gardens with stone lanterns, bonsai trees, bridges, bamboo, a meandering stream, and a teahouse. The hours are odder still—the place is more often closed than not. A reservation here is a good thing so the park managers can get busy and open the gate. Call (818) 756–8166.

Slightly south of the park is the ***Los Encinos State Historic Park,*** located in a hard-to-find residential section. It's a sleepy old park with a fenced-off duck pond and the skeleton of a Native American settlement that later became an adobe hacienda preserved from its 1849 origins. Now the settlement houses an office for park employees and a little local nature museum. Locals use the area to stage their weddings and watch their children play. 16756 Moorpark Street.

At the northernmost point of the San Fernando Valley between freeways 405 and 5 lies the mission that started it all: ***Mission San Fernando Rey de Espana*** at the confluence of four major freeway systems. The seventeenth mission established in California by the Franciscans in 1797, it managed to hold up until an earthquake took it down in 1971. Good as new now, it charges a $4.00 fee to wander the gardens, check

Mission San Fernando Rey de Espana

out the pottery, tools, and furniture that were spared, and try to re-create what D. W. Griffith saw in the mission that was used as a set for *Our Silent Paths* in 1910. 15151 San Fernando Mission Boulevard, www.californiamissions.com/cahistory.

Not to be missed among Valley parks is ***San Vicente Mountain Park,*** just 1.7 miles west of the intersection of Mulholland Drive and the San Diego Freeway 405 off a 7-mile stretch of Mulholland that has failed to get paved all these years. But perhaps there was method in the madness: the park is actually a converted Nike missile defense site that from 1956 to 1968 housed all that stood between Los Angeles and her would-be attackers. The park has lots of remnants from the era explained through self-guided interpretative centers, although the terrain is mostly wild now and overlooks the Encino Reservoir.

An Ant in the Valley

Did you know that the ant farm was first invented here in the Valley? It was, and it all started because of one ant at the wrong time in the wrong place. That place was at a picnic in a San Fernando park on the Fourth of July in 1956. Milton Levine, aka Uncle Milton (to avoid Ant Milton), looked down and saw pay dirt. The ant farm was born and the onetime anything-salesman became a millionaire. The home of the ant farm is still the Valley, at Uncle Milton Industries in Westlake Village.

Continuing west, hit Topanga Canyon Road, which transforms from a flat, six-lane sprawl in the Valley to an incredibly scenic two-lane mountain path below the 101 freeway. This is the area where the rock movement of the 1960s got started, where a happy hippie nudist colony flourished for decades, where the Manson Family lived, where UFOs are believed to have found their favorite hover spot.

If ***Topanga Canyon*** has anything, it's lots of nature and lots of character.

Topanga State Park is a treasure trove of trails: 36 miles of them through open grassland, live oaks, and spectacular views of the Pacific Ocean. Maps, directions and guided hikes can be gained by calling the California State Parks system at (310) 454–8212 or (818) 880–0350; or visit www.parks.ca.gov.

Moving northward to Roscoe Boulevard west of Van Nuys, you'll find another city oasis with a little bit of history. ***Orcutt Ranch*** was built in 1921 as the vacation residence of William and Mary Orcutt. He was the vice president of Union Oil Company, and she was the perfect hostess. The ranch had a 3,060-square-foot house on 200 acres. The house is still there with its Mexican veranda and Bavarian wine cellar, but the grounds have dwindled to twenty-four acres of blooms, bushes, and arbors, meticulously managed by the city (which bought the ranch in 1966) and free to the public.

The estate was known originally as Rancho Sombre del Roble, which means "ranch shaded by the oak," and indeed, a 700-year-old oak spanning 33 feet around its trunk still stands. Statuary was not ignored by this society duo: A life-sized replica of *The Three Graces* gets a lot of attention here. The trimmed hedges and 500 kinds of rosebushes line up in a good mile of garden pathways that can be easily negotiated. Scattered among the trees, citrus groves, and flowers are stone statues, brick walkways, grottoes, urns, benches, and stone walls.

Tours of the house and gardens are conducted the last Sunday of the month (except during July and August) between 2:00 and 5:00 P.M. Orcutt Ranch Park is open daily sunrise to sunset. 23600 Roscoe Boulevard, (818) 883–6641.

While searching for waterfalls, earthquake faults, and the most perfect view in these mountains and canyons, a few off-trail spots of interest call. At the upper reaches of Topanga Canyon Boulevard in the Valley, find ***Stoney Point,*** an eerie outcropping of rocks ascending from jagged heights rising out of the flatlands and a convenient favorite for the bouldering and climbing crowd. You might recognize it from one of more B westerns you might have caught.

Pancake Heaven

Don't let anyone tell you otherwise. The indisputable fact is that the A-framed chain of the International House of Pancakes started in the San Fernando Valley—at Toluca Lake in 1958.

At the lower end of Topanga where the streets wind around neighborhoods of tree houses, the ***Will Geer Theatricum Botanicum*** is Grandpa Walton's legacy to the theater arts. The venerable actor, who died in 1978, established the stage when he was blacklisted for refusing to testify before the House Committee on Un-American Activities and essentially barred from the studios in the 1950s. The classically trained actor then devoted his art to Shakespeare and his life to growing vegetables on his spread here. The theater stages professional productions during the summer; recent repertory offerings included *King Lear, Skin of Our Teeth,* and *A Midsummer Night's Dream.* 1419 North Topanga Canyon Road, (310) 455–3723, www.theatricum.com.

As mountains head to the sea on Old Topanga Road, think of Neil Young, Spirit, Canned Heat, and other 1960s rock bands rooted in these sycamore-shaded hideaways. Still honoring the music scene is the ***Topanga Banjo Fiddle Contest and Folk Festival,*** held every May in a remote, oak-shaded clearing, in these canyons called Friendly Acres.

Since 1961 pickers have been coming here and going for the gold. Contact (818) 382–4819 or www.topangabanjofiddle.org.

As neighborhoods taper and chaparral takes over, ***Inn of the Seventh Ray*** can be found about 6 miles north of the Pacific Coast Highway. This idyllic spot of aged cedar shingles, stone walls, and gardens under the oaks and sycamores is the perfect setting for a meditative lunch in the outback. New Age books and supplies can be managed at the adjoining ***Spiral Staircase*** bookshop. Contact (310) 455–1311 or www. innoftheseventhray.com.

Fair There

If the folks in the Valley know how to do one thing, it's celebrate. There's a fair somewhere in the San Fernando at least every week. A good old-fashioned fair to try is the ***San Fernando Valley Fair*** *in June, where you'll find home-cooking contests, gardening competitions, 4-H in full swing, and the rodeo riding again. It's all held at Hansen Dam in Lake View Terrace in the central upper reaches of the region. Call (818) 557–1600.*

As the Valley extends to the west along Mulholland Drive toward Calabasas and Ventura, you're suddenly not in L.A. anymore. The area is so countrified and remote, it could be Korea or Colorado. Here's where ranches and horses rule, although development is edging in at a galloping pace.

Continue westward along windy, scenic Mulholland Drive and the mountains get higher and craggier, the meadows more pastoral and desolate. Just south of Mulholland off Las Virgenes Road lies ***Malibu Creek State Park,*** 4,000 acres with nothing on it but a few tents and cabins, an inviting system of trails, and a mountain range that looks strangely South Korean. The state purchased the land from Paramount in 1976, and with it came the *M*A*S*H* set—or at least the natural portion of the set, which made such a perfect background for the hit television series. But then it could have been Africa as well, at least according to studio executives, who thought the sycamore-and-oak-shaded streams make perfect spots for Tarzan to traverse via swinging vine. Campers are welcomed here, and the place is pet-friendly. 1925 Las Virgenes Road, Calabasas, (818) 880–0367, www.parks.ca.gov.

Tooling along on a westward course on Mulholland, which eventually runs into Leo Carrillo State Beach in Malibu, make a segue to ***Paramount Ranch*** off the highway. The scene is Old West here. In fact it's a hot set much of the time, it's two blocks of saloons, livery, laundry, and grubs serving as a backdrop for any number of period films today. Television classics like *The Rifleman, Have Gun Will Travel,* and *The Cisco Kid* were filmed here. It was San Francisco in the film *Wells Fargo,* colonial Massachusetts in *The Maid of Salem,* and ancient China in *The Adventures of*

Smashing Pumpkins

Although L.A. doesn't get much weather, and gets even less of it in the fall, the city of Calabasas goes all out at Paramount Ranch with an annual ***Fall Pumpkin Festival*** *in October. The food, the booths, the face painting, and all the pumpkins you can grab are here, although smashing them may not be on the intended agenda. Call (818) 225–2227.*

Marco Polo. More recently it was home to the *Dr. Quinn Medicine Woman* series. When it's quiet today it's a veritable ghost town, with trails leading into the mountains beyond, shaded picnic areas, and lots of green meadows. Trails lead to other abandoned film sites. Come on the first or third Saturday of the month at 9:30 A.M. and take the guided walk through the ranch's history. Guided 6-mile hikes can be arranged at this time as well. 2813 Cornell Road, (805) 370–2301.

Around the corner as the crow flies is ***Peter Strauss Ranch,*** at the intersection of Troutdale Drive and Mulholland. The ghostly estate, named for its most recent owner—an actor perhaps best remembered for his leading role in the *Rich Man Poor Man* mini series, was built in 1926 as a ranch house retreat for a carburetor magnate. The stone house and aviary he built are still here, although empty but for a pair of peacocks that call the ranch home. He also constructed a stone lookout tower—not to be outdone by the next owner, who built a dam and a lake as well as what was at the time the largest swimming pool on the West Coast, large enough for pool parties of 3,000. The trails here aren't all that impressive—about 0.6 mile around the ground—but the eerie wanderings around this hideaway provide their own adventure. (818) 597–9192.

From here all roads lead to the coast, about 12 miles of winding scenic paradise. Do take time to go north and hit Calabasas, home of bland stucco residential developments, strip malls—and the ***Los Angeles Pet Memorial Park.*** You'll find here the final resting places for Rover, Hopalong Cassidy's horse, Toper, Petey the ring-eyed bulldog from *Our Gang,* Rudolph Valentino's dog Kabar, and the pets of Harry James, Spanky MacFarland, Suzanne Pleshette, Steven Spielberg, Gloria Swanson, and Mae West. The cemetery has been in operation since 1928. Plastic flowers and lawn ornaments are encouraged. 5068 North Old Scandia Lane, (818) 591–7037.

Places to Stay in the San Fernando Valley

Luxe: $250+
Deluxe: $150–$249
Good deal: $79–$149

Anabelle Hotel
2011 West Olive Avenue, Burbank, (818) 845–7800, www.anabelle-safari.com. The Safari's (see below) more glamorous sister offers big rooms, terry robes, a morning newspaper, and other nods to luxury. Good deal.

Beverly Garland's Holiday Inn
4222 Vineland Avenue, North Hollywood, (818) 980–8000 or (800) BEVERLY, www.beverlygarland.com. Owned by a former star of the *My Three Sons* series, the hotel has spunk and character with a number of complimentary amenities. Deluxe.

Radisson Valley
15433 Ventura Boulevard, Sherman Oaks, (818) 981–5400 or (800) 333–3333, www.radisson.com. A sleek high-rise in the valley's commercial district with large rooms and balconies and a rooftop pool, all sitting conveniently at the junction of the 101 and 405 freeways. Good deal.

Safari Inn
1911 West Olive Avenue, Burbank, (818) 845–8586, www.anabelle-safari.com. Cute affordable rooms in a motor inn near the Burbank Airport. Some rooms have refrigerators and kitchens, but you can also splurge at the Italian bistro on the premises. Good deal.

Sheraton Universal
333 Universal Terrace, Universal City, (818) 980–1212 or (800) 325–3535, www.starwood.com. Sited a stone's throw from the theme park and entertainment promenade, this hotel features great views, upscale brand rooms, a health club, a spa, and dining. Deluxe.

Universal City Hilton and Towers
555 Universal Terrace, Universal City, (818) 505–2500 or (800) 445–8667, www.hilton.com. A great location steps away from Universal Studios Hollywood and CityWalk, with classy modern rooms and a wonderful seafood buffet dinner, plus brunch on weekends. Deluxe.

Places to Eat in the San Fernando Valley

Expensive: $25.00+
Reasonable: $15.00–$24.00
Bargain: $8.00–$14.00

Arde's
4315 Riverside Drive, Burbank, (818) 729–8463. Fresh wraps, kebabs, and salads in a cottage-style setting near Universal Studios. Bargain.

Asanebo
11941 Ventura Boulevard, Studio City, (818) 760–3348. Considered a midpriced Matsuhisa, this gem in a Studio City strip mall specializes in creative, fusion sashimi and traditional Japanese classics. A favorite with the hip foodie crowd. Reasonable.

Caioti
4346 Tujunga Avenue, Studio City, (818) 761–3588. The guy who gave Puck the potion for California pizza is doing it himself here with the most unusual and varied pizzas on the planet, including a spicy sausage concoction popular with the late-pregnancy crowd because it somehow helps induce labor. Reasonable.

Chili John's
2018 West Burbank Boulevard, Burbank, (818) 846–3611.
This gingham-curtain-and-ancient-Coke-sign kind of place has been serving the best chili around to Angelenos for the past fifty years, with the interior decor to prove it. Bargain.

Delmonico's Seafood Grille
16358 Ventura Boulevard, Encino, (818) 986–0777.
Fancy and pricey old-style surf-and-turf with gourmet service and a lean toward Old World ambience. Expensive.

Saddle Peak Lodge
419 Cold Canyon Road, Calabasas, (818) 222–3888.
Wild game served under stuffed trophies in a hunting lodge setting looking over the hills of Malibu. Expensive.

Author's Favorite Places to Eat in the San Fernando Valley

Inn of the Seventh Ray
128 Old Topanga Canyon Road, Topanga
(310) 455–1311
(see page 147 for more information)

Saddle Peak Lodge
419 Cold Canyon Road, Calabasas
(818) 222–3888

Delmonico's
16358 Ventura Boulevard, Encino
(818) 986–0777

Caioti
4346 Tujunga Avenue, Studio City
(818) 761–3588

Pasadena and Beyond

If Los Angeles is the rebellious teenager that finds purpose and identity in everything flamboyant, then Pasadena is the conservative parent firmly dressed in white-gloved mores and rooted in what is enduring. Pasadena was its own enclave when wealthy industrialists from the Midwest settled it in the 1880s. They came for the orange blossom climes and brought with them their fine heirlooms, conservative traditions, and money. Southern California's first freeway, the 110 linking Pasadena to Downtown L.A., did not open until 1940, and until then Pasadena was a city of its own, devoted to its opulent architecture, massive front lawns, and the reign of the rose.

Today the city is home to some 140,000 people, not all of them wealthy, and the air has changed considerably from a century ago to sport some of the worst smog in the southland from its mountain-framed location. But the culture endures, right down to the meticulously preserved mansions and gardens and the ubiquitous presence of auxiliary clubs and ladies who lunch. In Pasadena it's possible to time-travel, whether that means back to the 1970s with Nixon as president and cafe culture keeping the cool; to the 1960s with Jackie hats and waist-cut knit suits; to the 1950s with a quiet main street and Ozzie-and-Harriet neighborhoods; or even to the 1900s with the finest California Craftsman architecture mixing with mansions that might look comfortable in Versailles.

But for all its pomp and circumstance over a glorious past, Pasadena has a smart present. It's one of the few areas in Los Angeles reachable by fast and easy public transportation, with a walkable and entertaining commercial center and free ***ARTS buses*** to ferry those who prefer to ride. In July 2003 the ***Gold Line*** metro light rail began taking commuters from Downtown Los Angeles past Chinatown, Dodger Stadium, and tourist spots in Highland Park to six stops in Pasadena on a ride that lasts about thirty minutes from Union Station. L.A.'s most treacherous freeway need no longer be the great Pasadena impediment.

With entree to Pasadena as easy as a hop, slide, and token, here are some of the highlights to put on your play list.

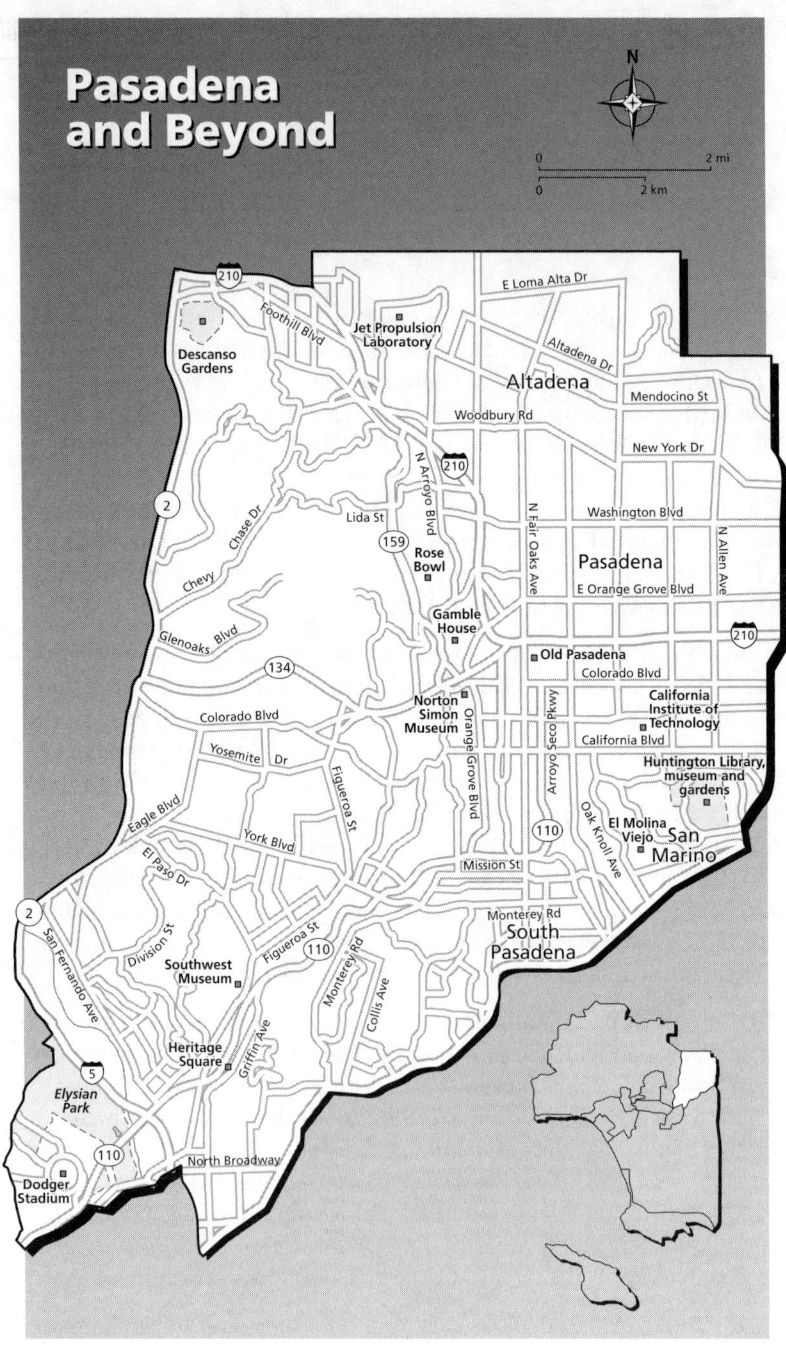

Pasadena and Beyond
N
0
2 mi
0
2 km
E Loma Alta Dr
Foothill Blvd
Jet Propulsion Laboratory
Descanso Gardens
Altadena Dr
Altadena
Mendocino St
Woodbury Rd
New York Dr
N Arroyo Blvd
N Fair Oaks Ave
Washington Blvd
Lida St
Chase Dr
Rose Bowl
Pasadena
N Allen Ave
Chevy
E Orange Grove Blvd
Gamble House
Glenoaks Blvd
Old Pasadena
Colorado Blvd
Norton Simon Museum
California Institute of Technology
Colorado Blvd
Orange Grove Blvd
Arroyo Seco Pkwy
California Blvd
Yosemite Dr
Figueroa St
Huntington Library, museum and gardens
Eagle Blvd
York Blvd
El Molina Viejo
San Marino
Oak Knoll Ave
El Paso Dr
Mission St
Monterey Rd
South Pasadena
San Fernando Ave
Division St
Figueroa St
Southwest Museum
Monterey Rd
Collis Ave
Griffin Ave
Heritage Square
Elysian Park
North Broadway
Dodger Stadium
210
2
159
134
110
5

Author's Top Picks in Pasadena

Norton Simon Museum

Vroman's Bookstore

Huntington Library's Japanese Garden and Tea House

Huntington Library's Rose Garden and Tea Room

Elysian Park

Well out of the way but worth the drive is the ***Banana Museum,*** in nearby Altadena, a by-appointment-only experience—but an experience it is. A call or e-mail is the price of admission, and it buys you entrance to a street-level store stuffed with everything banana, mostly collected from yard sales. The store is dedicated to "extolling the virtue of the bright, yellow elongated fruit from the herbaceous group that curves in the shape of a smile," says the owner Ken Bannister, who calls himself TB for Top Banana and has been tending this "museum" since 1976. Divided into areas like "Hard Section" and "Soft Section," the exhibit items—some 20,000 of them—range from huge stuffed toy bananas, to dainty porcelain salt and pepper shakers, to a framed petrified rotten banana mounted in a frame on the wall. A $5.00 donation gets you lifetime membership into the Banana Club and a T-shirt. 2524 El Molina Avenue, (626) 798–2272, www.bananaclub.com, bananasTB@aol.com.

Let's get back to central Pasadena.

The city's halcyon days in the early part of the twentieth century have been painstakingly preserved in many of its buildings and mansions, many allowing tours and others noted during walking tours. ***Pasadena Heritage Tours*** is a volunteer docent-led enterprise that offers walking itineraries around Old Pasadena (see next page), cottage and bungalow

Sig City

The 1944 Los Angeles freeway system brought asphalt geniuses to the table to try to figure out how to manage traffic and keep the flow going when different directions are involved and cars heading off the Pasadena Freeway need to access these directions. The result: Pasadena's 47-foot-high, four level Downtown Interchange that brings together the Hollywood, Harbor, and Pasadena Freeways. Before it was opened in 1950, the ultramodern engineering was attracting the attention of Hollywood crews, who used the interchange as the scene of a Martian attack in the original War of the Worlds. *The term* Sigalert, *which is commonly coined now in traffic reports around the country to connote a hopeless traffic snarl of thirty minutes or more, originated in L.A. with the help of Loyd Sigmon, who worked at KMPC Radio and used the alerts, usually describing the interchange at rush hour, to attract listeners.*

areas, and other neighborhoods where Craftsman and visionary architects were at work. The classic Old Pasadena Tour costs $5.00 and lasts ninety minutes. Contact (626) 441–6333 or www.pasadenaheritage.org.

Shopping, dining, browsing, and exploring is all the stuff of ***Old Pasadena*** (626–666–4156, www.oldpasadena.com). Once a series of run-down blocks presenting bars and vacuum cleaner repair stores, it's now a bustling restored twenty-two-block monument to early-twentieth-century architecture containing boutiques that specialize in hip. Bordered by Pasadena Avenue and Morengo Avenue, with Colorado Boulevard acting as Storefront Central for four blocks, this area rocks with designer aromatherapy stores, luxury chocolate counters, and folk art boutiques that feature international cottage industry crafts and send profits back to the villages. You do have chain stores here, of course. What's a neighborhood without a Starbucks and Barnes & Noble? But you also have back alleys where stores and cafes feature hidden courtyards, and out-of-the-way galleries can be happened upon.

One back-alley find is the ***Twin Palms*** restaurant and nightclub, which was part of Kevin Costner's divorce settlement to his ex-wife Cindy. The cafe is outdoors and makes generous use of muslin tenting. The food is California fusion, and "the scene" starts at 9:00 P.M. when the band comes on. 101 Green Street, (626) 577–2567.

Another spot is ***Rag Row,*** a series of resale stores on Union Street here in a town where one cannot be seen in the same haute couture creation twice. Between 93 East Union Street and 110 East Union are Clothes Heaven, Bailey's Designer Resale for Men, Bailey's Backstreet for Women, and Silent Partners to be plundered.

Shopping and dining can be combined with some serious art appreciation at the ***Pasadena Museum of Art (PMCA),*** which opened in June 2002. Located at 492 Union Street, about five blocks east of the clothing resale stores, it brings 30,000 square feet of space dedicated to the spirit of Left Coast creative vision: the art, architecture, and design of California from mid-nineteenth century to present. At press time a retrospective of California photography was on display with 200 rare images from the Oakland Museum of California's permanent collection, focusing on innovative work by Dorothea Lange, Edward Muybridge, Ansel Adams, Robert Frank, Richard Misrach, and Carrie Mae Weems. A vast rooftop terrace caps the space and allows an aesthetic moment of art and city appreciation. The hours are Wednesday through Sunday 10:00 A.M. to 5:00 P.M.; Friday to 8:00 P.M. Admission is $6.00. 492 East Union

The Chip Revolution

The Pasadena area is home of the first potato chip. Yes, it's true: The chip belongs to one visionary salt-and-oil-loving potato slicer named Laura Clough Scudder who, with her husband, Charles, discovered the delights of mixing high fats with high carbs and salt and selling it to an addicted public. They built a chip factory next to their home, but by the time they got it rolling the word was out and the taste was in: Some two dozen other companies were making chips and serving them up. So the Scudders did one better. They figured out how to package and market these calorie monsters and get them into every kitchen in America.

Street, (626) 568–3665, www.pmcaonline.org.

The odd yet historically significant 112-year-old ***Castle Green*** was once a downtown hotel but is now a residence. The lobby is open to the public and worth the look. One for the National Register of Historic Places, it's a six-story "castle" in two parts, connected by the "Bridge of Sighs" over Raymond Avenue and the epicenter for serious parade-watchers who may or may not know that President Taft once viewed the Rose Parade from this very bridge. Considered an eccentric interpretation of Moorish-Mediterranean styles mixed in with a little Classical column activity, its verandas and balconies in greens, oranges, and gold make it engaging to gaze at outside as well as in. The lobby sports a parlor room, a Moorish room, a card room, and a downstairs ballroom, preserved in pristine shape and the backdrop for more than a few films. 50 East Green Street at Raymond.

The ***Pacific-Asia Museum*** is a strange fixture in this quintessential American town. Located on the east side of Old Pasadena, its green tiled roof protecting the premises from evil sprits with upturned corners and pagoda dragons, it was the lifelong project of a wealthy resident who traveled widely and wanted a place to house her Far Eastern collections. Whether or not feng shui was considered in the design when it was built in 1924, the museum does have an authentic Chinese garden, rumored to be the only such undertaking in the United States (but soon to be rivaled by a grander one at the Huntington Hartford). Meanwhile, the koi fish beckon and the courtyard is a tranquil place to rest and think. The fee is $5.00; it's open 10:00 A.M. to 3:00 P.M. Wednesday through Sunday, and to 8:00 P.M. on Thursday. 46 North Los Robles Avenue, (626) 449–2742.

Another spot to meditate is just up Los Robles Avenue, where the ***Fuller Seminary Prayer Garden*** presents a public respite in a patch of green surrounded by vintage houses and Victorian Gothic accents. 135 North Oakland Avenue, (800) 236–2222, www.fuller.edu.

For another art-loving walkable jaunt, backtrack a bit to the ***Norton Simon Museum,*** about four blocks west (instead of east) of the downtown core. The halls of Rodins, Rembrandts, Picassos, Goyas, van Goghs, and Raphaelite works—2,000 years of Western and Asian acquisitions—is an easy and worthwhile part of any exploration. The exhibition rooms and grounds are compact and easily seen in ninety minutes or less, and the catalog of works is superb, collected item by item by corporate crusader and failed U.S. Senate candidate Norton Simon and his wife, actress Jennifer Jones. Open Wednesday through Sunday noon to 6:00 P.M. Admission is $5.00. 411 Colorado Boulevard, near the Colorado Street Bridge, (626) 449–6840, www.nortonsimon.org.

For those corporate millionaires who find their stock is worth pennies these days, the aforementioned ***Colorado Street Bridge*** on Arroyo Boulevard has provided a convenient jumping-off spot for many in need of escape. This 1913 span, standing 150 feet high and curving 1,467 feet between banks, runs high above the Arroyo Seco—a popular hiking spot today that was once the site of both orange groves and a bohemian movement of artists, architects, and craftspeople who created the vision of the city. The bridge is locally dubbed "Suicide Bridge" for its use during the depression years.

Any tour of Pasadena should include the ***Gamble House,*** not far from the Norton Simon Museum. It was designed with Japanese influence by the fathers of the Craftsman movement, brothers Charles and Henry

An Auspicious Beginning

The first Tournament of Roses Parade and games were held on January 1, 1890, at the Pasadena Valley Hunt Club, where members decided to stage a parade of flower-doused horses and buggies. This was followed by turn-of-the-century all-American games in which participating men competed in footraces, tugs-of-war, and a jousting pageant in which horsemen sporting 12-foot lances tried to spear three rings hung 30 feet apart while galloping at top speed. What with the rings, the floral displays, and the tournament spirit, the Tournament of Roses became a tradition, and competitions broadened to include chariots, ostriches, even elephants. But football took a dominating role when the first Rose Bowl was played in 1902 and the University of Michigan creamed Stanford 49–0.

Zippety Doo Dah

No one does parades better than Pasadena, but a number of local paradegoers feel that such pageants should be open to all queens, not just some special young women with the traditional assets. So the ***Doo Dah Parade*** *was invented in the late 1970s as the people's answer to the Rose Parade. Every November a colorful line of costumed participants snakes down Colorado Boulevard for what has become a major event in this otherwise quiet town. A queen is chosen weeks earlier from some two dozen contestants, mostly men dressed in outrageous costumes competing for the crown. Recent years have featured Mutiny Spears in a blue wig and twinkling body lights, and Oxygen Tank Lady—awaiting a lung transplant and just "dying to be queen." Belly dancers, vampiresses, blues singers, and cartoon characters show up, too, along with people impersonating animals, animals impersonating people, and even a box of cremated ashes. Any and all participants welcome. Call (626) 440–7379.*

Greene, and lived in by heirs to the Procter & Gamble fortune, David and Mary Gamble. Tours take about an hour and allow you to wander through sunlit rooms of dark woods and colored-glass panes with furnishings ranging from the 1920s to the 1950s. An outdoor sleeping solarium overlooks Arroyo Seco, a popular feature in the days when the Pasadena air was clear and scented. The clever ways that designers created closets, dorm space, and storage space aid in making these nooks and crannies interesting. But unless you ask, the docents don't talk about the ghost of Aunt Julia, the maiden sister of Mary, who came to live at the Gamble House in her early twenties and never left, literally. Open Thursday through Sunday noon to 3:00 P.M. Tours run every fifteen minutes and cost $5.00. 4 Westmoreland Place, (626) 793–3334, www.gamblehouse.org.

The well-known ***Rose Bowl,*** a bit farther north in Arroyo Seco, is of course the scene of the annual January football games and frequent home challenges for the UCLA Bruins, but on the second Sunday of the month the bowl becomes a bargain pit bar none. The ***Rose Bowl Flea Market*** runs from 9:00 A.M. to 4:00 P.M. on those Sundays and is one of L.A.'s prime events. It's possible to find rare antique jewelry pieces, colorful purses from Guatemala, and the delicate handcrafted one-of-a-kind brooches that usually only show up when somebody dies. There's a $2.00 tariff. 991 Rosemont Boulevard, (323) 560–7469.

By the way, if it's the ***Rose Parade*** you're looking for but don't want to have to camp out overnight for a spot or wade through a million people to see these feats of flowers and imagination, special ***pre-parade tours*** can be arranged in the month of December. For $5.00 a person (which includes two site visits) you can see the hoops and the draping and even a few cogs and widgets—though you may have to wait for New Year's Day to see all the blooms. Call (626) 449–4100 or a twenty-four-hour information line at (626) 449–ROSE to find out where the tours are taking place. No appointment is necessary.

A short walk down a long block in an area southeast of the Rose Bowl that's generally regarded as ***Millionaires' Row*** is the ***Pasadena Historical Society and Museum*** at ***Feynes Mansion.*** This eighteen-room 1905 homage to the Beaux-Arts tradition is one of the few preserved spectacles of a period when wealth was attached to the color of your hemoglobin. Original antiques, Oriental rugs, tapestries, and impressionist artworks adorn the abode, and you can even peruse Eva Feynes's twelve-volume compendium of amateur watercolors. What's odd about this place is the house next door. A separate building on the grounds curves in the shape of a nineteenth-century Finnish farmhouse and houses three rooms depicting such noteworthy items as an authentic Finnish sauna, a re-created smokehouse with an open hearth and iron utensils, and another room filled with myriad Finnish folk art pieces. What this has to do with the price of roses in Pasadena is that Eva Feynes's daughter Leonora married the Finnish consul in 1946 and created the Finnish consulate from the mansion and grounds. While the Finns have gone their way, the house stayed and was given to the Pasadena Historical Society in 1965, was placed on the National Register of Historic Places in 1985, and has been meticulously groomed and preserved ever since. It's open Thursday through Sunday from 1:00 to 7:00 P.M.; the admission fee of $6.00 includes a forty-five-minute tour. 470 West Walnut Street, (626) 577–1660, www.pasadenahistory.org.

On your walk you'll pass through what's locally considered ***Little Switzerland.*** This is a fairyland of sorts with wide avenues and hundred-year-old oak and sycamore trees dedicated to the architectural visions of ***Greene & Greene*** and built between 1901 and 1907. A ***Pasadena Heritage Tour*** (see above) will provide the missing details; otherwise you can casually amble past the ***Cole House*** next to Gamble House, now a Unitarian church; the ***Ranney House*** (440 Arroyo Terrace); the ***F. W. Hawks House*** (408 Arroyo Terrace); the ***Van Rosem-Neill House*** (400 Arroyo Terrace), which has the added design element of "clinker brick" or a decorative boulder wall; the ***White Sisters House*** (370 Arroyo Terrace)—the sisters were the architects' in-laws; ***Charles Sumner Greene House*** (368 Arroyo Terrace), designed, built, and lived in by one of the

Greene brothers; the ***Duncan-Irwin House*** (240 North Grand Avenue); and the ***James A. Culbertson House*** (235 North Grand Avenue), with its Tiffany-glass-paneled front door.

Farther south on Orange Grove Boulevard, it's impossible to miss the white gleaming balustrades of the Italianate mansion of one ***William J. Wrigley.*** Built by the emperor of gum upon his exit from Chicago, it is now the stately headquarters of the Tournament of Roses. House tours are offered free on Thursday from 2:00 to 4:00 P.M., February through August. The gardens, with 1,500 varieties of roses, are open to the public daily during those months. A tour will take you through sweet moments of Rose Bowls past and throw in some of the original Wrigley family furnishings and China to ogle. 391 South Orange Grove Boulevard, (626) 449–4100.

Just east of this neighborhood, between California and Del Mar Boulevards, is Pasadena's one and only winery. Most people living in Pasadena don't even know there's a winery here, but somewhere amid the palms and the scrubs a group of friends got together in 1996 and opened the ***Black Rock Wineworks.*** The grapes aren't grown here, but cellars store the wine and spirits. For the $5.00 tasting fee, you can have a tour of the winery and even pick up a logo glass and picnic corkscrew,

Headquarters for the Tournament of Roses

compliments of the wine tender. The winery specializes in Sauvignon Blanc, Grenache, Zinfandel, and Petite Syrah but also has some grappa and brandy in the barrel. It's open Saturday only, from 11:00 A.M. to 5:00 P.M. 171 Waverly Drive, (626) 844–8796.

The ***Oak Knoll*** area on the eastern edge of the town might be considered a wealthy suburb of Millionaire Row. Developed in the 1800s to attract some of the wealth teeming along Orange Grove Boulevard, the Oaks attracted architects and craftsmen who gave the neighborhood distinction. Crowning the spot is the grande dame of sprawling nineteenth-century resorts, the ***Huntington Hotel,*** now the ***Ritz-Carlton Huntington Hotel.*** (It was originally the Wentworth for the Civil War general who built it.) Since its opening in 1906, it has accommodated Albert Einstein, Theodore Roosevelt, Prince Philip, and a host of other notables. Henry Huntington took it over in 1914 and added twenty-three acres of designed gardens to the grounds, including a Japanese garden and a covered bridge—America's only Picture Bridge, with thirty-nine panels of original paintings of California scenes across the roof beams by artist Frank M. Moore. Ritz-Carlton spiffed up the rooms, added a full-service day spa and salon, and kept everything else as it was, including the swimming pool—California's first Olympic-sized watering hole, with bar and whirlpool attached. 1401 South Oak Knoll, (626) 568–3900.

While you're in the area walking the pristine avenues, you may wish to stop for coffee—preferably the kind that doesn't cost a month's salary. ***Euro Pane,*** east of Oak Knoll at Lake Avenue and Colorado, is Pasadena's answer to Paris. The croissants here get the lords and dames of Orange Grove and Oak Knoll out of their gardens for an hour, and the scones, cinnamon rolls, and specialty breads keep the counter and few sitting tables packed on weekends. 950 East Colorado Boulevard, (626) 577–1828.

The streets around Euro Pane—namely Colorado, Mentor, and Green—converge into a sort of artsy theater enclave where trendy coffeehouses, chic cafes, and cheap eats mix with playhouse theaters. The ***Pasadena Playhouse*** at 39 South El Molino (626–356–7529, www.pasadenaplayhouse.org) is a 1917 stage landmark that attracts star talent and first-rate direction, and definitely benefits from its Los Angeles anchoring. ***The Ice House*** nearby at 24 North Mentor Street is Pasadena's answer to the Improv. More than a few mega comics have put in their time on this stage, including Jay Leno, David Letterman, Steve Martin, and Robin Williams. Pre- or postshow munchies can be downed at ***Crocodile Café*** (140 South Lake near the Green Street intersection, 626–449–9900), which is always crowded because the food (salads, pastas, pizzas done California-style and locally labeled "Spago for the People") is so inexpensive and the service so uneven. Head for the quieter patio seating option if you can; forget about reservations. When pasta is too fancy for your fancy, feed your food habit at ***Pie 'N Burger*** nearby at 913 East California Boulevard at Lake (626–275–1123). It doesn't get more American, more basic, or more comforting than french fries and a patty—and the pecan pies are killers.

If you feel like upping the experience with some Hollywood dishes, Jennifer Lopez recently opened ***Madre's.*** The style is anything but casual: white linens and lace ruffles on the tablecloths, crystal chandeliers, fine woods, and even an in-house cigar maker. Still, the food is anything but formal—home-style Puerto Rican and Cuban cooking, "just like Mama." J.Lo's friends are bound to show, and the show is good. 897 Granite Drive, toward the Cal Tech campus, (626) 744–0900.

Truly upscale diners will want to test the fare at ***Bistro 45***—atmospherically Art Deco, conveniently located next to the playhouse, and likely to put you out a good day's wages, at least if you're a regular working stiff. The menu is part California, part French, part North American, and part New Zealand. Try pan-roasted New Zealand John Dory or Roasted All Natural Quebecois Veal Loin. The chicken is free range, of course, and the prime rib cut from holistic cattle. 45 South Mentor Avenue, (626) 795–2478.

Continue south for a block or two and come to ***Rose Tree Cottage*** at

Book Break

It's fitting that a city whose university has spawned twenty-two Nobel laureates also possesses the oldest and largest independent bookstore in southern California. ***Vroman's Bookstore*** *at 695 East Colorado Boulevard (626–449–5320, www.vromansbookstore.com) has been selling books to Pasadena gentry for nearly a hundred years and a decade. On any given night at 7:00, celebrated authors are giving their words and their autographs, from George Foreman and his new health message to Dexter Scott King discussing his childhood; on other nights, open groups gather for enlightened discussions. The Colorado Boulevard location is spacious and modern with lots of places to hide out with a prized tome amid the two floors of shelves. Still, it's* ***Vroman's Bargain Books*** *that commands the most attention. This separate store at 340 South Lake Avenue (626–396–1670) is a hip and cavernous space where overstocked, damaged, discontinued, and remnant titles are shelved and displayed with dignity and logic and given new life.*

East California Boulevard and Lake. Rather than a great place to chow down, this is a good place to relax and have tea—in another country. The Tudor-style cottage is part of a courtyard of little cottage specialty stores selling gifts and soaps and notions from Great Britain. Tea is served on Royal Doulton bone china and tableclothed settings surrounded by rattan chairs and English roses by the window. Cucumber finger dabs, fresh scones (with real Devonshire cream), and Rose Cottage shortbreads await. There are plenty of homemade berry and fruit jams to dollop. Three seatings only, folks—Tuesday through Sunday at 1:00, 2:30, and 4:00 P.M., reservations required. The fare for this affair is $22.50 per person. 828 East California Boulevard, (626) 793–3337, www.rosetreecottage.com.

Continuing east on Colorado and then south on Wilson, the ***California Institute of Technology*** (Cal Tech) puts a lot of East Coast into this Mediterranean-climed metro. It's enough to know that Einstein ambled these hallowed grounds when you explore the campus. Indeed, the university has produced twenty-two Nobel Prize laureates, many teaching members of the faculty. Italian Renaissance–style buildings complemented by blooming wisteria, all surrounding sculpture gardens and lotus fountains, instill a cloistered feeling where it's possible to find the peace you need to think. 1201 East California.

The south side of the institute empties into ***San Marino,*** another exclusive suburb of Pasadena—a dry town where making a right on red is verboten and the home of the ***Huntington Library, Art Collections and Botanical Gardens.*** The attraction for most is the art—among other treasures you'll find the 1770 *Blue Boy* by William Gainsborough and the 1794 *Pinkie* by Thomas Lawrence here—what's outside may be a little more Off the Beaten Path.

The railroad and real estate baron Henry Huntington might be singly responsible for creating what is now L.A. and linking it to the rest of the world with his work on the Southern Pacific Railroad and his creation of the Pacific Electric Company, which ran bright red trolleys from Downtown L.A. to the ocean until a man called Armand Hammer came along with his Occidental Petroleum company. When Huntington and his second wife, Arabella—who was also his aunt by her previous marriage to Collis Huntington, to whom she bore a son out of wedlock—came to California, the price was high for Henry. The newly widowed Arabella preferred the parties of Paris to placid pastures of Pasadena, and to keep her happy, Henry had to build her a palace. The grand Beaux-Arts establishment contains one of the finest archive collections

Huntington's Conundrum

Many a newspaper writer attracted by the idea of a wealthy society widow marrying her wealthy society nephew churned copy around the wedding of Henry to Arabella, the surviving wife of his dear Uncle Collis. This ditty in the July 18, 1913, issue of the St. Louis Republic *summed it up:*

He Becomes:

His Own Uncle.

Nephew of His Wife.

Brother-in-Law of His Mother-in-Law.

Great Uncle of His Own Children.

Step-Grandfather of His Own Children.

And She Is:

Her Husband's Aunt.

Cousin of Her Adopted Daughter.

Sister-in-Law's Daughter-in-Law.

Step-Mother of His Own Great Nieces.

And in Case She Has Children She Will Be Their Aunt.

of British and American history, literature, and art from the eleventh century on. Similarly, both were avid art collectors—he of American masterworks, while Arabella had a taste for European traditions.

But the 207 acres of meticulously landscaped gardens are the precious remnants of another era—and country. Flora can be categorized into 14,000 species, 2,000 of them in the rose family alone. The Japanese Tea Garden gets the most attention with its Zen meditation corners, but the grounds also offer a meditation and prayer labyrinth such as monks used in the Middle Ages. Unlike other labyrinths found at spas, cemeteries, and churches, this one lies in the shadow of a Louis XV statue and is defined by paths and bumps in the grass. The most fragrant of roses are in the arbor leading up to the ***Rose Garden Café and Tea Room,*** where teas are served in fine china cups with the appropriate finger sandwiches, tarts, and scones doused with crème fraîche on white-clothed tables. If you have a feathered hat, this is the place to wear it.

Docent tours around the estate are complimentary but need to be reserved in advance. Highlights include the Huntington Mausoleum and what is colloquially called the stink plant—a rare 6-foot orchid from Malaysia that blooms as rarely as once a century. When it does open, however, the monstrous bud becomes a stand-in for Little Shop of Horrors, letting off an odor that rivals rotting flesh.

The Huntington Rose Garden

The museum and gardens can be found at 1151 Oxford Street (between Orlando and Euston) in San Marino. Open Tuesday through Friday, noon to 4:30 P.M.; from 10:30 A.M. on weekends. The Huntington is closed Monday. Admission is $8.50, and tea menus run around $25.00 per person. To arrange a docent garden tour, call (626) 405–2127 or show up after 1:00 P.M. Reservations are advised for the tea room: (626) 683–8131.

Heading southward on El Molino Viejo or Old Mill Road, the destination is, well, ***The Old Mill.*** The 1816 mill built by the Gabrieleno Indians under the auspices of Franciscan padres settling the mission at San

Gabriel had plenty of grist for the water-powered wheel—the first in southern California—until 1823. That was when another mill was built on the grounds of the mission, rather than several miles away as this one was. What stands is a preserved, bilevel Spanish Mission–style adobe that has been used subsequently as a golf resort clubhouse and historical society headquarters. It's now a museum open from 1:00 to 4:00 P.M. daily and free for the exploring. What the caretakers and pamphlets don't mention is the rumored tunnel that lies under the adobe as a hidden, underground passage that linked the mill with the mission and hid the cache. 1120 Old Mill Road, (626) 449–5450.

Out from Pasadena along the Gold Line from Downtown is a stop in Highland Park that brings some very off-path—but possibly soon to be discovered—campy L.A. surprises. In unlikely low-to-middle-income neighborhoods in the shadow of Dodger Stadium, look for the neatly mythic Elysian Fields in ***Elysian Park,*** a 600-acre sprawl that was set aside for preservation and public use when the pueblo was founded in 1781. The park is a mélange of hiking trails shaded by giant sycamore, eucalyptus, and oak trees and open fields where soccer games and BBQs happen most weekends. Dog-friendly and surprisingly picturesque, this would be L.A.'s answer to Central Park, if L.A. had a center.

In ***Highland Park*** on the road to Pasadena via exit 43 off the 110 northbound or light rail, explorers can sniff around a mostly Hispanic neighborhood until they come to the hidden cul-de-sac (road signage ample) of ***Heritage Square,*** a strange abandoned theme park of sorts comprised of turn-of-the-twentieth-century Victorian houses moved from Bunker Hill. Tours happen hourly; for a $6.00 charge you can walk around seven domiciles and a church. Museum hours are 10:00 A.M. to 3:00 P.M. Friday, and from 11:30 A.M. Saturday and Sunday, with tours beginning at noon. Grounds close at 4:30 P.M. 3800 Homer Street, Highland Park, (818) 449–0193.

Nearby, across the freeway, are two other largely ignored gems: the Charles Fletcher ***Lummis House*** known as ***El Alisal,*** and the ***Southwest Museum.*** The 1898 Lummis adobe is significant because it was built by hand by a man who walked to L.A. from Ohio and then became the *Los Angeles Times*'s first city editor. The house was built with the goal of creating a gathering place for all those in love with Native American cultures and the mystique of the West. The sycamores that grow around the site shadow the home, which was built from boulders brought up from the Arroyo Seco, iron rails from the Santa Fe Railroad, and stray telegraph poles. Hours are Friday through Sunday noon to 4:00 P.M. Admission is free. 200 East Avenue 43, (213) 222–0546.

The ***Southwest Museum*** on its perch on a hill near the Lummis adobe and overlooking the freeway gets few visitors—but those who do come get treated to a collection founded in 1907 and dedicated to the preservation, display, and study of more than 250,000 items of Native North, Central, and South American life. If you like baskets, ceramics, textiles, and artifacts, they're here in quantity and can be observed and studied in both the museum and library. Four floors of glass displays and dioramas provide as much inspiration as the grounds and view. A small store sells all manner of dream catchers. The hours are Tuesday through Sunday 10:00 A.M. to 5:00 P.M. Admission is $6.00. 234 Museum Drive, (323) 221–2164, www.southwestmuseum.org.

Our final stops are a bit far-flung, but well worth the trip. Heading out of Pasadena toward the northwest en route to Glendale, ***Descanso Gardens*** calls to camellia lovers like sirens to sailors. The eighty-acre rolling retreat near the intersection of the 2 highway and the 210 freeway at 1418 Descanso Drive is nearly always in bloom. The presiding twenty-two-room Georgian-style mansion, meanwhile, provides in personal collections of art an indoor attraction as engaging as the outdoor offerings. The estate was once the rancho of *Los Angeles Daily News* owner and publisher East Manchester Boddy, who built the home in a spot where little could grow in the acidic soil. Then along came the camellia, and the newspaper magnate had found his métier. Today some 100,000 camellias adorn the gardens in 600 varieties—the largest such cultivated site in the world. And then there's the rosarium, a five-acre floral wonderland of some 7,000 species. The birding is great here, too, and to make the point the local Audubon Society built a Bird Observation Station on the grounds. Tired bird-watchers and rose sniffers can take five at the Japanese Tea Garden or ride the "Enchanted Railroad" through a bed of blooms. The gardens stay open daily except major holidays from 9:00 A.M. to 4:30 P.M.; admission is $5.00. The train runs weekends only and costs $1.50. Tram tours run Tuesday through Friday at 1:00, 2:00, and 3:00 P.M., and you can add an 11:00 A.M. tour on Saturday and Sunday. Cost is $2.00. 1418 Descanso Drive, (818) 952–4401, www.descansogardens.com.

Lastly, if you head off into the foothills of the Angeles National Forest above Pasadena, you might get a better appreciation for the earth you're on if you step into the ***Jet Propulsion Laboratory (JPL).*** The facility itself, visible from the 2 highway, is a sprawling glass-and-steel apparition in an otherwise spare chaparral that's now a landmark on the National Historic Register. This is where the term *rocket scientist* was coined, and it has been in the business of space and aeronautics engineering since 1944 when it was founded as a division of Cal Tech. It currently operates at full bore as one of the nine NASA centers. The good news is the public is invited, at least for the 2-cent—actually, free—tour. These run an average of two hours and include a promo movie about JPL's contributions to conquering the space frontier. Scientists here contributed *Voyager* in 1977, for instance, which captured noise and light from Jupiter's moons, Saturn's rings, and Neptune's mantle. You can also see *Magellan, Explorer 1,* and *Galileo* before taking off to another building that houses the space communications area, which tracks all the objects still left in the sky. The tours are not formal or set, so reservations are needed to get a space and time. 4800 Oak Grove Drive, (818) 354–9314, www.jpl.nasa.org.

Places to Stay in Pasadena

Luxe: $250+
Deluxe: $150–$249
Good deal: $79–$149

Artists' Inn and Cottage Bed and Breakfast
1038 Magnolia Street, South Pasadena, (626) 799–5668 or (888) 799–5668, www.artistsinn.com. Twelve quaint themed rooms (think Impressionist Room, Italian Suite, van Gogh Room, Gauguin Suite) in a Cape Cod–like cottage in a quiet Pasadena neighborhood. Breakfast and afternoon teas are included. Rates average $160. Deluxe.

The Doubletree Hotel Pasadena
191 North Los Robles Avenue (at Walnut), (626) 792–2727 or (800) 222–8733, www.doubletree.com. Great location in its proximity to Old Pasadena and all the cafes and nightlife to be found. Spend Sunday brunch on the hotel patio with the gourmet buffet. Pool, spa, gardens, fountains, and a Spanish Mediterranean flavor add comfort and ambience. Deluxe.

Hilton Pasadena
168 Los Robles Avenue, (626) 577–1000, www.pasadena.hilton.com. This hotel is above standard in its elegance and service, which are both given much attention in this old-wealth location. The added bonus is its nearness to Old Pasadena. Deluxe.

Old Pasadena Courtyard by Marriott
180 North Fair Oaks Avenue, (626) 403–7600 or (800) 321–2211, www.courtyard.com/laxot. Here's a Courtyard that wants to be a Hilton. Its

Author's Favorite Places to Stay in Pasadena

Ritz-Carlton Huntington Hotel
1401 South Oak Knoll Street
(626) 568–3900
(see page 160 for more information)

Doubletree Hotel Pasadena
191 North Los Robles Avenue
(626) 792–2727

Artists' Inn and Cottage
1038 Magnolia Street
(626) 799–5668

stately presence in the heart of a historic district of mansions and Craftsman homes makes it a cut above the Courtyard name. Custom-decorated guest rooms include ten suites, nine spa kings, and three boardroom suites surrounded by a neighborhood of wide streets and hundred-year-old oaks. Good deal.

Pasadena Inn
400 South Arroyo Parkway, (626) 795–8401 or (800) 577–5690.
This hotel is convenient for its simplicity: a standard hotel setting around a swimming pool convenient to Old Pasadena, the Norton Simon Museum, and the Pasadena Convention Center. Rooms come with complimentary coffee and rolls. Good deal.

Sheraton Pasadena Hotel
303 Cordova Street, (626) 449–4000, www.sheratonpasadena.com.
Large rooms and suites, each complete with a coffeemaker and complimentary Starbucks and Tazo tea. The Club Room serves light breakfasts, while a year-round outdoor pool and fitness room complement the offerings. Good deal.

Places to Eat in Pasadena

Expensive: $25.00+
Reasonable: $15.00–$24.00
Bargain: $8.00–$14.00

Arroyo Chop House
536 South Arroyo Parkway, (626) 57–PRIME.
Unassuming on the outside, the inside here assumes a lot. This chophouse is all 1920s Deco with dark mahogany walls and an Art Deco–inspired mural. Entertainment is via piano and singer, and the food is simple: beef, with half a dozen cuts to choose from seared lightning fast in a broiler that climbs 900 degrees to lock in the flavor. Wine sample pairing is possible with every course, which are all ordered and served a la carte. Expensive.

Bistro 45
45 South Mentor Avenue, (626) 795–2478.
Expensive. See page 161 for more information.

Café Bizou
91 North Raymond Avenue, (626) 792–9923, www.cafebizou.com.
Café Bizou owes its success to the three Gs: good prices, good-tasting entrees, and great $1.00 soup and salad accompaniments. The menu tends toward California comfort with items like Crispy Potato Scaled Salmon, Spicy Chicken Fettuccine, and Beef Short Ribs. The atmosphere is noisy upscale bistro. Reasonable.

Clearwater Seafood
168 West Colorado Boulevard, (626) 356–0959.
This is a fun fish house in a great location with a menu that takes its lobster as seriously as it does its oyster selection: twenty-seven choices of oyster by bay and location. Chowders, pastas, and salads as well. Reasonable.

Crocodile Café
140 South Lake, (626) 449–9900.
Bargain. See page 160 for more information.

561
561 Green Street (at Madison), (626) 583–8275.
Located in a renovated historic building in the

Pasadena Playhouse district, the Craftsman look here prepares you for the skilled execution ahead. The cuisine is created and served by the professional staff and students of the famed California School of Culinary Arts. The adventurous menu brings game and elite sea creatures, blended soups, and mushroom spinach salads with a twist. Expensive.

Madre's
897 Granite Drive, (626) 744–0900. Expensive. See page 161 for more information.

Pie 'N Burger
913 East California Boulevard, (626) 275–1123. Bargain. See page 161 for more information.

Raymond Restaurant
1250 South Fair Oaks Avenue, (626) 441–3136. It's worth getting out of the heart of the town for a meal in this historic Craftsman cottage, home of a former caretaker for the long-disappeared Raymond Hotel. The decor is Victorian with a fireplace for added coziness. Dishes like sautéed rainbow trout, apple cobbler, tomato and bacon soup, and "cream tea"— with double Devon cooked cream—are on the menu. Ten percent of the tariff goes to preservation of the Gamble House. Expensive.

Twin Palms
101 Green Street, (626) 577–2567. Reasonable. See page 154 for more information.

Indexes

General Index

N

O

P

Museums Index

Accommodations Index

Restaurants Index

About the Author

Lark Ellen Gould is an award-winning journalist living in Los Angeles, whose recent travel industry expertise comes out of an eight-year tenure as western regional bureau chief at *Travel Agent Magazine.* As a freelancer she has covered famine and war in Africa, economic development in the United Arab Emirates, and social issues in India and Nepal for international newspapers and magazines. She continues today as Pacific-Asia editor for *Recommend Magazine*. When not on a plane she can be found testing sidewalk dives around L.A. looking for the best chili dog combos with and without fries.